Creative Training

A Train-the-Trainer Field Guide

By Becky Pike Pluth

Foreword by Ken Blanchard

Creative TRAINING

Becky Pike Pluth

A TRAIN–THE–TRAINER FIELD GUIDE

foreword by Ken Blanchard

My dear Raegan, Brody, Gabe and Lucas,

How quickly you have grown up during the writing of this book! Daily you show me the wonder and joy of doing something for the first time. I practice the principles in this book on you regularly and am richly blessed by having you in my life. You have challenged me to be a better teacher and mom and have allowed me to fail enough to find success sweeter.

Mom

Endorsements

What a treasure of proven training insights! Three hundred years of experience at The Bob Pike Group delivers tried and true methods that get results. Every nugget of knowledge is backed by research. Every gem of advice pushes you closer to being the competent trainer you desire.

—Elaine Biech, author of *Training and Development for Dummies*, editor of *ASTD Handbook*

Becky Pluth effectively combines the research and the practice behind Instructor-Led, Participant-Centered training. The book also blends the design and delivery of training in an engaging and effective manner.

—Sivasailam "Thiagi" Thiagarajan, author of *Interactive Techniques for Instructor-Led Training*

In her newest book, Creative Training: A Train-the-Trainer Field Guide, *Becky Pike Pluth has combined decades of personal training experience with excellent brain research about how to train easily, successfully, and effectively. She makes sure the reader understands the important, brain-based reasons for using ILPC (Instructor-Led, Participant-Centered) training strategies. Even better, Becky imbues the book with her own delightful stories and sense of humor as she shows you how to teach in ways the human brain learns best. Becky's book is a "must" for any trainer's bookshelf!*

—Sharon L. Bowman, author of *Using Brain Science to Make Training Stick* and *Training from the BACK of the Room*!

If you're particularly drawn to adult learning theory, you'll find what you're looking for between the covers of this book. If you enjoy the research behind the theories, you'll find it, too. Or if you are more of a learner who wants specific research-based techniques you could use in your training tomorrow, they're here in abundance. Something for everyone from the novice to the seasoned trainer. Quite a book.

—Dave Arch, author of *Transforming Leaders The Sandler Way*

This Field Guide is a practical, hands-on guide to the decades of real-world experience that has formed the Creative Training methodology. Becky's done the hard work, distilling all of it—and the cutting edge neuroscience behind it—into a single page-turner-of-a-book. Now, it's up to you to implement these concepts into your daily activities in order to engage learners at a higher level.

—Jeb Brooks, president and CEO, The Brooks Group

Over the last decade or more, I have had the pleasure to witness and participate in BPG's training sessions and boot camps. One thing that always stands out is BPG's great ability to strip away preconceived notions/habits and get to the heart of crucial, every day training behaviors that one can apply instantly. Becky Pluth and her capable staff are also not afraid to embrace learning technology and effectively show how to use new tools—with gusto!

—Paul Keller, C3 Softworks

Creative Training: A Train-the-Trainer Field Guide

Credits
Cover Design by Studio 810
Internal Layout by Alan Pranke
Edited by Liz Wheeler with assistance from Sara Davis

Publisher
Creative Training Productions LLC
14530 Martin Drive
Eden Prairie MN 55344

For additional books or quantity discounts, contact:
The Bob Pike Group
Phone: 800-383-9210 and 952-829-1954
Fax: 952-829-0260
Email: info@bobpikegroup.com

Contents

Nice to Know

Appendices

Where to Go

ACKNOWLEDGEMENTS

Being around people is life-giving to me while solitude is not. Thank you to those who traveled with me on writing weekends to help encourage, edit, research and scare away the solitude for me. Because of that, you gave this book life.

Sara Davis, I thank you for being my cheerleader and critic. I have found a kindred spirit in you; everyone should be so lucky. Thank you for those first few words, "I hope your book is research-based enough." They pushed me to read far more neuroscience journals and research more than I might have otherwise. Your prayers are coveted, and once again, I have benefited from having a doctor in the family as you reviewed this manuscript multiple times. I love you.

Liz Wheeler, thank you for standing by me, for being well-read, and for lending your writing ability to this project. Thank you for knowing me so well and using my own stories to fill in the gaps. An editor's job is not an easy one, and you continue to say yes to working with me while knowing the challenges that a "flexible" writer brings to the project. Thanks for laughter when you noticed my dictated content had clearly come out wrong. Darn autocorrect! I love and respect you so much.

Kate Larsen, you are a catalyst in my life. You loved on me from the inception of this book by allowing me to find my words at your cabin, and you gave me valuable neuroscience research highlighted with notes on how it relates to Creative Training Techniques®. You cheered me onto completion when I would drag my feet; I am grateful for your gentle guiding. You are an amazing role model and mentor to me in this field and as a female business owner but even more so in marriage, parenting, and faith.

The Bob Pike Group team and licensees: Rich, Doug, Priscilla, Janice, Adrianne, Scott, Michelle, Erin, Sandi, Becky, Greg, Tom, Vicki, Keith, Jim, Brandon, Mark, Cindy, Karen, Marc, Jason, Anthony, Ayako, Hisham, Zeinab, Ken, Susan, James, and Emily. This book wouldn't be here today without all of your insight and wisdom. Thank you for reviewing chapters, doing edits, challenging my thought process, reminding me of tips I had long since forgotten, finding gaps, believing in the process for decades, sharing content and praising the result. Your input and passion have helped form these methods which set the standard for how training should be and are changing the way people train around the world. This book would not exist if it were not for each of you.

Elaine Biech, Kathy Dempsey, Jim and Naomi Rhode, Sharon Bowman, and my brothers Rob, Andrew, and John Pike for your friendship and encouragement. Thank you for creative ideas from writing to brainstorming book titles. I am richly blessed by each of you.

My father, Bob Pike, began this work nearly four decades ago. Many of the concepts I teach originated with him, and those methods are now backed by neuroscience that didn't exist then. I have had the privilege of working with the "Trainer's Trainer" for twenty years and am grateful to have found what God created me to do in teaching Creative Training Techniques. I took the helm of The Bob Pike Group in 2013 and am thrilled to continue what he began.

Mom, you have always been there for me. As I wrote this book, you provided a place to write, ongoing childcare, encouragement, meals on so many occasions, and late night conversation to give me a much needed "study break." I am so grateful. I love you.

Ken and Margie Blanchard, thank you for allowing my family to know you and learn from you. Thank you for challenging Brad and me in our personal relationships with Christ, in our marriage, in business and even in our physical health. I have learned a great deal about business, life and becoming who God wants me to be by spending time with you. You two are amazing.

Pat Webb, thank you for enjoying a cup of Earl Grey with me that lovely day at Camelback Inn talking about growth strategies and intellectual property. You showed me how powerful it is to be prepared as you presented your research, and I took that and applied it to this book. In the past two years, you have transformed my thinking as a business owner and consultant. In that time, however, the biggest challenge you gave me was to strengthen my CORE starting at home. My family thanks you, and I am blessed to call you friend.

Tom Richards, thank you for saying yes to going on this journey with me as my COO and friend. Thank you for teaching me to be more expressive in storytelling versus just fact-telling. You have already made a big impact as you advance the organization and keep us on track. You have helped me make the complex simple.

To my best friend and husband of fourteen years whom I deeply love and respect, thank you for being consistent in your devotions and praying for us, me, the company, and this book. I admire your thirst for knowledge and dedication to learning. You challenge me to take the time to learn and apply new ideas. I am honored that you have adapted, adopted and applied these methods to teaching golf which demonstrates Creative Training Techniques works in any industry. I am so blessed to be at your side doing life together.

To my Savior and Lord Jesus Christ, who has bestowed on me undeserved grace as I grow into the woman you desire me to be. You are the true CEO of my life and The Bob Pike Group. Thank you for being my safety net; in you I place my trust.

"The LORD lives! Praise to my Rock! May God, the Rock of my salvation, be exalted!"
2 Samuel 22:47 (NLT)

FOREWORD

I'm a big fan of Becky Pluth. Not only is she a fabulous human being, she is also a great trainer and bestselling author. As chairman and chief training officer of The Bob Pike Group, Becky is an expert in Instructor-Led, Participant-Centered (ILPC) training.

In *Creative Training*, Becky illustrates exactly what ILPC is and why it is effective. Training is so much more enjoyable—and memorable—when it is a dialogue, not a monologue. In fact, Becky and I agree that during training, the person who does the most talking does the most learning. This Train-the-Trainer Field Guide walks you through implementing creative training in your workshops with your content as it demonstrates how engaged your learners will be when you involve them rather than lecture them.

Becky takes on the myth that building in interactivity requires more time to design and execute than does traditional, trainer-centered teaching. In fact, using methods in this book, trainers can actually cut their design time in half. Many trainers also find that classroom time is reduced because ILPC training focuses on what learners need to know and provides other resources for the nice-to-know.

Other topics covered in the book include: effective learning retention strategies, methods for increasing participation and interaction while focusing on content, needs assessment and analysis tools, and how to work the room to diminish difficult participants. You will find bonus chapters on creating PowerPoint slides for both classroom and online instruction as well as implementing ILPC in the virtual arena. If that's not enough, Becky includes brief articles (sidebars) from industry leaders like Jennifer Hofmann, Sharon L. Bowman, Neen James, and others.

Need I say more? When you use the interactive learning processes in *Creative Training*, your learners will not only retain more, they will be able to instantly apply what they've learned back at the worksite. Thanks, Becky. You're the best.

Ken Blanchard
Chief Spiritual Officer of The Ken Blanchard Companies
Coauthor, *The New One Minute Manager®* and *Leading at a Higher Level*

INTRODUCTION

I was seated next to my younger brother Rob on a plane en route to Toronto. I was a high schooler on the third plane ride of my life as we joined my dad, Bob Pike, on one of his business trips.

The first night, we visited the Eaton Center, which wowed us with its indoor skating rink, and had dinner at the CN Tower. The next day my dad gave a presentation, and my brother and I watched from the fourth row. Looking back, I have no idea who was in the audience or what the keynote was all about, but I remember that every single person in the audience was hanging on his every word.

As I looked around the room, I saw faces smiling, heads nodding, some people laughing, others intently taking notes. They were completely engaged and ready to learn. When my father was done speaking, the listeners gave him a standing ovation. Many people lined up to talk with him afterward. It was at that moment that I thought my dad was really good at whatever he had just done. I remember wanting to be that good at something someday.

So here we are, more than two decades later. I followed in his footsteps, made a name and career for myself in the training industry, and now provide vision to The Bob Pike Group.

I've had the opportunity to learn from a training industry thought leader and from dozens of men and women who are the best and brightest trainers in the country (many of whom contributed sidebars in the pages to follow). And all the while, I've absolutely loved my work!

Australian productivity expert Neen James once told me how she decides when to say yes and when to say no to work. She said, "I work with people I love, in places I love, doing what I love." This is what I have had the opportunity to do.

Why do I love my work so much? Because the training methods I've learned over the years make training so much more enjoyable. It becomes a dialogue, not a monologue, and the participants learn and retain so much more. That's why I want to share these Creative Training Techniques with you.

These methods also save time and money. How?

- According to the Association for Talent Development research (Kapp 2009), designing one hour of classroom instruction takes between 40 hours on the low-end and 185 hours on the high-end. I will show you how, on average, to cut your design time in half.

- Your learners will be able to retain at least twice as much as before in training.

- Because learners can remember more, they are better able to adapt, adopt and apply the training back on the job. This also results in improved performance and outcomes.

- With less time spent in the training room, learners have more time to be productive in their jobs.

And if that's not enough, the icing on the cake is that less ongoing review of training is necessary when employees learn the content the first time and remember it later, which opens the door to expanded training offerings.

The methods in this book have been developed, refined, and proven to work as a result of over 300 years of combined training experience at The Bob Pike Group. We have tested these methods and principles time and time again and always see the same amazing results. In this book, I break down everything you need to know about Instructor-Led, Participant-Centered training. It is not only an art, it is a science that is repeatable in virtually any training environment.

So now that you know that the methods in these pages could save you hundreds of hours of design and classroom training time, I hope you will invest a few of those hours in reading this book. Once you have grasped what Instructor-Led, Participant-Centered training is about, this book will be a valuable reference later as you design new training that implements these techniques.

Part 1

NEED TO KNOW

Chapter 1

WHAT IS INSTRUCTOR-LED, PARTICIPANT-CENTERED TRAINING?

It was my first day at the local community college. I felt small and somewhat intimidated as I attempted to navigate those hallowed halls of learning. I funneled into the large amphitheatre for my first class, found a seat somewhere in the middle and sat down. As the professor began, we went through the syllabus and discussed the textbooks. Then he started in on a lecture.

Growing up with Bob Pike meant attending workshops where I was involved in learning activities or engaging in conversation with other learners as a way to more fully assimilate the information. So after the first class, when the only active thing I had done was take notes, I was shocked that apparently not everyone believed in making learning more engaging. And once the newness of college wore off, I was really bored.

In today's marketplace, companies are faced with many workforce problems. Three of the biggest? Companies have to contend with employees that lack the right skills, balance training costs against the bottom line or the inefficiency of no training at all, and tackle an increasingly disengaged workforce of employees told to do more with less.

The Instructor-Led, Participant-Centered training model (ILPC) or Creative Training Techniques® addresses these problems by helping employees learn twice as much in half the time. Unlike my typical college experience (and probably yours), this method creates more buy-in and enthusiasm, successfully changes behavior, significantly improves employee engagement, drastically increases skill application back on the job, and ultimately saves time and money.

There is a direct and positive correlation between ILPC methods and learning, retention and application. So, conversely, less ILPC equals less—less of everything companies are generally looking for when they spend money on training their workforce.

This method incorporates social learning and small groups with interactive activities and engagement using methods based on brain science to create a repeatable process. By using ILPC, you can cut your design time in half and know that your training was designed right the first time. And less time is spent in the classroom (or learning environment) as people "catch" what is taught the first time. For 35 years we, at The Bob Pike Group, have been implementing these principles for ourselves and for our clients and benchmarking the results.

Several years ago, an oil company with more than $2.5 billion in net income came to us with unacceptable levels of injury and death on the job. They suffered from a rate of 0.61 injuries per 20,000 hours worked, a rate considered to be unacceptable in the industry. This relatively high rate was attributed to a training curriculum that lacked participant engagement, which led to a less than ideal retention of safety information.

To reduce the number of injuries and deaths on the job, The Bob Pike Group, along with experts from the oil company, designed and developed the Life Critical Skills Training course. Our consultants facilitated results-based design meetings to identify learning objectives and content based on previous knowledge, skills, and abilities of future participants.

To support the learning objectives, we incorporated interactive learning activities.

To facilitate participant engagement, we created a leader guide and participant guides including PowerPoint decks, scripted activities, and support materials.

In redesigning the training curriculum, we also conducted a pilot program and subsequently edited the program to address feedback. To ensure participant engagement in future training, we also delivered train-the-trainer programs to prepare the oil company's instructors to deliver the new course.

The oil company saw an increase of success in their Life Critical Skills Safety Program; participants were much more engaged in training and retained more information. The oil company also noticed a consistent understanding of the procedures across diverse organizations along with high test scores and positive feedback. After working with us, they saw their previously high rate of 0.61 injuries per every 20,000 hours worked drop to their best-ever personal safety record of 0.45 injuries per every 20,000 hours worked.

We also worked with them on several other design projects. For example, we helped them identify and segment "need-to-know" and "nice-to-know" content. "Need-to-know" information was then shared in class while necessary but not mandatory "nice-to-know" information was communicated in other ways outside of the classroom. As a result, courses that were previously running at ten to fourteen days in length were reduced by half, while maintaining the necessary high test scores!

Another client who saw dramatic results by implementing an ILPC training program was an Oklahoma bank with $325 million in assets. The family-owned bank came to The Bob Pike Group with a need for formal teller training to optimize procedures within their business. A lack of consistency, failure to meet customer service objectives, and lack of uniformity plagued the bank and negatively impacted their revenue. The bank estimated it was losing $500,000 each year due to proof errors and other suboptimal procedures.

After analysis, our consultants, using content provided by the bank, created an ILPC training program for them, complete with training manual and job aids. We also utilized our expertise in adult education to train the one-on-one trainers selected by the bank.

After just three months of working with our company and implementing ILPC methods, the bank saw an average of 99.54% proof accuracy bank-wide, which effectively saved the bank a half million dollars a year. In addition, tellers showed more confidence, pride, and understanding in their roles and duties while trainers showed greater efficiency.

These are just two stories out of hundreds of clients who have implemented these dynamic methods and have reaped the benefits. While some might argue that interactive training costs more or takes more time, these examples show that interactive training actually saves money, reduces training time and, in some cases, also saves lives.

Why Train?

The purpose of training is to increase learners' knowledge, build their skills or change their attitudes. This must not be confused with a presentation or facilitation, which are opportunities to inform or have a subject matter expert lead learners through a process. (For more specifics on the role a presenter, trainer or facilitator plays in the workforce, see Appendix B.)

The primary goal of a trainer is to make sure that when the learners leave the room, they are able to apply the information they just acquired. Another way to think about transfer is this: learning has truly occurred when behavior is changed. We, as trainers, foster this crucial transfer by allowing practical application time during our courses, giving learners time to move their new knowledge from working memory into long-term memory. Through skill-building and skill practice, we allow learners a chance to apply content in a safe environment. The more they apply it in class, the more it will stick.

ILPC is sometimes called active learning or creative training, but whatever name it might be given, this method of training and learning has become a way of life for me and is the gold standard in the training industry. These ideas have been taught at every conference *Training* magazine has sponsored since 1980, reaching across the globe to over 50 countries on all six inhabited continents. This method crosses over not just geographic borders but generations, industries, and topics.

The active nature of instructor-led but participant-centered classes helps participants learn more easily and with better content recall because they have applied or interacted with the information.

ILPC works because the learner is involved in the learning process in a variety of ways. Put another way, the learner is doing the work. By placing the learner in the co-pilot's seat, his or her knowledge, comprehension and rate of retention is increased. "Instructor-led" means that the presenter is the "guide on the side, not the sage on the stage." He or she is guiding or facilitating the learning process for the learners, not standing on the stage verbally depositing information into the brain banks of the silent learners. ILPC instructors take a step back and recognize that the instructor is only one piece of the learning puzzle, and that, ultimately, the one doing the talking is the one doing the learning. An instructor-led trainer lectures only when she must, not simply because she can.

There are three different styles of teaching that are most frequently used in a classroom setting: one-way communication, two-way communication and three-way communication.

One-way communication is primarily lecture-based. The instructor is the subject matter expert and shares from knowledge and life experience with others.

Reducing Tension in Two-Way Communication

I'm sure you can think of a teacher or professor who would call on students during the lesson and ask specific questions to see who was paying attention or who had completed the lesson.

Asking impromptu questions directed at one individual is what we call the "mystery call on." It increases anxiety in the learner. Research shows that when anxiety is increased, retention of information in our working memory is decreased (Darke 1988, Owens et al. 2014). Other studies showed heightened anxiety inhibits verbal ability, which is why you may have seen nervous presenters stumbling over words, misspelling words or forgetting facts or statistics.

If you are going to use two-way communication, I recommend finding ways to use instructor-student communication in a positive and reinforcing manner and not for purposes of testing, because if you reduce tension in the classroom, you increase learner retention.

Two-way communication is when an instructor not only talks about content and concepts but also provides opportunities for learners to interact with the instructor. Examples of this style include a presenter asking a question and having the audience respond or a panel discussion. This style can be used in the midst of lecture to engage learners, as long as it's being used as an engagement technique, not as a testing method.

Three-way communication is what ILPC training is all about. It occurs when the instructor uses a mix of presenting time, trainer-and-student interaction, and student-to-student interaction. Having a balance of all three allows for different learning preferences—reflective versus participatory, direct versus indirect, specific versus general—and it provides variety which helps maintain interest in the content.

ILPC trainers do not have to be subject matter experts that know everything about the topic they're training. With ILPC, the trainer needs to know just a little bit more about the topic than the people in the room, and the training will be effective because, with ILPC, the instructor is just one piece of the training puzzle. Learners are gaining, retaining and transferring their knowledge through participant-centered (not speaker-centered) learning. And the learners themselves are responsible for drawing upon previous experience in sharing with the group.

Why Not Lecture?

Because of all of the benefits of active learning, we at The Bob Pike Group, with our more than 300 years of combined experience, discourage lecturing for more than ten minutes without an interaction or an activity. The average learner doesn't learn best just by listening, and lecture alone can cause a listener's mind to wander and disengage. Lecturers typically talk *at* an audience and don't allow learners time to practice and apply what is being learned. Lecture usually also has a focus on theory versus application, which results in lower transfer of skills back on the job.

I was keynoting at Turning Point Technology's Annual Users conference in 2010, where Dr. Eric Mazur, Dean of Applied Physics at Harvard University, was also keynoting. At dinner, we talked about ILPC, and he recalled when he first stumbled upon interactive learning. "I asked the students to talk to one another about a question I had been trying to explain. It was chaos, but within just a couple minutes, my students had figured out what I had just spent a quarter of an hour explaining," he said. Using this discussion method tripled his students' gains as measured by assessments. Dr. Mazur's research shows that, when teaching interactively, both males and females gain more, but women gain disproportionately more although there is not yet definite research on why that is.

I don't want to completely write off lecture, but in an ILPC setting, we have guidelines for its use. Like PowerPoint, lecture can be used appropriately for good, or it can be overused and abused. When done in ten-minute stints or less, lecture can be an effective way to provide background information, knowledge or detail that will help the learner get an overall picture. Examples of when you might use one-way communication in an ILPC setting include telling a story, setting up a scenario, giving a keynote presentation or speech, or when teaching a topic in which safety is of concern or money is at risk.

Bloom's Taxonomy

A person who takes notes during a lecture increases the chances of recalling information exponentially because multiple modalities are being used to learn. If a learner is taking notes *and* organizing them as he goes along, he is processing the information as he writes; because of this, he will find the information easier to recall later. In Benjamin Bloom's taxonomy of learning, which was later revised by Lorin Anderson, a former student of Bloom's, this note-taker is moving from knowledge to comprehension, or put another way, is moving from remembering to understanding (Bloom et al. 1956, Anderson et al. 2001). This transition requires higher order cognition.

ILPC training encourages this deeper level of cognition. In a lecture, the instructor is hoping or assuming that intrinsically motivated students will engage with the information on their own. But an ILPC instructor takes the time to link known information with new content. When she groups or "chunks" the content in an organized way, she is helping learners compartmentalize the information, one step in moving from knowledge to comprehension. This process can be accomplished in a lecture format. However, when a trainer immediately allows learners to interact and do something with the information instead of only listening, she is allowing learners to use higher cognition processes that move that information into long-term recall. Put simply, a kind of "muscle memory" is gained by immediately engaging with the information.

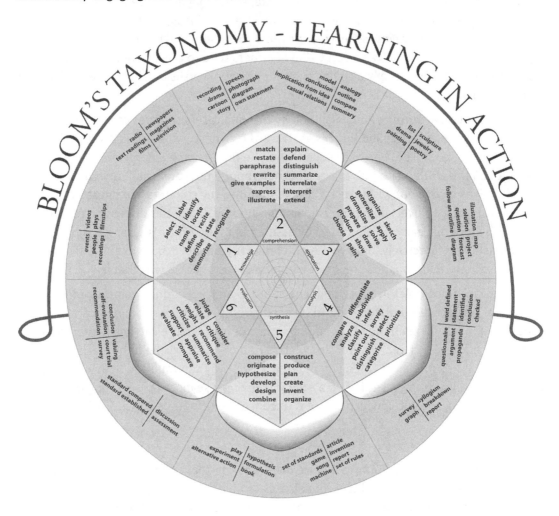

A full-color version of this Bloom's Taxonomy by John M. Kennedy T. can be viewed at http://bit.ly/26og9S9.

It is like a file folder system on a computer. You have the main folder labeled ILPC; once you click to open the main folder, sub-folders like "Working Memory," "Active Learning," and "Laws of Learning," appear. The more clicks it takes to get to the information, the more your memory has to work to recall the information. But if we can help learners organize and store the information in the working memory better, it becomes far easier to access those file folders later. That's the overall job and purpose of ILPC training: *making it easier and quicker for learners to retrieve file folders in the brain so the information can be applied back on the job and accomplish what we call training transfer.*

Something for Everyone

In this fast-paced, high activity form of training, we certainly recognize that there are some personalities that will prefer to work on their own—and a well-designed ILPC course takes those personalities into account. For example, every exercise or activity does *not* need to involve the entire group. Individual exercises also work well in breaking up chunks of lecture. In the chapters to follow, I will list individual, partner, and group activities that serve as openers, closers, revisiters, and energizers that are all designed to break preoccupation, engage participants, increase and lock in learning, always with the goal of boosting retention and transfer of learning back on the job.

While this book is static, the ideas are dynamic, allowing you to adapt each to your different topics, industries or platforms. My hope is that the ideas, methods and research in this book challenge, grow and empower you as a trainer. We cannot do "business as usual" as trainers. We have to be perpetually growing in our craft to better meet the needs of an ever-changing workforce. Otherwise, we may find ourselves, as John Peatling says, "the well-meaning antiquarians of the day after tomorrow (Peatling 1983)."

If this is your first introduction to active learning, I encourage you to read this book through to understand the art, science, and execution of Instructor-Led, Participant-Centered training. If you already have a firm foundation for implementing ILPC methods into your training, feel free to read the chapters with the most relevant information for your current challenge.

Chapter 2

THE FUNDAMENTALS OF ILPC

Why does ILPC work? What is it about this method that shortens training time while still increasing retention and training transfer back to the job?

Over the course of the next few chapters, we will look at the learning FUNdamentals, theories, and laws we use as a framework for our Instructor-Led, Participant-Centered content. These tenets are what allow us to increase retention while decreasing time in the classroom. In this chapter, we will look at our FUNdamentals which are based on behaviors we have observed, testing metrics and brain science. While these FUNdamentals have been implemented in all of The Bob Pike Group programs for over three decades, it's exciting to better understand why these work with positron emission tomography (PET), functional magnetic resonance imaging (fMRI), and other technological advances now available to us!

FUNdamental One. Doing=Learning. Action Planning=Retention.

The person that is doing, practicing and applying content and information is the one that is learning the most. And the brain that is doing the talking is doing the learning, so it is time that we get our learners' brains talking and processing information. Today, Tiger Woods remains the most famous athlete, followed by Peyton Manning. What makes them so good at their sports? Focused practice. Research on the top athletes, musicians and chess players finds they require a minimum of ten years of practice to reach their peak performance (Ericcson 2006)! It obviously requires more than just practice to be Woods or Manning, but practice is a big part of what takes them from being a possibility to reaching their potential.

"Practice" in the training classroom can be a specific assignment, responding to a question, a reflection with written response. Practice requires the learner to do something. Focused practice allows the learner to get feedback on the assignment and make changes to improve. The amount of practice in the classroom is dependent on what other tools are available for further learning, like job aids. And if money or safety are at stake, increase the amount of practice.

Then be sure to set aside time for learners to create an action plan for what content they are going to apply first back on the job to increase the probability of them using the information. Action planning is usually done on specific blank planning pages in a student workbook; at The Bob Pike Group, we also use a "Concepts to Capture" or an "Adapt, Adopt Apply" chart in several of our courses where learners can post their top take-aways and ideas they plan to use right away. Then we have participants read what others have posted and "steal shamelessly" any ideas they think they could use. It's a powerful way to learn and requires the learner to think critically about the information and how they can use it.

Learning Styles Versus Learning Preferences

For years, books and workshops promoted the importance of training while using a learner's learning style whether that be visual, auditory or kinesthetic. In the last few years, however, it seems that mindset has drastically changed and training Twitter feeds are filled with vitriol for trainers who still use the idea that there are indeed learning styles and that teaching to those styles increases retention.

So which is it? And how can we come to such completely warring conclusions?

When I graduated from college, I began working as a substitute teacher, then taught night school at an alternative high school and attended graduate school full-time. My whole world was filled with educational theories, models, and best practices. I learned how our brains work in class, and I learned more by practicing learning theories each day with my students. For every single theory, I found an equally interesting and compelling opposite. So where was the truth?

In Ruth Colvin Clark's *Evidence-Based Training Methods,* she said sometimes researchers look for information to prove their theories, while others find different results that lead to new conclusions. For example, in the 1930s and 40s, smoking was becoming quite prevalent and even a majority of doctors were smokers. Cigarette companies started using images of doctors in their print advertising saying more doctors smoked their brand. Some doctors were even endorsing smoking for their patients to clear up coughs and sore throats! Now you will find studies showing smoking's direct correlation to cancer and other diseases in addition to what is estimated at $92 billion worth of lost productivity annually.

In 2014, Paul Howard-Jones, a professor of neuroscience and education at Bristol University, wrote that this particular learning styles "neuromyth" came as the result of misunderstanding, misreading or misquoting scientifically established facts (2014).

The idea of learning styles has been around for decades. In 1955, Joseph Left and Harry Ingram created the four panes of the Johari Window, a model designed to map out personality awareness: known, hidden, blind, and unknown. In the early 1980s, Howard Gardner theorized the concept of Multiple Intelligences, the idea that each person learns, remembers, performs and understands best through one of eight modalities: logical/mathematical, verbal/linguistic, visual/spatial, bodily/kinesthetic, music/rhythmic, interpersonal, intrapersonal, and naturalistic. However, neither of these methods, despite some testing, has proved to increase retention or the ability to learn.

For years, books and workshops promoted the importance of training while using a learner's learning style whether that be visual, auditory or kinesthetic. In the last few years, however, it seems that mindset has drastically changed and training Twitter feeds are filled with vitriol for trainers who still use the idea that there are indeed learning styles and that The conclusion I have come to is that a learning style is more of a learning preference and doesn't have much, if any, impact on learning retention. [I am discussing only learning styles here, not the benefits of interactive learning.] So why bother with multi-sensory experiences if just lecture will do?

1. Because the learners will enjoy the training more.

Over the course of the last decade, we at The Bob Pike Group have used a personal learning inventory to help identify people's preferred style of learning: reflective or participative. Our research show that over seventy percent of people profiled prefer participative learning where they engage in the process versus just listening to lecture. Even if some adults cannot tell you their "learning style," they do know whether they like working alone or in groups. They know if they like to read with music on or in silence. Because people come to training with so many different preferences and personalities, a multisensory experience helps everyone feel more at home and increases the enjoyment of the training for both learner and trainer. As a very tiny bonus, while individuals can effectively learn through any of the three modalities, there is supporting research that concludes that learning in your preferred style slightly increases educational outcomes (Kratzig and Arbuthnott 2006).

2. Because you, as the trainer, will enjoy it more.

Building in activities that provide for visual, auditory and kinesthetic learners is being interactive, which is the foundation of Instructor-Led, Participant-Centered training. I have found that a one-hour keynote, where three-way communication is limited, is way more exhausting than eight hours in the training room. Even a class that I have taught perhaps a hundred times can still be very novel to me as the participants in the classroom add their voices, their stories, their experiences to the material, thereby giving the content new life. And adding in that interaction among participants, which plays to these different learning preferences, gives me an opportunity to listen in on their learning and thought processes, take note of especially good ideas to have them share with the large group, or get the next module prepped for a seemingly seamless transition.

3. You'll make connections with your learners faster.

4. You'll get better workshop evaluations.

Trainers that allow for interactivity and engagement receive higher evaluation scores as do trainers that are friendly and personable. While participant evaluation scores do not necessarily tie to stronger retention, they do suggest that the participant was more open to learning and more engaged in the process (Sitzmann et al. 2008).

When we allow learners in our classrooms to write, speak, demonstrate or practice new content or skills, we use the brain's neuroplasticity, or its ability to change, to improve the odds that this information will get used once class is over. And when they action plan and commit to using the content, the probability they will do just that is increased significantly.

FUNdamental Two. People don't argue with their own data.

Tap into your learners' prior experience and expertise in the classroom as a natural springboard for faster buy-in to your content. Drawing on the participants' knowledge not only honors their experience but taps into their beliefs.

Let's say I am teaching on characteristics of a coach, and I have a list of fifteen attributes. I might choose to have small groups brainstorm on their personal whiteboards the most effective coaches they have known and the characteristics that made them effective. Groups usually come up with twelve out of the fifteen. I then fill in the knowledge gaps, but now I am only lecturing on a few characteristics instead of all fifteen! And persuading a group to believe the small portion of content I am providing is a lot easier than getting buy-in for every one of the traits.

By having the participants share, I am allowing them to critically think about past coaches and analyze what made that person a great coach. This requires higher-order cognition or more cognitive processing than just absorbing and listening to the information.

FUNdamental Three. People retain more when they have fun, have the power to choose and have a sense of belonging (Glasser 1998).

When I was in training and development for a large U.S.-based retail company, I used ILPC methods. Shortly after one class I taught, I was called into the vice president's office and asked what had been going on. While I was training, another executive had heard the class laughing and "being loud" and went to the VP stating that learning should be happening in our classes.

The truth is that when the fun is eliminated from the classroom, a portion of learning is also eliminated. When I say fun, I don't mean joke-telling or games for their own sake; everything needs to have a purpose. When I say fun, I'm talking about enjoying the process of being involved in the learning and being with others which then creates a powerful, positive energy and classroom environment which makes learning quicker, better, and easier. When participants are engaged in the learning, it increases internal motivation for learning, which in turn reduces stress and anxiety and learning flows through the affective filter allowing for the "Aha" moments to be developed (Krashen 1982). These Aha moments come from learners making their own connections and discovering the learning for themselves, not from an amazing lecture (Kohn 2004). (Neuroimaging through PET and fMRI indicate activity levels in the brain and make it possible for us to study the brain without first being dead! We are able to actually "see" when a person is about to have an "Aha" moment.)

FUNdamental Four. People have different learning preferences.

Over the years, I have been exposed to a myriad of learning theories, styles, and approaches. Some talk about dominant style or the nine multiple intelligences. Some follow behavior theorist Howard Gardner and his buckets of multiple intelligences, and others a neurosurgeon, George Ojemann, who has done electrical stimulation mapping and has studied over 100 brains and written over 300 research papers. He thinks there may be millions or billions of intelligences (Ojemann et al. 1989).

I believe Ojemann's research, which indicates no two brains are wired the same. Brains are not identical, but we all have preferences, and we all have ways in which we prefer to learn. As trainers, it is vital to understand preferences to create learning experiences that are engaging for the masses.

Over the last two decades, we have had tens of thousands of our participants, who are usually teachers or trainers, participate in a Personal Learning Insights Profile®. We found that Learning Purpose, Learning Structure and Learning Activity preferences for our clients fall into the descriptions below no matter what industry sector they were in or continent they were on. Based on this data, we are able to create train-the-trainer courses that meet individualized needs and can adapt to needs in the moment.

LEARNING PREFERENCES CONTINUUM

Name of Participant: _____

Informative Learner ◄─────────────────────────────► **Practical Learner**

Give informative learners a lot of additional "nice to know" information, such as extra examples or more reading material.

Give practical learners just the "need to know" information that will help them learn the specific content you are teaching.

Specific Learner ◄─────────────────────────────► **General Learner**

Create a lot of structure for specific learners. Let them know your agenda and objectives, give them specific time frames for the class, and give them a sense of the flow of information and exercises.

Give general learners a global overview of what you will be covering, but allow them the opportunity to structure the information in such a way that works for them.

Reflective Learner ◄─────────────────────────────► **Participative Learner**

Allow reflective learners time to study and learn on their own when appropriate. Let them read and reflect on the material, and then you can answer questions they might have.

With participative learners, have a lot of discussions and activities to keep them engaged.

Used with permission from SCORE: For One-on-One Training, volume 6.

Learning purpose is why you want to learn. If you are like me, you are practical in nature and learn just in time to use the information. For this book, I have been reading a lot of journal articles, all of which are directly related to how the brain works and how we learn. I want to be able to apply what I have learned and prefer not to be tested.

Or you may be like Bob Pike or my husband Brad who are both interested in learning any type of new information even if there is no immediate application. If it looks interesting or informative, they will listen to, watch or read it. On social media, they have taken every type of Test Your Knowledge quiz so they can measure what they know.

Our data consistently shows that the distribution of practical versus informative learners is a bell curve with a majority of trainers falling in the middle with a good appreciation for both practical *and* informative. Neither Bob nor I fall into the center of the bell curve; we are outliers.

Learning structure is how information is organized. It is either specific and step-by-step or flexible and more general in nature. I fall into the general category and prefer to have an overview of what will happen. I'm also flexible in that I don't mind if we jump around in a workbook as long as the information is useful.

In a training course, it works well to give me time to do my own thing and solve the problem without a bunch of directions. Trial-and-error gives me a chance to test my ideas out versus relying on solutions and strategies others have developed. Several of the other Bob Pike Group trainers fall on the specific side, which is great for balancing out our training team.

Specific structure means having clearly defined objectives and clear directions. I can usually tell whether my learners are specific or general after the first activity. I call them The Quick and The Analytical. The "quick" (general structure) begin creating and implementing or designing before I have finished the instructions while the "analytical" (specific structure) are looking at the "quick" and thinking, "Wait, she isn't done giving all the instructions!"

Specific learners like to hear and see a demonstration, samples of the task, or an example of what their project should look like. Our data consistently shows that the distribution of specific versus general is a fifty-fifty split. I am also an outlier here so it is especially important for me to remember to give clear directions, have an agenda for each day and consistently give an example of what I am looking for.

Learning activity is how actively engaged a learner prefers to be in the learning process. It does not correlate with whether you are an extrovert or introvert. It is purely an engagement preference. Some prefer to actively participate (participative) while others enjoy taking in the information and taking time to ruminate and ponder (reflective). As a participative learner, I love being able to think out loud and brainstorm ideas with others. It helps me to think through problems, strategies, and issues while better understanding the concepts being taught. Working in a group provides me with immediate feedback and suggestions which can help give me direction and focus. I also like anything hands on.

Making the Link Between Activities and Your Content

by Janice Horne

Have you ever participated in an activity in a training that left you wondering, "What did we do that for?" Here are six things to keep in mind when planning your activity so it effectively bolsters your point.

To keep on task and your audience engaged, every activity must have an intended purpose. While some activities point to the new learning, others may have learners revisiting with prior content. Perhaps the activity is merely designed to get participants comfortable with each other. Whatever your intent, never do an activity just because you want interaction

When considering which activity, run it through twin filters of time and budget. Sometimes one activity may make our point perfectly, but it takes too long. Search for an activity that would make the same point in less time or adapt the activity so it takes less time.

Consider your audience. Engineers aren't too big on coming up with a skit, whereas sales reps don't get too excited about brain teaser puzzles. So plan your activity with your audience in mind.

And plan it to involve all of your participants. Any time you don't have the whole class actively doing something, you may lose their interest and their attention.

Keep the focus of the activity on the learning, not the activity itself. The activity should always add value to the training.

Verbalize the link between the activity and your content or message. Then participants won't have to wonder what the connection is. You want your participants walking away remembering the exact point that you wanted to make with the activity .

Janice Horne is a master participant-centered trainer at The Bob Pike Group and helps businesses and organizations improve results through the training function by focusing on training design and delivery.

Don't talk about an experiment. Let's DO the experiment. Bring on the practical application, study groups, or games that teach.

Meanwhile, we also have reflective learners in the classroom who prefer to study independently, read a book or other written materials, and work on their own projects. They often enjoy lectures over hands-on activities and are more likely to recall information they have had time to think about. Neither of these is better than the other; it's merely a preference.

Our research shows that there is a 75/25 split with seventy-five percent of those surveyed landing on the participative side. Remember, if you have ten participants, seven may like the games and activities, but there are three that also need time for reflection and digestion of material through reading, self-study or the like. Build in exercises that fall into both styles.

Recognizing that people have preferences for how they want to learn, how information is structured and how they like to be involved helps us remember that all people learn differently, and we need to use a variety of methods and activities to meet their varied needs.

FUNdamental Five. The brain doing the talking is the brain doing the learning.

When learning new content, you can more quickly synthesize it by expressing it in your own words. The more thoroughly you can verbally explain the way your new learning relates to your prior knowledge, the stronger your grasp of the new learning will be. This process of elaboration, or giving new material meaning by expressing it, strengthens new messages for a learner (Brown et al. 2014). You may have heard this concept called linking, when we connected new ideas to concepts we already knew.

How might this look in the classroom? When it comes to reviewing content, don't be the trainer who says, "Let me summarize," and then regurgitates what she just said. If the trainer is doing the talking, then it's the trainer doing the most effective learning. Instead, encourage your learners to revisit the material. A revisit is when the learner is the one expressing what he heard and learned and is recalling and making links and connections for himself. [See the chapter on Revisiting for activity ideas on how to continuously revisit content in a variety of ways.]

Let's look at the brain doing the talking in action. At The Bob Pike Group, we were working with a Women to Work Program in Florida, which equips women with new skills to increase their employability. At the same time, a local fiberglass boat company was having a hard time retaining employees after training. The work was redundant and done outside under tarps in the sun and humidity. When we learned they had a need, we asked if they would be open to hiring women in a male-dominated industry. Although wary, they were receptive to the idea because their average employee was only retained for thirty days after training.

The women we trained had never built fiberglass boats. Matter of fact, many had never even been on one! But they had other experiences to which we could link the boat-building information.

We used cake baking as a metaphor for boat building to link knowledge and make it easier for the women to verbally compare and contrast the two. For example, in both baking and boat building, there are wet and dry ingredients. They need to be measured and added at the right time. In contrast, though, while a cake needs to cool before it gets frosted, a fiberglass boat needs to be buffed out quickly before it dries. And while there was redundancy in both activities, there also was artistry and a sense of pride in the completion.

Along the way, the women verbalized the content regularly through activities like pair shares and peer teaching and demonstrations to make sense of it and create meaning for themselves. The concept was incredibly simple, and it worked. The women were hired and stayed on the job 120 percent longer.

Chapter 3

THE LAWS OF LEARNING

When learning something new, it's helpful to have the experience, then an awareness of what you just went through, and then the theory. Knowing the theory behind why you did something will help you adapt, adopt and apply the knowledge from the experience to other projects.

So in the last chapter, we began tackling the "why" behind Creative Training by examining the FUNdamentals of Instructor-Led, Participant-Centered training. Now, let's look at some basic learning laws established by research that need to be followed for any training to be effective. We'll also look at how you can follow those rules in an ILPC classroom.

Learning Law #1—Readiness

People learn best when all other basic needs have been met such as rest and food, and extreme mental or emotional distress is not present (Thorndike 1911). Glasser supports this as survival, the concept that in order for learning to take place all basic needs must be met. Glasser defines basic needs as food, clothing, shelter, breathing, personal safety, and security.

Part of readiness is also being motivated to learn. Motivation affects how well we are able to comprehend material (or how hard we are willing to try). It can also enhance performance (Ormrod 2008). The phrase "What's In It For Me?" (WIIFM) stems from this. Just as you want to understand the "why" behind creative and interactive training, participants must understand the why behind the training in which they are participating and be given time to buy into the value of the training.

To help bolster this motivation, give participants a strong purpose, a clear objective, and a definite reason for learning something; this helps learners prepare mentally, and they make more progress than they would otherwise. Take the time to design strong objectives (I give some guidance on writing these in the chapter on Needs Assessment and Analysis) and a clear agenda, and then share the structure with the class. Half the class may not care about structure, but the other half does, and this helps create meaning for those learners. When students are ready to learn, they meet the instructor at least halfway, simplifying the instructor's job.

A focus on the content also helps with readiness. One element of really comprehending and digesting the content is the need for participants to be tuned in and paying full attention. Psychologists Mitchell, Dodson and Schacter (2005) found that the original "encoding" of information matters. Giving your full attention when learning something for the first time makes a difference. We don't want our learners walking away misremembering information and later recalling it inaccurately because we didn't create an environment where focused attention to learning could happen.

To help gain the focus of learners, break preoccupation early on with a relevant opener so the learners begin to focus on the learning and what value it holds for them. By focusing their minds on the learning, you increase their interest in the content, and they are less likely to become a difficult participant for you later.

To help create interest and buy-in and overcome some of the distractions, take one or more of these steps to engage learners and get them ready for learning:

- Allow learners time at the beginning of the workshop to flip through the workbook and flag content in which they are interested in learning more.
- Give them time to write out goals they want to accomplish by the end of the workshop.
- Allow participants to use their own content for project work.
- Use an opener to break preoccupation (outside concerns fade away).
- Create exercises from relevant, need-to-know content instead of inserting a game for the sake of a game. If you need templates for activities that use your content, purchase any of the *SCORE for Training* books.

Learning Law #2—Exercise

As the presenter, it is my job to repeat important information at appropriate intervals. Psychologist Edward Thorndike's law of exercise states that ideas often repeated are best remembered. Instead of the fire hose approach of sharing all about a topic at one time, I attempt to be more like a sprinkler and provide bits and pieces throughout a training. The law of exercise also focuses on allowing participants to practice and process the information they are learning. The chapter on revisiters provides many examples of what can be done to reinforce learning without repeating yourself. Get your learners doing the talking and practicing what they have learned.

Learning Law #3—Effect

The law of effect was first put into words by Thorndike who said that positive reactions to certain scenarios increased the likelihood that that specific behavior would be repeated when the same scenario was presented.

This ties into our learners' motivation. When the process of learning or the outcomes of the learning is pleasant, then motivation to continue learning or repeat that behavior is increased. This could be as simple as positive reinforcement by the trainer or the learner's manager, or a feeling of satisfaction when the learner has demonstrated the ability to complete a new task.

On the flip side, negative reinforcement can also decrease the learner's desire or motivation to learn; it is to the trainer's benefit to help the learner see evidence of progress and have real successes along the way. Let learners know that success is achievable and expected.

To set up a positive learning environment:

- Use praise, encouragement and approval often.
- Have participants thank one another for working together or sharing by giving high fives, a hand shake or a knuckle bump.
- Reduce tension to increase retention.
- Think of the spirit of the law versus the letter of the law and show grace when learners are late or make mistakes.
- Chunk content into manageable pieces for learning successes.
- Create curiosity. Use humor and imagination, and allow for participants to take calculated risks.
- Honor their experience. At The Bob Pike Group, we do this by asking participants to write their number of years of experience on their name tags. We then explain to the class that we will learn not only from the facilitator and the content, but also from one another.
- Encourage linking content to something they already know or can do to make it easier, such as connecting words with pictures and ideas with music and so on.

Learning Law #4—Primacy

What happens first often creates a strong impression. The information with which you start your session is far more memorable than what you cover in the middle of the presentation (see chapter on Seven Ways We Remember Anything). That is one reason we create a lot of beginnings and endings during ILPC trainings—as a way to create more "primacy" moments to help learners retain content. Start your session with a relevant opener for retention instead of opening with housekeeping details or something off topic.

Learning Law #5—Recency

If you have just met five people, you are more likely to best remember the first person you met (primacy) and the last person you met (recency). The principle of primacy states that things learned first are second-best remembered while things learned most recently are remembered best. Capitalize on those endings—those times before breaks or at the end of the day—to cover key information that needs to be remembered. Don't close with an evaluation.

Learning Law #6—Intensity

Intensity is the idea that the more dramatic and the more closely tied to a real situation, the more memorable the learning is to a student. Examples and sample problems practiced in the class that are similar to what would be encountered back on the job are far more memorable than something more distantly related to the actual job. For example, a trainee's job is to repair iPhones, and in class they learn how to repair similar or identical Apple products to maximize the learning. We also call that near transfer. If an iPhone repairman is in a class on fixing Samsung products, the intensity will be limited as the direct correlation and application is reduced for the learner. This is an example of far transfer where what you are learning is somewhat different than what will actually be done back on the job. In the case of far transfer, the trainee is required to critically think about the process and apply it back to the job. Far transfer in general is more successful with topics like communication, sales training or general leadership training where the same skills can be used in diverse situations.

Learning Law #7—Freedom

The law of freedom states that learners learn best when they are allowed to choose what to learn (Glasser 1998, Weibell 2011). When a topic is forced upon a learner, a wall goes up; the pre-frontal cortex of the brain shuts down and so does the willingness to learn (Arnsten 2009, McEwen and Morrison 2013). The more choices a learner is offered, the greater the learning. The Bob Pike Group's Social Element of Learning states that a sense of control along with a feeling of inclusion by the learner brings about an openness to participate and take risks. As an equation, it looks like this:

Control (Choices) + Included = Open to Participate/Learn/Take Risks

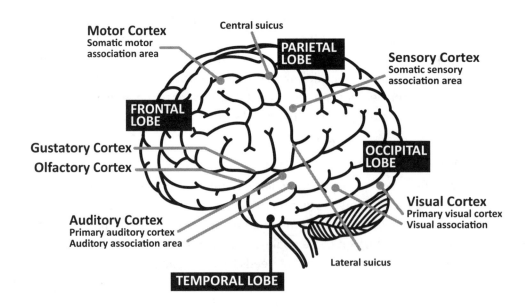

To weave freedom into the classroom, have learners:

- Vote on the topics they want to spend the most time covering
- Choose their own learning goals
- Select a learning partner instead of assigning them one
- Create their own content that is relevant to their job by using job-specific simulations versus scenarios that are from another industry

Give learners choices all throughout the day. These could be small choices such as where they sit or bigger choices such as what task they want to work on. There are hundreds of choices that can be made each day in a session; allow learners to make as many of them for themselves as possible.

Learning Law #8—Application

In adult learning, application requires a participant to put something into operation. It means that things that are most often repeated are best remembered. Throughout an ILPC class, there is time to apply what is being taught. It is all about taking the knowledge, comprehending it, *and* doing something with that information to move it from short-term memory into working memory and on to long-term memory. This goes beyond just practicing the skill or using the knowledge in class; it's actively working to apply the concepts back on the job. Participants should leave class with the confidence that they can do or accomplish something with their new knowledge.

To ensure learners have this confidence, have:

- Participants create projects in class that are relevant and apply the skills to their job
- Learners take an active role in role-play scenarios
- Learners practice skills in class
- Simulation experiences

Chapter 4

SPACING AS A RETENTION TOOL

Motivation and application help your learners remember better what they have learned. "Spacing," or reviewing information at spaced intervals, is another way to improve content retention.

As I reflect on all my years of school, I consider the methods I used to memorize and learn in preparation for tests or to transfer the information to life in some way. It didn't matter the content: math facts to history dates to scripture verses. Some of the standard ways I used to recall information were writing it out on paper, creating flash cards, singing it in a song, using an alliteration or mnemonic device, creating cheat sheets, rote memory, color coding, mind mapping, group study (a favorite but not as productive!), and simply by watching something being done or modeled. One method I didn't practice very often was spacing the learning and spreading the studying out over time, a significant element in learning retention.

Spacing out training to increase learning retention

Spacing is the idea that learning occurs over time. There are two ways to space. The first is by changing the context and reactivating an idea after more time has passed. Usually, this is a day or more after the initial learning. It affirms what many of your high school instructors probably encouraged you to do: review your notes every night, don't just wait for the night before the test. Looking over the information periodically helps your brain better grasp and file the data, whereas cramming doesn't help you retain the information in the long run.

In one study, seventy-two percent of the students felt they learned more when cramming. However, in actuality, only ten percent did equally well or better with cramming versus ninety percent who did better with spaced review (Kornell 2009).

Multiple studies show that cramming is actually associated with low achievement (Hartwig and Dunlosky 2012). Yes, cramming can be effective if the goal is for high scores on a test but not so for long-term use and true learning. When learners can percolate on a concept over time and then build on the concept at a later point, the learning bonds, and there is stronger connection and attachment. In our jobs, it is more common that the knowledge needs to be transferred back to our work and used over time, thus spacing out the learning is far more effective for the kind of end results we want as trainers.

The second method of spacing is during rest (Bell et al. 2013). What is happening during rest between learning segments can actually strengthen the learning and contribute to making the memory last. Sleep helps our minds forget the minutiae and irrelevant information while relevant information is stored and moved into long-term memory (Bennion et al. 2013). It goes along with the idea of letting an idea "bake" for awhile.

A study published in *Applied Cognitive Psychology* separated learners into two groups (Rohrer and Taylor 2006). One group did their studying all at once while the other spaced the studying into two sessions a week apart. Both groups scored in the seventy percent range a week after the studying was complete. However, one month later, the two groups were tested on the same information again. The participants that had spaced out their study had retained a significant portion of knowledge with scores at sixty-four percent while the other group scored about half of that!

If spacing training out isn't possible, create touch points after the class to extend the learning. Using a product like Mindsetter® or TrainBy Cell allows you to program content that can be digested over a period of time and can be used as a follow-on to your course. Or have managers meet with the participant after the course to review key concepts and content.

What should spacing look like in our training sessions? It is best to create learning that is scheduled with time in-between. For example, instead of one six-hour class day, it would be better to allow sleep in-between the modules. Teaching three hours one week and then three hours a week later is better. This is especially true for complex content. Memories grow over time; therefore, time needs to go by in order for new neurons, the brain cells that carry information, to be made.

Building Space into Class

There are three generally recognized types of memory. The first is immediate memory, or sensory, which includes sight, sound and touch. It is what grabs our attention. Working memory takes the immediate memories and begins using them to make calculations. These memories can last from thirty seconds to a few days. Finally, there is long-term memory. Long-term memory is created when the concepts learned during the class are consolidated and enhanced with sleep. These memories can last up to decades.

For example, I am writing this chapter while staying at a bed and breakfast in Iowa. When I arrived, I met the innkeeper; this was the immediate memory. When this memory moves into my working memory, certain details are lost such as background noise, weather, people that may have been in the room, what book she was holding. The loss of these unimportant details helps make my working memory more efficient.

To increase long-term retention in our classes, spacing should be built into your design. When I was getting my master's degree, one of the activities we would do in class was five minutes of meta-cognition. It is a fancy way of saying "reflection time." We would allow our brains to slow down and process information following the What, So What, Now What method. As a trainer, I have used this model and have further refined it by asking specific questions to help structure the process for my participants and produce better results. For each of the questions shown in the graph heading, there are other questions learners answer to help further process the learning.

Reflection	What?	So What?	Now What?
Description	Learners describe the experience.	Learners describe the difference that it made.	Learners describe how this applies to their job for the future.
Possible Questions	• What happened? What did you observe? • Why does the structure and hierarchy exist? • What is your initial reaction?	• Did you learn a new skill or clarify an interest? • How is your experience different from what you expected? • What did you like/dislike about the experience? • What did you learn about the other learners? • How did the experience relate to your job?	• What else is currently happening to address the issue? • How does this impact other departments in the organization? • What learning occurred for you in this experience? • How can you apply this learning?

What? Learners describe the experience. This is the shortest of the reflection elements. I usually spend just thirty seconds answering a couple of questions about what really happened in the exercise, experiment, practice time, etc. These questions are usually extrospective. This could include the conditions or environment in which the learning took place and a brief description of what was done.

So What? Questions should take learners into introspective thoughts on how the learning was important. If you want the learner to get into a level of higher order thinking, ask questions that begin with "how."

Now What? This is all about what is going to be done with the new information and what impact it will have. This requires analyzing, synthesizing and evaluating the experience which is much harder than just talking about what was done or what happened. Allow the most amount of time to be spent on these questions. Additional questions you can use to help get learners started could be:

What learning occurred for you in this experience? How will follow-up be done to address issues and concerns? If you could do the experience again, what would you do differently?

If time outside of class is restricted, but you still want to use spacing as a retention strategy, which is highly recommended, try adding elearning into the mix. Perhaps a training module or two is done asynchronously within a certain time frame. You could also add in a couple of short webinars or podcasts to revisit key points of content. Tapping into the power of social media (see chapter on Using Social Media in Training for ideas) can extend the learning. You can also use mindsetter.com, an easy tool that allows you to send automated learning prompts that can trigger self-reflection and increase learning retention at your pre-determined intervals. Of course, the learner needs to actually click the link to benefit, but if you have laid the groundwork and shared what is in it for them and the reasons behind the spaced learning, the number of those clicking the link, doing the work and retaining the information will be significantly higher.

4 More Ways to Study Smart
They are NOT What You Think!

By Sharon L. Bowman

Go the extra mile with your training participants. Besides reminding them to review what they've just learned from your class or training, give them a study aid to take with them. Later, when they have time to look over the training content, they will have a few extra "Study Smart" tricks up their sleeves to help them review and remember information longer.

1. **Drink a lot of water.** Why? Because dehydration sneaks up on you. You might say, "Oh, I'm not thirsty right now." Or, "But I've been drinking coffee/tea/sodas all day." Substances with caffeine are diuretics—they actually make your body shed water. In addition, two of the most common symptoms of dehydration are sleepiness and headaches, not feeling thirsty. To use this strategy: Have a large bottle or glass of water handy and take regular sips while you're studying. That will help keep your brain awake and alert.

2. **Take a short catnap.** Why? Because medical research indicates that a short nap (about ten to twenty minutes) improves the brain's short-term alertness. Even a five–minute rest inserted into a study hour can have a positive effect on the brain's ability to stay awake and focused. **To use this strategy:** If possible, stretch out flat on your back, with your legs resting on a footstool, pillows, or some other source of elevation. That way you take all the pressure off your back and surrounding muscles. Put a small pillow or rolled towel underneath your neck to support your head. Then, take a few deep, slow breaths to begin your short catnap. Your body and brain will feel refreshed and alert afterwards.

3. **Use body parts to boost your memory.** Anchoring—a neurolinguistic memory tool—simply means touching a part of your body (example: your shoulder) while reciting a specific thing you want to remember. Do this at least six times over the course of a couple of hours. The repetition of information while touching the chosen body part will help move the information into long-term memory. **To use this strategy:** Assign the most important concepts you're learning (say, six of them) to six body parts (knee, hip, waist, shoulder, elbow, top of head). Recite each item as you touch the body part to which it is assigned. Then repeat this procedure intermittently during the study time or day. Over time, you will remember the information with ease.

4. **Explain it to someone.** When you explain the information you're studying to someone else, your brain will have processed the information three times:

1. When you first heard or read the information

2. When you thought about how to explain it in your own words, and

3. When you actually verbalized it.

To use this strategy: Tell a family member, friend, your cat, dog, or an imaginary person what you're learning about. It's that simple.

Sharon Bowman is author of Using Brain Science to Make Training Stick *and* Training from the BACK of the Room!

Chapter 5

Seven Ways We Remember Anything

When I tell you to, close your eyes and imagine a blank black screen and on that screen an apple. Once you have that in your mind's eye, you can open your eyes and continue reading. Don't read to the bottom until you have done the assignment first! So go ahead, and close your eyes, and imagine the blank black screen and an apple.

Did you imagine the letters A-P-P-L-E? Or did you picture an apple?

Most people see an actual apple. Was your apple black or was it in color? Most people see a red or yellow apple.

This illustrates that our brains think in color and in pictures. So as we go through the seven ways we remember anything, let me introduce you to another useful tool to help you remember: the window pane.

In each pane, there is an image and a key word that helps trigger the concept represented in the image. Note it is a representation of a concept, not a duplication. The pictures should be easily reproducible so that learners can draw the icons or images and recreate the pane in their handouts. This window pane introduces our seven ways we remember anything.

7 Ways to Remember

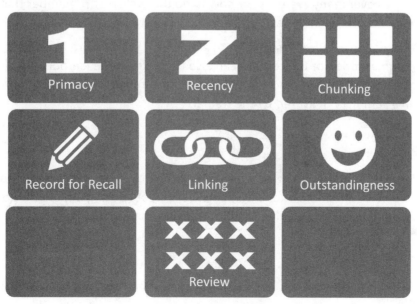

Primacy and Recency

When you meet a lot of people at the same time for the first time, you might remember the first one or two people you meet, and then perhaps the last few people you meet. Somehow, the others in the middle just don't seem to stick. This is the idea behind the Primacy–Recency Effect which says we disproportionately remember things that are first and last in a series, with the most recent items being remembered best (Morrison et al 2014). It is also called the serial position effect. Items at the beginning and ending of a list are distinct and don't have to compete for space in the working memory, unlike words in the middle which compete for space with other words in the middle (Strickland 2001). This is true for our classrooms. Our learners will have an easier time remembering what we covered first and last better than what we cover in the middle.

This means we want to create multiple beginnings and endings in our classes. The start of the day would be one beginning, and therefore one opener, and right before going on a break would be the first ending or close. When you re-start class after a break, you have another opportunity to open or start and before lunch would be another opportunity to close the session. In a typical day, there will be four opportunities for opening and closing or for creating beginnings and endings to increase retention. And Tony Buzan, in his book *Use Both Sides of Your Brain,* actually encourages even more small breaks in-between so as to create additional opens and closes (Buzan 1983).

When starting class at the beginning of the day, you have twelve seconds to grab the participants' attention. Preparing an opener that breaks pre-occupation, allows networking and is relevant to the content is important for gaining and keeping the participants' attention. This makes your early content memorable.

Ending with impact also helps cement your key content into learners' minds, so end training with a closer that requires the learners to put their new knowledge to use; it is more memorable than ending with Q&A or filling out an evaluation form. In the chapter on Closers, we cover many examples of how to do this well. Just remember that your closing few moments are valuable real estate and should cover concepts that are significant.

While information acquired last (recency) generally is remembered best; frequent revisiting and summarization of the content can also help fix it in the learners' minds. Retention is most successful when revisiting activities or self-reflection is done by the learners rather than a summary delivered by the trainer.

Chunking (7 +/- 2)

In the 1950s, Bell Labs was up against a growing problem of people misremembering phone numbers. At the time, phone numbers were created using mnemonic devices such as TRemont 3106. You would pick up the phone and tell the operator your number, TR3106.

But Bell had figured that, with the exponential growth of people needing phone numbers, they needed to switch their methods. So they commissioned Professor George Miller of Harvard University to help justify leaving the mnemonic system and persuade popular opinion that this was the right move (Roemmele 2012).

Miller's paper argued that people could, on average, remember about seven bits of unidimensional information at a time (Miller 1956). He also said we could remember exponentially more bits if we had a way of "recoding" the data and chunking them together.

Bell Labs took this information, along with other internal research, and created the North American phone system with which we are familiar today (excluding the three-digit prefix). The seven digits are broken into two chunks of three and four digits to make the numbers easier to remember.

To tie this back to training, if you look at the example window pane, you will see that there are nine panes available, but in this instance only seven will be used. If there were only six bits of information there would just be two rows with three panes in each row.

If you have a very large amount of content to train, first take the time to chunk each piece of information into manageable pieces. Consider Michael Lotito who has eaten everything from televisions to a Cessna 150 aircraft. How did he do it? Little by little over the course of two years.

Record to Recall

Have you ever written a grocery list and then left it at home? Did you discover that, because you had written it down, you were able to recall most, if not all, of the items on it?

In The Bob Pike Group workshops, we provide time for learners to handwrite information into their workbooks by filling in the blanks. Why? Because writing in a workbook and taking notes by hand increases retention (Mueller and Oppenheimer 2014). While taking notes on a laptop or smart device is becoming more popular and increases how many notes you can take, it's been shown that this kind of note taking is actually detrimental to retention. It doesn't matter if learners are writing out thoughts in a journal, workbook or on a flip chart. The pen is still mightier than the laptop.

Linking

When learning something new, we naturally try to fit what we are learning with something we have learned or experienced in the past that may help us more quickly understand a principle. As a trainer, it is my job to help find ways to create these learning links (Song et al. 2016). For example, when teaching how to build a fiberglass boat, it makes sense to use the analogy of baking a cake, as we mentioned in chapter two. By using this metaphor, we made the technical aspects of boat-building seem less daunting. For a twist, have participants create their own metaphors for the content they just learned. This is a quick way to allow participants to reach a higher level of cognition and move new content into long-term memory.

Another way to link is through the use of concrete props or visual aids. For instance, I use a magic trick and relate it to all the details that go into designing an effective debrief, or a time for asking questions and gaining information after a completed project. When a training has been well planned, it is seamless and may seem to be an illusion. Then I reveal the steps to the trick, and learners see that designing the debrief also has similar steps. Whenever possible, have enough props so each person in the room can have one such as a juggling scarf or card from a deck.

Outstandingness/Intensity

The more outstanding or intense the material that is taught, the more likely it will be retained. A sharp, clear, vivid, dramatic, or exciting learning experience teaches more than a routine or boring experience.

The principle of outstandingness indicates that a student will learn more from the real thing than from a substitute. For example, a student will get more understanding and appreciation of a book by reading it versus seeing the movie version. Participants in a class will have a greater understanding of tasks by doing them rather than merely reading or listening to a lecture about them.

Real world applications that integrate procedures and tasks will make a vivid impression on the learners.

How to create outstandingness:

1. Emphasize important points of instruction with gestures, showmanship, and voice.

2. Demonstrations, skits, and role-playing (skill practice) increase the learning experience of students.

3. Use examples, analogies, and personal experiences to make learning come to life.

4. Make full use of the senses (hearing, sight, touch, taste, smell, balance, rhythm, depth perception, and others). Smell=smelly markers; touch=table toys; sight=posters, slides, etc. Sense of smell is the biggest trigger to memory.

5. Make it memorable.

Curiosity is a part of intensity, which is why we want to create curiosity. In fact, researchers performed a meta-analysis of data from about 200 studies with a total of about 50,000 students and determined that curiosity did indeed have a significant influence on academic performance, about the same as conscientiousness (Association for Psychological Science 2011).

As instructors, we can only attempt to create curiosity for learners, but it is worth the effort. Here are some examples of what could create curiosity in the classroom:

- Colorful posters on the walls
- Upbeat music playing when participants walk in

- Unusual props (we use raw potatoes in one of our examples)
- Tactile objects on tables for kinesthetic learners to fiddle with instead of clicking their pens or playing with change in their pockets
- Fill-in-the-blanks in the workbook because participants want to know what the answer is and whether they guessed correctly
- Pleasantly scented markers
- Field trips to a different part of the building or outside where you conduct a segment of the class
- Show everyone that it is good to volunteer or share answers by awarding prizes to those who volunteer or share first
- Announce that there will be a guest speaker but do not say whom
- Choose unusual times to start and stop breaks (e.g., lunch at 11:38, or offer a thirteen-minute break)
- Let participants earn points but do not share what the points are for until the end of class
- Trial and error processes that allow learners to explore and wonder
- Creatively confuse participants—because participants are not curious about what they already know, but they are curious about the unknown
- Allow opportunities for critical thinking and not just questions and answers

Sometimes it makes sense to allow questions while you train. Other times, it is more helpful for people to hold onto their question until a given point, because you may end up covering the material anyway. We use a "Parking Lot," a poster board on which people can place questions on sticky notes for later discussion, or an "Ask-it Basket" where questions can be submitted any time. Both of these methods give the instructor the flexibility of answering questions at a time that is appropriate and helpful for everyone.

Repetition: Revisit six times six ways ✗✗✗ ✗✗✗

Repetition, drill and practice is the foundation for all skills, and concepts most often repeated are best remembered. Students learn best and retain information longer when they have meaningful practice and repetition. Keep in mind that reviewing or revisiting content in a variety of ways makes it far more interesting and creates curiosity. Saying, "This is so important I am going to cover the content six times. Time number 1..." is not creating an environment where learning takes place. It creates anxiety. Instead, use several approaches to cover the same content.

It is clear that practice leads to improvement only when accompanied by several key elements. Last year, my daughter Raegan was learning her multiplication and division facts. She'd been doing the study by rote memory and flashcard use because knowing the facts was required. She felt she had no use for the information and continued to test poorly on it.

However, a little later, we got a multiplication facts app on the tablet. She scored points for accuracy and speed, and she got to select categories and compete against herself.

Within one week, she was able to learn and recall far more than in months of practice with the flashcards that I had painstakingly created and laminated. Why?

- She chose it. Buy-in makes the learning more meaningful.
- Raegan was able to compete with herself and assess immediately how well she did.
- It was repetitive but in a fun way.
- The app provided positive reinforcement through earning coins which she could use to build cool aquariums and buy fish and food with her earnings.

The human memory is fallible. The mind can rarely retain, evaluate, and apply new concepts or practices after a single exposure. Participants do not learn complex tasks in a single session. They learn by applying what they have been told and shown. Every time practice occurs, learning continues.

As the trainer, you must repeat important items of subject matter at reasonable intervals, and provide opportunities for students to practice while making sure that this process is directed toward a goal.

Ways to make this happen might include:

- Having learners discuss the concepts with their table groups
- Allowing participants to choose which method they use for revisiting the material
- Having participants create quiz cards or review games
- Using mnemonic devices, which is a pattern of letters, ideas, or associations that assists in remembering something. One example is an acronym like EAT = Experience, Awareness, Theory.
- Using products and tools, like mindsetter.com, that allow your learners to revisit content after the workshop to improve retention and skill transfer back to the job.
- Creating PowerPoint games or using pre-made games to revisit content. For the highest level of participation, each person in the room should have his or her own clicker, or audience response system. This creates more focus and attention and drives learning. (See PowerPoint chapter for a list of free websites with games for learning.)

Our window pane here was two-fold: to introduce you to the memory tool and to have it serve as a visual overview of the seven ways we remember. While all seven methods are valid, it can be overwhelming to know where to start. It is like putting up Christmas decorations. It seems daunting when you are looking at ten bins, but if you do it one bin at a time, the task is far more joyful and manageable. So don't try to include all seven memory methods at one time. Review the window pane step-by-step, and then choose one new method at a time to design into your class.

Chapter 6

SELF-COMPASSION AND POSITIVE THINKING

As instructors, it is our job to create the best possible atmosphere for learning. Part of that means helping our learners have accurate thoughts about their abilities to use and apply the information they are learning. According to Mayo Clinic, low self-esteem impacts nearly every facet of a person's life, which would include the ability to learn. Perhaps it's not so much the self-esteem as it is self-compassion, or the ability to cut yourself some slack and show yourself some grace (Neff et al. 2005). I have found that most adults are harder on themselves than they deserve. As a trainer, I take steps to encourage self-compassion and positive thinking in the classroom as a way to quiet our harshest critic: ourselves. Many times this comes naturally, but for those of us who want to make sure it happens, here are a few ideas.

When you are training others, give yourself a lot of grace. Our minds are powerful tools that can believe emphatically what we tell them to believe. If you think your presentation is not going to be your best, you might stumble through it. Your negativity might create a self-fulfilling prophecy.

Don't apologize. More times than not, people will not even notice what went wrong. Encourage your participants to do the same. If you embarrass someone in front of the rest of the group, that is a different story. Then it is time to humble yourself and apologize to that person in front of the group. As the offense was public so should the apology be, and it reassures other participants that you will not embarrass them next. Everyone makes mistakes—and mistakes are not a permanent reflection on your character or work. Mistakes are isolated moments in time, and we all have our moments.

Use hopeful statements. We may need to give participants statements to repeat throughout our courses that help to motivate. For example: "Even though it's difficult, I can handle this situation." Research shows that what students believe about their abilities and intelligence "can powerfully influence their learning success (Mangels et al. 2006)."

Avoid "should-ing" on your participants. When I was in college, a particular instructor would always say, "You should do this," or "You should do that." Stop using "should" and "would" and replace them with words that present a choice for learners to make for themselves. Instead say, "You can do this" or ask "How can you do this?"

Reframe thinking. When learners have a difficult time with a concept, stop the group and ask, "What can we think and do to make this less stressful?" I once had the opportunity to spend time with Dr. Srinivasan Pillay, a professor at Harvard Medical School. Pillay's research uses brain magnetic resonance imaging (MRI) and functional brain imaging (FMRI) to better understand the landscape of how unconscious fear affects brain function. The increase in amygdala activity disrupts the functioning of the anterior cingulate cortex (ACC). The ACC monitors decisions for errors and conflicts.

In his book, *Life Unlocked: 7 Revolutionary Lessons to Overcome Fear,* Pillay says, "Reframe your fears as things that you will overcome. This stimulates the ACC, which monitors for fear and, in its role as an attentional center, redirects your attention away from the fear and toward the solutions offered." An interesting side note he shared was that, based on clinical studies, women are more fearful than men, something I keep in mind when teaching.

Focus on the positive. Have learners focus on what they can control instead of what is out of their control. Sometime trainers complain they don't have a decent training room or "These activities work for you, but I work with engineers." Instead, take the concepts and ideas from this book on Instructor-Led, Participant-Centered training, and start implementing what will work. I've used openers, closers, revisiters and energizers with success with all levels of learners from frontline employees to CEOs. You may need to modify the way you address and approach an activity, but the concepts remain the same.

How can I design positive thinking into my workshop?

1. Action idea page. Have learners write what they CAN do on an action idea page. Revisit that page often throughout class and have them verbally share with a partner what they will start doing.

2. Calm thoughts first. As the class goes along, have participants reflect on what will be the easiest element to apply. By starting with the areas that are easy, it brings a sense of calm into their thought processes that reduces fear and anxiety.

3. Visualizations. Have participants take a few minutes to visualize themselves back on the job using the information successfully. The room should be quiet and still—I usually walk them through a visualization as practice first. I use an example of Pluth's Four Ps of training design: Planning, Producing, Performing, and Perfecting. Plan how you will implement the training. Produce job aids to help you perform the task. Then keep improving on your execution of the skill until it is perfected. For the visualization, I might say something like, "See yourself planning to implement what we learned. See yourself prepared with your questions answered and tools in place for work tomorrow. You have created any materials needed for success including checklists, job aids or cheat sheets. Visualize yourself waking up the next morning ready to apply the new learning. See yourself successfully completing the new task and the smiles of co-workers celebrating in your success with high-fives, smiles and laughter. After the day is complete, watch as you head back to your workspace and make a few notes on what you will do to

improve." Have them do this on their own with some of the new concepts they have learned during your time together. Encourage them to repeat that same visualization until it comes to fruition back on the job. Then it is time to look at their list of action ideas and select a new concept to tackle. They should then come up with a visualization around that particular concept.

4. Write down three positives. One of our trainers, Priscilla Shumway, has learners write things on the back of a $100 bill (play money). She has them put their "money" in their wallets in front of the credit cards they use most often and read their three positives each time they use that credit card. Using this example, you could have learners write down three positives about themselves as it relates to the concepts they learn with you. One month is a start but to truly unlock fears, three months would be better. Shumway connects with some of her past students at our conference each year, and several of them have pulled out the hundred dollar bill and showed it to her. Powerful!

5. Hope or fear? Change your lens to one of hope. When learners get back on the job, there will be moments with negative feelings that stem from change or the new process. Encourage learners in the classroom to change their lens to one of hope and to practice that in their lives.

Positivity must be grounded in reality, and negativity cannot be ignored. If we are not in touch with reality, false optimism will result in counter-productivity. Sharing in small groups is important as it helps bring balance.

Beginning Intentional Instructor-Led,
Participant-Centered Design

Chapter 7

NEEDS ASSESSMENT AND ANALYSIS

Now that we have covered a lot of the philosophy and research behind Creative Training, let's begin looking at the practical steps of designing a course that is participant-centered using ADDIE.

You are probably familiar with the ADDIE training design model: Analysis, Design, Development, Implementation, Evaluation. When I first started designing training, I skipped the analysis and assessment stage and even objective writing and dug right into the development stage! For me it was truly the "Ready. Fire. Aim!" approach.

As I edge toward a significant birthday, I am planning a trip to New Zealand with my husband and two friends. If you decided to go on a big trip overseas, would it work out well if you decided where you were going once you got to the airport? Or attempted to book a room after reaching your destination? It might be more adventure than you had bargained for! Prior to our trip, we will be doing a needs assessment to ensure we gather all the data we need to make wise decisions and ensure a fun trip that is memorable for the right reasons.

A needs assessment, which really is just gathering information and analyzing it, may seem overwhelming, but it doesn't need to

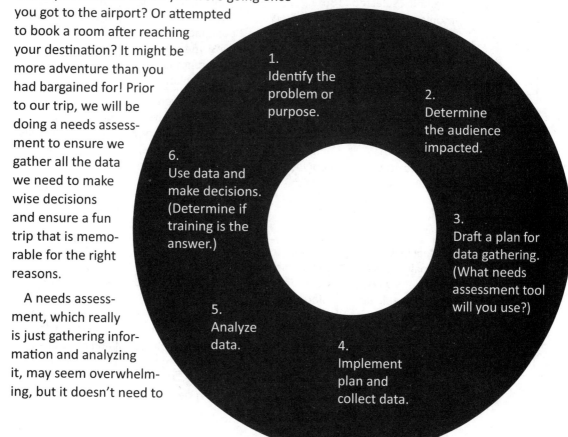

1. Identify the problem or purpose.

2. Determine the audience impacted.

3. Draft a plan for data gathering. (What needs assessment tool will you use?)

4. Implement plan and collect data.

5. Analyze data.

6. Use data and make decisions. (Determine if training is the answer.)

be. It's one step in the analysis process to identify the underlying issue that training might solve. Here is a simple overview of the cycle.

Doing some form of needs assessment helps us determine the issue's current state versus desired state and where there are gaps. When courses are quickly designed without due diligence in analyzing the need, courses often must be re-designed after launch based on feedback from participants.

Many times we assess the same way we always have. If our company is familiar with surveys, we create surveys, even if we know we won't get the number of responses needed for it to be accurate. Every needs assessment is unique and different. Each time a project is in front of you, think about which tools are best. Consider using the method that best suits the needs of the project versus what you know. I recommend using two or more of these tools that give non-repetitive data.

There are many ways to gather the information you need. Here are the most common ways along with the three-step process we have developed called Results-Based Design™.

	Definition	Purpose	Pros	Cons
Interviews	Asking questions of and talking with individuals to gain information around a selected topic	To obtain "real" current information and observe the strength of feelings related to that issue	Valid data from a broad range of people, find out behavior information, opinions and attitudes and can be done face-to-face via Skype or visual conference call or even by phone.	Time constraints, must train interviewers to ask questions in similar format, interviewer bias, easy to lose sight or get off track, can be expensive
Instruments	A number of assessments often completed by an individual that offer quantitative data of a topic under observation	Measures progress and growth and determines differences in a population	Typically it requires less time off the job, it's confidential, easy to score, a large population of people can take it and little administrative time is required	Opinions change based on time and circumstances and language barriers
Focus Groups	A tool in which a small group of people engages in a roundtable discussion of selected topics of interest in an informal setting	An intimate environment to share ideas and information	High response rate, efficient and economical, stimulate others' creative thinking, structured guide, face-to-face, and has the ability for clarification	Fosters conformity, intimidation, moderator control, moderator skill required, qualitative data and not statistically significant

	Definition	Purpose	Pros	Cons
Observations	A tool whereby individuals or groups are directly observed in various settings in order to get behavioral data about processes and interactions	Determine roles to form concepts prior to an interview. Validate preconceptions	Accurate behavioral data, can be unobtrusive, moderate cost, confirm findings, understand the process	Trained observers, bias behavior, observer bias, and time-consuming
Tests	An assessment intended to establish what an individual knows in relation to other people as well as relate knowledge and skills to the expectations of a given role	Determines basic knowledge and skill level. For pre- and post-measurement	Identifies current skills, provides a baseline, valid data, uses measurable criteria, efficient and cost-effective	Test are not always well written, logic and reasoning isn't visible, requires planning and monitoring, need for a proctor and often tests are out of context
Surveys/ Questionnaires	Research instruments that contain a series of questions intended to gather statistical data from respondents	Gathers information from a large population	Cost effective, easy to administer, addresses a large audience and is consistent	Survey must be developed, technology for administering, respondents require response time, need statistically significant response numbers (if polling ten people, nine must respond) and often it doesn't uncover challenges or gaps.

Non-Repetitive Measures

Non-repetitive measures look at the same information in more than one way. It doesn't repeat itself like a pre-test and post-test, which may be identical, but instead it looks at the same content or concepts from two different angles.

When we were helping one client design sales training, we asked if they had done a needs assessment. They provided us with a survey the sales team filled out that showed the perceived need or training gap was in the areas of time and territory management and closing the sale. We could have created a course based on that survey alone, but we would have been missing a huge gap that was identified only when we went on a ride-along observation with high and low performers.

During those ride-alongs, we found that both sales reps used similar methods for time and territory management and again when closing the sale. The difference between the two was actually in overcoming objections. The high performer on average overcame objections six times before moving into closing the sale while the low performer overcame just two objections.

By taking the time to assess needs using two different methods, we helped design a course that met both perceived and real needs by spending a majority of the time on the real need, overcoming objections, while just one-sixth of the time was spent on the perceived need of time and territory management and closing the sale. It is important to teach to both perceived and real needs, but spend the majority of the time on the real needs identified. By teaching to both real and perceived needs, we are gaining buy-in and support from our learners and thus getting better results.

Selecting the Right Assessment

When a new project crosses my desk, there is a tidal wave of thoughts and questions as I determine which of the above tools to use to uncover the need. Here is a list to consider when deciding which tools, process or method would be best to use. Once you've answered the questions, looking through the pros and cons will help eliminate methods that don't meet your parameters.

Management Buy-in: To what degree are they willing to participate? How important is the project? Is the project visible?

Time: How quickly does this need to be done?

Performance Analysis: Is the issue a skill deficiency? How can the deficiency be assessed?

Money: Is there budget for assessments, hiring a facilitator, bringing people in from across the country to take part in a meeting?

Audience: Are they local or spread out? How many people are going to be a part of the needs assessment? Is there a gap in knowledge between respondents?

Resources: Is there a survey and usability expert to help craft questions? What technology is available?

Confidentiality: Does it matter? Be sure to share with respondents if the assessment is anonymous. Generally respondents are more forthcoming when they have the choice to put their name on their responses or leave it off.

Statistically Significant: Does the data need to be reliable and significant?

Work Interruption: To what degree can employees be away from productive work?

Determine Whether Training Is the Answer

Once you have concluded your assessment and analysis, determine whether creating and executing a training will actually solve the problem. Sometimes, as trainers, we are order takers. Someone hands us the assignment and off we go without questioning our task. This described me years ago!

Returning to my company after maternity leave, I found the corporation had "reorganized" and that I was moving from leadership training onto the technical training team.

My first project was completely different from anything I had ever done, and I didn't know anything about the systems for which I would be designing training. I dove into developing training on this brand new software that would be rolled out in six weeks.

I spent many of those next few weeks working until midnight and away from my newborn, which was difficult. When the roll-out date approached, I had a meeting with the director who requested the training and asked a few questions about what other software systems would need to be plugged into this one to make it work. The director had an "A-ha" moment, realizing there were gaps in one of the software systems this product needed to be plugged into to make it work. In that moment, I realized the work of the past six weeks was effectively wasted. The first problem we had—a systems issue—would not be solved with training. The training I developed would never be rolled out during my time at the company.

The Performance Solution Model (explained in Appendix C) will help you look at six different areas within your organization and help you determine what the root cause of your problem is. Is it systems? A recruiting issue? Or maybe the solution really is training. The questions in the Performance Solution Model provides questions to narrow down:

What is the need: a deficiency, a desired improvement, or future planning?

Who is impacted by the need: the entire organization, a division, a department, an individual or a job position?

How should the need be addressed: with a systems correction, with organizational development, with placement, with coaching, with recruiting or with training?

Tom Peters says, "A new employee within two to three weeks, will treat employees as they are being treated." This Golden Rule also applies to patterns in the workplace. That's why I feel strongly that we, as trainers, must ask the hard questions when someone says to us, "We need training." There needs to be a shift from trainers merely being training providers to trainers becoming trusted advisors. If someone pushes for training, push back and discover whether the training is needed. Avoid training malpractice and the potential that the training won't deliver results because it's not fixing the underlying problem.

If I had understood and known how to use the Performance Solution Model, I would have saved myself six weeks of late nights and hard work and saved the organization money and rework time. If I had just taken a moment up front and asked about other systems, we would have realized that training was not the first step and instead worked on getting all of the systems working. It is now one of the most valuable tools in my belt and something that I use in every discovery and design session.

In addition to the Performance Solution Model, you can also look at AWA. Psychologist Bob Mager says, "If you put a good employee in a bad system, the system will win every time." If you can't say yes to all three of the following questions, then your system is broken and your training will be for naught. AWA is able, want, allowed.

- Are the learners **able** to do the task? Do they have the skills and knowledge to do the job? (If not, do some training.)

- Do they **want** to do the task? Do they have the right desire or attitude? Adults want to understand "why" when they are asked to do something. (If not, utilize coaching, recruit someone who does, or move the person into another position.)

- Are they **allowed** to do the task? If the employee needs to be able to do something in order to perform his or her position, but the system forbids it, look at correcting the system or creating an organization development program.

Unpacking the Results Based Design™ Process

Once you've completed the assessments and determined that training is the right solution, it's time to get the managers and stakeholders on board as you continue your issue analysis. I know it seems crazy; we haven't even designed anything! But "training is a process, not an event," and the process begins before the training.

Including the most senior stakeholders and their direct reports in a Results-Based Design™ (RBD) session ensures their "voice" is heard, and the focus is on the right path. When trainers move forward with what they think is needed versus extracting the information and needs from those doing the job, any number of random objectives can be added to a program and only after months of implementing the training and reviewing evaluations is it revealed that learners didn't need some of the content. This is costly, not only because re-design needs to happen, but also because there were all those trainees in class learning content they really didn't need! That time could have been better spent applying or practicing. An RBD session takes guessing out of the equation and is our first choice in conducting a needs assessment.

A huge selling point for using RBD is that it gets manager buy-in, which is critical. Broad and Newstrom's research in *The Transfer of Training* shows that the manager before and after class has the greatest impact on whether a learner uses what is taught in class. Managers have the influence before the class to get learner buy-in and help prepare learners for what is to come. After the class, the manager can encourage implementation of learning and can continue the learning process for greater transfer back on the job.

RBD is a sixteen-step process that needs to be completed in order. As I walk through these steps, I will also be expounding on each so the steps are spread throuogut the rest of this chapter.

To begin the RBD process, have a meeting and invite stakeholders, managers, a few people who have been in the role a long time or are high performers, at least one person new to the role, and trainers and designers that will be working on the project.

Definition	Purpose	Pros	Cons
A meeting of five to fifteen people that includes stakeholders, trainers and frontline workers that follows a process to gain alignment on gaps and needs	Provides a platform for a variety of people to share perspective and come to agreement on key needs	Effectively cuts down on additional meetings, speeds up design time, buy-in established quickly, repeatable process, and by the end of the meeting there is clear direction	Requires a trainer facilitator, requires time from stakeholders to attend, at times process seems ambiguous, takes time to complete (two to three days)

Key stakeholders are only in the meeting for the first three steps in the process and return at the end of the session to review the rest of the project and add any additional thoughts to the process.

1. Identify the business goal of a course or its purpose. One of the biggest mistakes that trainers make is forgetting about the big picture and tying the training to an overall business objective, goal or need. The purpose of the training should be clearly laid out by key stakeholders within the business unit and the training team.

2. Define success. After aligning the training with business objectives, determine how success will be measured. If there is a real business need for a course, there will be a way to measure results to show training had a positive impact whether it increased revenue, reduced errors or costs or got a product to market faster. When this is done well, the training team is viewed as a strategic partner rather than an order taker.

3. Create metrics that will help to show a return on attendance (evaluation metrics). This step further clarifies what success is by determining which measurements exist or need to be created to compare the training "before and after." These metrics help provide evidence that the training impacted the business purpose for which it was designed. When a training can provide these metrics and evidence, it becomes easier to sell the investment of training.

4. Identify the audiences to be trained and gather information about them. The needs assessment phase (which comes just before you begin the Results-Based Design phase) and analysis phase is a good time to identify your audience and learn whatever you can about your participants. The model that helps us better understand who will be in the room and for whom we are writing objectives (step five) is the KILI model: Knowledge, Interest, Language and Influence.

Learner Knowledge (K)

Many of the questions outlined in our Rapid Design (pages 60-62) will help you identify how much education or experience participants will bring to the classroom. A sampling of questions might include: how well can they read, listen, communicate with others or even write? Do they have social skills? What is their baseline of knowledge around the content? Do they have rote knowledge of facts and details or an overall understanding of the process? To what degree do they need to know the content? Here are four options:

Awareness is a basic understanding and requires the lowest level of cognition. It is simply recognizing things when they see it. Awareness can come after reading an article or being instructed.

Familiarity means that there is some degree of recall. The learners know how to trigger the information and access it when needed.

Competence is the ability to apply what has been learned. Competence doesn't occur until behavior has changed. Typically this will not occur during a class, unless the course is over 66 days, which is the average amount of time it takes for a new habit to form (Lally 2010).

Mastery is the ability to teach others the same information and skill. Just because you practice something for hours on end doesn't mean you will be the next Tiger Woods or Yo-Yo Ma (Hambrick et al. 2014, Hambrick et al. 2016). Deliberate practice is one-third of the formula to becoming an expert. Other factors that influence mastery include using the training or concepts on the job and for fun (dominant-relevant experience), starting and spacing the learning over time, and having natural ability. Passion for what you are mastering and your personality also play a role.

Learner Interest (I)

It is difficult to master a topic if an attendee feels forced to be in a training room or is disinterested in the topic in general. These are "prisoners" in the room: people who'd rather be doing anything but sitting in this class. An attendee could also be a socializer, someone who is there simply for the people aspect. Or you may encounter the know-it-all who doesn't feel the need to attend, so he can push back on one concept after another. Perhaps some are there as "vacationers" and got a business trip out of the deal. The goal is to move each of these participants away from these potentially disruptive mindsets to that of the engaged learner as quickly as possible. The first step in doing this is to gauge the participants' interest.

Learners' interest can usually be observed within the first ten-minute opener. I use a name tag activity at the beginning of my sessions which asks learners to write their name and an adjective that describes how they are feeling this morning on the nametag. Learners write all sorts of adjectives from "tired" or "excited" to "goofy" or "pensive." By looking at the adjectives chosen, I begin to better understand the interest in the room. Then I'm careful to listen and watch the participants meet and greet. In this way, I hear the socializers doing a lot of the talking, and I see the prisoners crossing their arms and sometimes wearing a scowl on their faces.

Learner Language (L)

Prior to a session, gather information surrounding language level. You don't want to patronize by using language that is too simplistic; and, you don't want to lose learners because you use unfamiliar jargon either. Even when you have identified that your audience consists of tenured employees, consider skipping the jargon or, at the very least, explain the terms or acronyms on first use. I once was presenting to a room of executives on the return on investment (ROI) of a course. At the end of the workshop, a director came up to me and thanked me for explaining ROI before using the acronym as she couldn't remember, having just returned from medical leave.

Learner Influence (I)

When considering what content to cover, discover what kind of support the learners are likely to receive back on the job and if they are able to influence others around them. If they have little authority, then put support systems in place prior to the training. This includes working with managers to help create accountability for the participant to follow through with the new content. Often in our culture, there is little time for managers to think through how they will do this, so I would suggest designing a follow-up question sheet to give to managers to use during status updates in the following weeks. It is like my husband and me with our four kids; when they learn something at school, church, cub scouts or sports, it is our job as parents to ensure those new skills are used and practiced. The more often we check in and encourage them in their new learning, the more they use those skills and feel even more confident the next time they are asked to recall or use the learning.

On the other end of the spectrum are those participants that have great authority. These decision makers can drive new programs quickly and can influence others to do the same. How can they be partners in promoting the learning as well as challenged by the training?

Finally, perceived authority can be different from actual authority. During a needs assessment, ask stakeholders how much authority participants have follow to through on the training and what supports need to be established.

5. Determine desired behaviors that learners will be applying back on the job and write objectives. Writing specific and measurable objectives are imperative if you want to show how the training impacted the business needs, so let me show you what well-written objectives look like.

ABCDs of Objective Writing

The ABCD method for writing objectives helps ensure that courses are designed with training transfer as a focus. Training objectives should be written so that you can evaluate the behavior while students are still in the class. Once a learner leaves the room, it is unrealistic that you would be able to determine if the objective was met. The ABCD method helps us to determine the goals or answer, "As a result of training, what do I want participants to know, feel or do?" Always design objectives with the learner in mind.

The ABCDs are Audience, Behavior, Condition, and Degree of mastery.

Audience: Who is in the room receiving the training (e.g., new hire sales representatives)?

Behavior: What do I expect them to be able to do differently? This is an observable behavior (e.g., modify a sales scenario).

Condition: What will the learner be expected to know from the training in order to accomplish the behavior (e.g., provide the IMPACT sales process)?

Degree: How much will need to be completed by the end of the course for course requirements to be met (e.g., accurately use all six measured by a peer)? The degree of mastery usually includes a number or a percent. In this case, all six steps are required or 100 percent mastery, which is measurable.

Put ABCD together and it looks like this: Given the IMPACT selling process, the new hire sales representatives will be able to accurately modify a sales scenario to follow the six-step sales process as measured by a peer using the IMPACT checklist. Based on this objective, all stakeholders—including you, your boss, your learner and your learner's boss—know exactly what will be covered in the training and what observable behaviors will be measured at the end of training. This objective is narrow, specific, and tangible.

Objectives are easiest to write for knowledge (cognitive) and skill (psychomotor) based activities. It is very difficult to judge feelings (affective) to determine a degree of mastery in change management (were feelings changed or improved by fifty percent?). Write knowledge and skill-based objectives first. Be sure to use action verbs that are measurable. Take a look at some of the objectives you have previously seen or written in different classes. Objectives that are poorly written might look like this: "By the end of the course, students will understand the IMPACT sales steps" or "At the end of the workshop, learners will know the three parts to the company's vision statement." But how do you measure "understand" or "know"? Objectives that use vague and immeasurable terms like learn, understand, think, or perceive should be re-written. Some well-written objectives might be:

1. Given an assortment of emergency medical systems (EMS) equipment from which to choose, the paramedic will select all of the equipment necessary to perform rapid sequence intubation without error.

2. Given a list of five performance objectives for a training program, participants will correctly label all of the parts as A (audience), B (behaviors), C (condition), or D (degree of mastery).

3. Given the corporate dress code policy, the employee will verbally convince a peer of the benefits of compliance.

On the next page, you will see a grid based on Bloom's updated taxonomy with verbs that are useful for creating effective and measurable objectives. The verbs on the left side are used to write knowledge-based objectives, the easiest level at which to obtain mastery. Each step clockwise becomes more difficult for the learner as all prior levels need to be mastered before moving onto the next step. For example, in order for comprehension to be reached, a learner must first know the information. The last step, "creating," is the most difficult because it requires mastery of all five prior elements.

The verb chart also provides ideas for each category of Bloom's revised taxonomy: knowledge, skills, and attitude (KSA). Knowledge is simply knowing or understanding something. Skills include anything with physical movement, motor skills, demonstration or hand-eye coordination. This could be working a forklift or modeling effective listening techniques. Attitude refers to feelings. These are the most difficult objectives to write because emotion and motivation are difficult to measure. I also refer to KSA as Know, Feel, and Do.

This list is not only good for writing objectives for courses, it is helpful for writing objectives for your personal learning goals at work, for sales proposals, and for many other tasks.

The next few steps should be self-explanatory and are not exclusive to ILPC training, so you should already be acquainted with these.

4. Brainstorm constraints keeping participants from being successful.

5. Determine knowledge, skills and attitudes (KSA) needed to perform the behaviors that were identified.

6. Create tools to measure whether participants have learned the material.

7. Determine the prior knowledge of learners. (KILI comes into play here, too.)

8. Draft a timeline that includes rough deadlines, dates to consider and when the pilot training session will be held.

9. Discuss resources available to help on the project.

10. List supports for the project that includes subject matter experts, project leads, champions, testers, etc.

11. Discuss restraints and how to minimize.

12. Compile a list of communications.

13. Define the budget.

14. Miscellaneous

If you don't have time to do a meeting with all stakeholders, managers, etc., then here is a sampling of questions we regularly use at The Bob Pike Group to do analysis for the upcoming training. These questions can also be used in our Rapid Design format which follows these questions.

- Why is this course important?
- Why are we developing this course?
- What are the business challenges you are facing that makes this course important?
- If we are successful in this venture, what will your employees be doing differently or better?

- What does success look like?
- Who will be impacted by this project?
- To what extent do they need to be involved? (in class, communication, webinar)
- For what employee groups is this training intended?
- Are there secondary audiences?
- What specific behaviors do you want to observe in the participants AFTER the training?
- What behaviors support the success and lead to stated business outcomes?
- Are these different for different audiences?
- What is the mental discipline of the learners? Short or long attention span? Are they new to the content or revisiting the content?
- How will we identify that the employees are behaving the way we want them to?
- How are they applying what was taught in the program?
- Are these different for different audiences?
- Why aren't our people behaving this way now?
- What is keeping people from having the level of success we want them to have?
- What specific knowledge, skills, attitudes do our people need to perform the behaviors identified?
- What do the participants need to know (knowledge), do (skills), or feel (attitudes) at the conclusion of the program?
- How do we measure that our participants have learned the material?
- Will there be a test (to measure knowledge and/or attitudes), an observation (to measure skills) or some combination of both?
- What do participants already know that can be reviewed but not re-taught?
- What prior knowledge do they need to have in order to be successful in this program?
- What deadlines do we need to be aware of?
- What design elements need a timeline to meet our end time goal? (layout, design, printing, SME, legal approval)
- Will there be Alpha, Beta and/or train-the-trainer courses?
- Who else is available to help with this project?
- What other resources are available to us?
- Is there pre-existing content?
- What equipment and/or facilities will be needed?
- Who or what can support us in this project?
- Who are the SMEs?
- Who is the project leader?
- What might get in the way of our successful outcome? And can we minimize them?
- Can we eliminate any restraints now?
- What, how, and when do we need to communicate in order to ensure the success of this project?

- What are the lines of communication?
- What tools are available and who will take the lead?
- What are the projected costs for this project?
- Are the funds already budgeted?
- What authority do we have to spend the money?
- Where do we go if we need more money?

Results-Based Design Fast or Rapid Design

Sometimes, a full-out assessment isn't needed, especially if it's a small project. Rapid Design is a short-cut, if you will, for RBD. It's not as exhaustive, and therefore may not get you optimal results, but if time is of the essence, this is an alternative.

While RBD needs to be done step-by-step and in order, we cut Rapid Design down to two mandatory, but detailed steps. In addition to these, you can choose other steps in RBD to supplement these, but these two must be done.

1. Identify the business goal of a course or its purpose.

2. Determine desired behaviors that learners will be applying back on the job and write objectives. Then choose content and select activities to teach desired behaviors.

If you desire to really dive into performance analysis or need great questions to help you get started, I highly recommend the book *First Things Fast* by Allison Rossett.

Chapter 8

FOUR PRINCIPLES FOR BUILDING AN ILPC WORKSHOP

So you have come to the conclusion that training is at least part of the solution, and you know the content on which you need to train. Now it's time to create the training session.

The following four principles will guide you through making sure you present your content in a way that utilizes the social component of learning and specifically plans in interaction so your workshop has increased motivation and interest while greatly improving content retention.

The four principles are CPR, CIO, EAT and 90/20/10. They provide a foundation for solid instructional design that keeps the focus on the learner.

CPR: The Breath of Life in Training

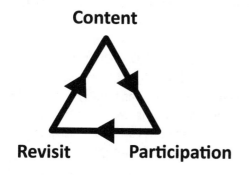

Content

Revisit   **Participation**

The CPR in ILPC training is **C**ontent, **P**articipation, and **R**evisit. Chunking the content, having learners participate in relevant activities, and building in revisits allows learners' brains to digest and reflect on the content. The concept of spacing we discussed earlier allows for us to touch on a concept in several places to increase retention. Each training module should be twenty minutes or less and should include teaching content, allowing for participation and providing an opportunity for revisiting.

The C stands for content, which is the information that needs to be transferred from you, the trainer, to the participants. When considering content, divide it into bite size chunks to make it more manageable for the learner to grasp and recall information.

Participation should occur at least once every ten minutes. There are hundreds of ways to engage learners but a few common examples are practical application, working with a partner, games and simulations, activities using card sorts, or chart paper diagrams.

Make sure that in each CPR module there is time built in for the learner to **revisit** what they learned in their own words. As I said earlier, the brain doing the talking is the brain doing the learning. Instead of the instructor saying, "Here is what we just did," it should sound like "Work with a learning partner and share the five fundamentals of learning in your own words." After learners have had time to revisit, you can then do a high level recap to make sure everyone caught what was taught.

Buzan, in his book *Use Both Sides of Your Brain,* noted that if content review took place at prescribed intervals, retention stayed consistently high, around eighty-five percent and higher. But if review didn't take place, as much as eighty percent of the detailed information would be lost within twenty-four hours! Obviously revisiting is essential. [If this is something that interests you, Hermann Ebbinghaus' learning curve and forgetting curve might be fascinating reading.]

No matter the content covered, it needs to be accessible later when the learner is back on the job. Saying "Let's review" is a trigger for people to check out and go on a mental vacation. Instead don't announce it, just do it.

Ask participants to write down their favorite new piece of learning on an action idea page throughout the session. At different points, ask them to highlight their top two takeaways and then find a partner and share those ideas. After listening to their partners, they should add any new takeaways to their action idea page. Then have learners go back to their table groups and share one new idea that others can add to their action idea list if they want. It is not cheating; it's consulting! Notice what happened: you looked at your list and highlighted. That is one revisit. You talked with a partner about your list and listened to theirs. That is revisit number two. You decided what to share in your small group. Revisit number three. You went around the table hearing even more ideas. Revisit number four. You added additional ideas to your action idea page. Revisit number five.

Revisiting information is key; just don't call it that.

CIO: The Social Component of Learning

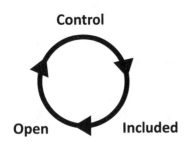

Control

Open   **Included**

Perhaps you have read about the trends in schools to move toward individual learning plans (IEPs) and individualized learning. In our classrooms, we as trainers can create an atmosphere where this can happen by having learners control their experiences through choice.

When structuring activities, consider the CIO principle: When we feel in **control** of what happens to us and our learning, and we feel **included** in a group, we are more **open** to taking the risks involved in learning new content and skills.

C = <u>Control</u> (of what happens to me)

Give the learners choices...lots of choices. These can be small like choosing the color of a marker, selecting their own seats, picking someone with whom to share, voting on the agenda, or allowing learners to write their own goals for the class.

People don't argue with their own data or their own choices. The more involvement and participation, the more learning is going to occur. Instead of telling and lecturing, put participants in situations where they can discover for themselves. If the trainer says it is true, the learners could say, "Of course she does, she is teaching it." If, however, the learners say it's true, it becomes fact because they came up with it. The participants take ownership. Through choices and developing their own opinions and thoughts, learning is embedded further.

I = Included (in a group)

Consider for a moment how many groups you are a part of in life. Book club, basketball league, golf league, running club, church Bible study, motorcycle group, crafting guild and so on. It is much easier to network in a small focused "team" and get to know a few people better over the course of two days than to look around a packed room and choose someone with whom to connect. People naturally want to know someone and feel a part of something, so we need to build that into the session and help make it more intimate and less overwhelming.

Today's adult learner is different from thirty years ago. They grew up on multiple devices and often were on more than one at a time. I look at my eleven, nine, seven and even my five-year-old, and see it is being taken to a whole new level as they have technology in their hands while also watching a movie and talking on the phone! We cannot compete with this kind of stimulation on our own; we must use the participants' energy to stimulate and mobilize the group's energy.

O = Openness (to learn)

When the "C" and the "I" have been intentionally built into the design of the program, the "O" naturally occurs in the participants—they become open to learning new content and exchanging ideas. We **must** establish a culture of freedom and choice where participants feel a part of the culture and class before participants will be open to learning.

The social component of learning means balancing games or large group exercises for the extroverts with opportunities for small groups and reflection for the introverts so all have a place in our classroom.

Ever asked a question of the large group and gotten no response? People are afraid to answer even an easy question in front of a large group. There is a fear of embarrassment. Using CIO can help you instead create engagement by asking questions to be discussed in pairs, triads or small groups of three to five people. An introvert is far more comfortable listening in a small group and is more likely to respond.

E-A-T, A-T-E or T-E-A?

Experience.

Awareness.

Theory.

Whenever possible in participant-centered training, attempt to design learning modules that follow in the format of E-A-T: experience something first, then gain an awareness of what happened during the experience, and finally receive an explanation of the theory behind the experience.

Neuroscience of Adult Learning states, "The more regions of the cortex used, the more change will occur (Johnson and Taylor 2006). Thus, learning experiences should be designed to use the four major areas of the neocortex (sensory, back-integrative, front-integrative, and motor). Our EAT (experience, awareness, theory) principle helps us engage the four major areas of the cortex simultaneously.

Providing an experience is a way for participants to actively engage in experimenting and trying out a task even though they may have never done the task before. It is often a trial-and-error approach.

For example, in a computer based training course, you might give learners five minutes to work through a job aid on an application and see how far they get. This can be done alone or in pairs. During this time, learners will review information, reflect on what they have read to make sense and meaning of the data, interpret the content and then apply it, in this case, to a software program.

The idea is that they are experimenting and getting familiar with the application and building an awareness of what is to come. At the end of the five minutes, you can then begin to share the theory needed to fill in gaps.

By giving learners an experience first, you draw on what they already know. One of the ILPC FUNdamentals is "People don't argue with their own data." If we allow for participants to engage with the content and then talk about it, they more quickly buy-in to the concepts because they have firsthand experience. They are engaged from the first moment and can come up with questions through the trial-and-error process that will be helpful for their learning. It also makes the lecturette (a lecture of less than ten minutes) more interactive because they have firsthand experience. To keep all cortexes of the brain engaged during this mini-lecture, consider including a variety of exercises from reflecting to creating their own job aids to practicing.

Comprehending new information requires us to link and build on what we already know. Linking requires the brain to draw on data already in the brain, formulate new thoughts, reflect on the new images and snapshots of information (the computer program) and constantly run through the information over and over again as the trial-and-error process continues. Experiences allow learners to be tested during the learning and not just at the end of a process. This takes time and is considered the slowest part of learning. During the theory portion, consider using guided reflection through a series of questions to help learners move through the process faster.

Another benefit to the EAT principle is that we learn more if we struggle first than if we are spoon-fed the information. Guessing or struggling assists the learning process by keeping attention and focus, and the learner is engaged because his or her brain desires completion (Zeigarnik 1927).

Think about when you can't remember a fact on demand. Many times it will surface later when you haven't even been thinking about it. Your brain keeps searching until the task is finished. Psychologist Bluma Zeigarnik's research showed that we have a tendency to remember incomplete tasks better than completed tasks and will more likely return to them at a future time to complete them. Zeigarnik's research was done in 1927; a re-examination of her work was done in 1991, and the results came back that her study was replicable and the results conclusive (Seifert and Patalano 1991).

A-T-E. Awareness. Theory. Experience.

A trainer would organize information in this order when learners coming in already have a basic understanding of the information. They may even be masters that are in class to refresh for forty hours to keep their license or certifications. They walk into the room already aware of the concepts, and it is much easier to link to the base line of information.

For example, a friend of mine is a hairstylist who just went through a re-certification. She already knows how to create updos and braids. The class didn't teach the fundamentals but linked to what she already knew and taught her new twists on age-old concepts. When teaching a group of people with a strong knowledge base, it is best to teach a bit of the concepts and then allow for practice, practice, practice.

T-E-A. Theory. Experience. Awareness.

The main exceptions to the EAT process in participant-centered training is when safety is a concern, money is at stake, or the learners have no prior knowledge of the content. Then switch it around and teach it in the TEA format. Instead of having learners jump into a pool with no experience, we teach the theory first and the basics of how to swim. This sets learners up for success in their experience. Yes, they can struggle a little, but not to the point of disaster.

In technical training, if there is only a live application that can be "practiced" on and where making mistakes could "break" the software, then this would be an example of "money being at stake." Instead, provide enough background, screen shots, case studies and examples prior to going live on the system.

If I have learners with no prior exposure to the content, I do a lecturette and then allow for practice. Follow this pattern throughout the segment of content that they have little knowledge in:

Content-Practice-Content-Practice-Content-Practice

For those with experience, it looks like this:

Content-Practice-Practice-Practice

Then repeat the cycle. Notice both types of learners have the same amount of practice; it is just chunked differently for greatest learning (Clark 2010).

If you can find ways to follow the EAT order in your training modules, even in these higher risk situations, I encourage you to do it. Even if the experience is not "live," it can still provide a way to create engagement with the content without risking money or safety.

When I was a corporate trainer at Target doing a software roll-out with no practice mode, I created cards with an image of the relevant keyboard keys and another card with what each key's function was. By taking a step back and finding a way to teach outside a system that might get broken, learners were able to begin recognizing images and words together through an experience, which tapped into their whole brain and increased their focus and learning.

90/20/10

Based on my years of experience and research, I know that participants can listen with understanding for about ninety minutes before a break is needed for recharging. No matter the individual, participants were becoming antsy and more distracted every minute I go beyond ninety minutes. Research shows that humans can only listen with retention for **up to** twenty minutes (Szpunar et al. 2013). Therefore, you need to build in a distinct change-up or change of pace every twenty minutes. This is why a CPR module is up to twenty minutes, which allows for content to be taught while learners participate and revisit all throughout. Re-set learners' attention by changing up methods and creating engagement every ten minutes. Interactive strategies could fall into categories like participant-generated questions, problem solving in groups, idea-generating exercises or practical application time.

Let's work backwards to see this principle in action. If you need to involve the learners every ten minutes, how many times will you involve them in twenty minutes? If the discussions or activities are short, it could be as many as three times; if the activity is longer, then one or two times. How many twenty-minute chunks of content will fit into a ninety-minute segment of training? If you consider adding in an opener and a closer that last five minutes each, that leaves time for four modules. Remember that we can retain information when engaged for up to twenty minutes so consider shortening a few of the chunks to fifteen minutes and having five or six modules in a ninety-minute timeframe.

Chapter 9

DESIGNING AND DEVELOPING INTERACTIVITY: A STEP-BY-STEP GUIDE

I've covered why you should design and execute training that is instructor-led, but participant-centered. I've also looked at the individual components and principles for designing ILPC training programs. Now I'm going to dive into the nuts and bolts of how to actually develop the training course. Because this is a repeatable process, I've also included several of the templates I use. To make it easy, let's first look at the steps and then dive deeper into each with examples. You will not need to use every template every time. *You will see a couple of different examples from which to choose based on your preference.*

Remember, at this point, you have done your needs assessment and analysis, and you know that training is the answer. You also know who is in your training audience. Now it's time to begin designing the actual workshop.

1. Determine your measurable objectives and insert the session objectives into your outline following a logical presentation order.

2. Determine which content needs to be covered and then determine whether it will meet the specified objectives. These modules of content should be twenty minutes or less (CPR, CIO, 90/20/10). Consider creating a mindmap, outline, fishbone or other graphic organizer to brainstorm content.

3. Identify activities to engage participants in the content. This includes openers, closers, revisiters and energizers. Examples include a role play, learning partners, matching games or other activities that teach. Use a variety. (EAT, CPR)

4. Ensure there are revisits throughout.

5. Draft your materials list.

6. Practice or pilot test the session with real participants to gain insight and feedback to make improvements to the session before rolling it out.

Following is my master checklist that takes me step-by-step through the development process. I use this in conjunction with the planning template (which helps me get nitty-gritty with each content module to ensure I know what information I'm going to cover and how I'm going to cover it).

Date	Design Checklist	Example	My Project
	Designing and Developing the Materials		
	Brainstorm content that meets learning objectives	Mind Map, Index Cards, Concept Web	
	Effective opener that breaks pre-occupation, allows for networking, relevant to content	Puzzles, Statistics, Quotes	
	Design ideas around the EAT (Experience, Awareness, Theory) model if possible	Experience goes first	
	Include learners by giving them control through the CIO (Control, Included, Open) model	Give choices and networking time	
	Chunk content into 20 minutes or less segments	Use actionable verb list	
	Select IL/PC activities that meet learning objectives	Select from list of 114	
	Confirm Content, Participation, and Revisiting during each chunk		
	Plan for a physical break at least every 90 minutes		
	Confirm participant interaction at least every 10 minutes	Use variety – lecturettes, group discussion, journaling, content application	
	Anticipate occasions for energizers	After lunch, late in the day, mid-morning	
	Allow learners to close before breaks with a closer (Action Plan, Celebrate, Tie Together)	Action Ideas, Lecture Buster Cards	
	Plan in clear instructions to facilitate activities	Start together, give clear steps to accomplish	
	Plan in carryover opportunities	Immediate, Next Day, 30/60/90 Day	
	Develop job aids that complement learning objectives	Observation checklist, Process flowcharts	

Date	Design Checklist	Example	My Project
	Designing and Developing the Materials		
	Create Learner's Workbook	Use color, fill-in-the-blanks, Need to Know/Nice to Know/Where to Go	
	Create Leader's Guide	Flow Overview, Timing, Objectives, Bullets	
	Theme the training as appropriate	Purchase items that enhance the course theme	
	Determine the best room layout for the session delivery	U-Shape, Rounds, Classroom	
	Design PowerPoint slides that enhance, not replace the message	Reduce words but keep the meaning, Use images, Design on paper first	

The Designing and Developing the Materials checklist provides step-by-step guidance as to what comes next when working on development. To the right of each step is an example of what might be done to trigger ideas or provide a helpful tip for that step.

Let's look at each step in-depth.

1. Determine your measurable objectives and insert them into your outline.

Once you have completed your needs assessment (chapter seven) and determined training is the solution to the situation, you will also know what outcomes you need to see as a result of the training. You will use that information to write objectives for your training course, which we also covered in chapter seven.

Early in my career, I designed my first manager training course for a fee—I was so excited! I poured my heart out to create an active and engaging course with opportunities for application and action planning. On a conference call with the client, toward the end of the design, they asked me what the objectives were for the overall course and by module. I quickly shared that I would email those over later that day. Why? I had to write them! I had a fatal flaw in my design. I didn't think about the end results before designing.

Goals and objectives are the heart and soul of clearly identifying what you want to accomplish and how you plan to get there. Goals are broad, general, and sometimes abstract while objectives are narrow, precise, tangible and concrete. Objectives are how we reach the goals.

An ILPC trainer should spend twenty-five percent of the design time on the needs assessment and getting the objectives right for the course. If you have four hours to plan, you will spend at least one hour determining the goals and objectives for the workshop.

Spending this time before designing ensures there is no rework later and that participants get the content the first time through.

So now look at your objectives and decide in which order they should be taught to give participants a logical flow that helps them catch connections.

2. Determine which content needs to be covered.

Keep in mind that content that won't be used immediately and isn't mandatory can be put in a Nice-To-Know section of the workbook or in other job aids. Then learners can use these takeaway resources for on-the-job use, so you don't need to cover that content in class. If they aren't likely to use it right away, they will lose it. Having a reference that covers it will allow for a more effective use of time in class teaching need-to-know material.

Creating a graphic organizer can be an effective way to deduce which content you want to include. Pictured here is a mind map, a visual way to brainstorm and connect information. Once you've completed your mind map, content web, or other brainstorming graphic, you can cross-reference the content with your measurable objectives to determine what is Need-To-Know and what is Nice-To-Know.

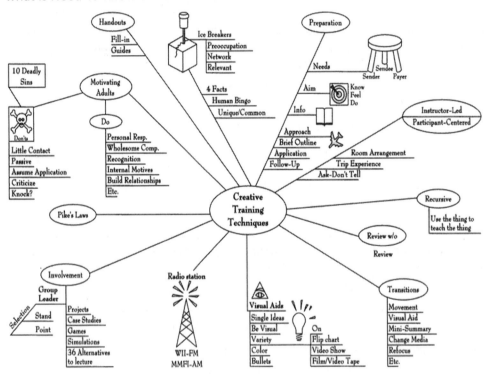

A mind map is a visual way to brainstorm and connect information. Start with your topic in the center. Then draw lines out to topics or subheadings. You can determine later if you want to include all topics or subtopics, but this will help get the ideas down on paper.

3. Identify activities to engage participants in the content.

Glasser, in *Choice Theory*, goes into detail on four components an instructor has control over to set adults up for successful learning. One of these elements is fun, which really resonates with me.

As an instructional designer, be sure to build in activities that are not your natural bent. I am an extremely participative learner. I like to engage and be social. When designing, I need to include a variety of exercises that allows for reflection, not just socializing. Reflection time, individually, in pairs, or in groups, is important and valuable for all types of learners because it allows us to assimilate and apply the information we just learned.

The following are two templates that I have used in designing my training sessions. First, I review my mind map, take a section of the content and work through up to ninety minutes in the high level planning template. Once I have completed this template, I then use the bottom portion of the second template, the session checklist, to double check my work (Know, Feel, Do and EAT).

Planning Template

Title/Subject:	Length of time:

Objective(s):

Time			Materials
	Opener:		
	(CPR In each <20 min.segment, include involvement every 10 min.)		
	△	C: P: R:	
	△	C: P: R:	
	△	C: P: R:	
	△	C: P: R:	
	△	C: P: R:	
	Closers:		

This session checklist can be used as a stand alone or in conjunction with one of the other planners. If used as a primary template, you will want to add in additional CPR sections based on the number of content modules. This template should be used for designing a segment lasting ninety minutes or less. Plan which opener you will use to start the session, which closer you will use at the end of the sixty minutes, and which energizer or revisiters you will include. For each twenty-minute learning modules, insert CPR (which stands for Content, Participation and Revisit). In the CPR sections, specify the content you will be covering, how you will build in learner participation and how the learners will revisit the content. Do the same for Know, Feel, Do, (KSA) and EAT. If you are designing ILPC training for an online environment, see the chapter on Virtual Training which also includes a planning template.

Session Checklist Example

4/16	1 Opener	Matching Game
4/22	1 Closer	Gallery Walk
4/24	1 Energizer or revisiter	Graphic Organizer
	CPR	
5/12	- Content	Vocabulary from workbook
5/14	- Participation	Paint a picture in their minds
5/15	- Revisiter	Describe with a partner
	CPR	
6/20	- Content	Model brainstorming descriptive words
6/26	- Participation	Brainstorm in small groups
6/27	- Revisiter	Create C.O.R.E. graphic organizer
	Know	Components of C.O.R.E.
	Feel	Confident, excited, able to implement
	Do	Use C.O.R.E.in their own training session

When I do the session checklist after doing the planning template, I do not literally write everything out again; rather I just mentally go through and make sure I have all the learning principles covered. I primarily use the checklist to ensure I have followed the EAT principle and that there is a Know, Feel and Do (KSA) component to the training.

The following CPR Session Layout Example is a good template if you prefer a more linear approach or if you are a specific learner. It still allows for the principles to be used but in a more traditional step-by-step approach. When I use this template at The Bob Pike Group, I have participants complete their own template and then have them highlight the Cs or content concepts, the Ps or where the variety of participation comes into play, and then the Rs or content revisits. This way the participant can visually "see" the CPR. In this example in step 1, there would be a C above examples of CORE and example of a "training session," Ps above "listen" and "paint a picture" and an R is above each instance of CORE (Closers, Openers, Revisiters, Energizers) because the participants were exposed to this content in the opener making subsequent engagements with CORE a revisit.

CPR Session Layout Example

Name: Becky Pluth

Audience: Project Managers

Topic: Participant-Centered Training

Length of time: (1) 60-minute session

Materials: *Creative Training Revolution,* Becky Pluth 2015, chart paper, markers

Objective: Participants will recognize C.O.R.E. (Closer, Opener, Revisiter, Energizer) and when to use.

Assessment: Oral Communication, C.O.R.E. Graphic Organizer

Opener: Play matching game with examples of C.O.R.E. and terms/definitions.

Step One: Invite participants to listen for examples of C.O.R.E. as the instructor reads an example of a "training" session aloud in order for them to "paint a picture" in their minds.

Step Two: After the story, invite participants to turn to a partner and share what elements of the story fall into each category of C.O.R.E.

Step Three: Instructor models the process of brainstorming C.O.R.E using a graphic organizer.

Step Four: Participants will brainstorm a list of C.O.R.E. in small groups. Each group creates a C.O.R.E. graphic organizer on chart paper placing concepts about their training inside each of the four areas in the circle.

Closer: Charts are posted on the wall for a Gallery Walk.

4. Ensure the content is revisited throughout. Using these templates will help you build in revisits, increasing your learners' retention of the content.

5. Draft your materials list. I think this one is self-explanatory. Be sure to include what may seem obvious but frequently gets forgotten.

6. Practice or pilot test your new ILPC-designed session with real participants to gain insight and feedback. Then make improvements to the session before rolling it out. This is especially valuable in helping finesse the timing, making sure you have activities that resonate with the audience, and finding any gaps in content.

In the checklist, I have the date that I fill in when the item is completed. I then have the step I need to take like "brainstorm content." Next to that is an example of an activity I might use to complete that step. Lastly, there is a blank where I pick which activity I will use and write it in. The activity can be one of the prompts from the checklist or something else which fits that purpose.

Once I have completed planning my content and my activities, I then create a timing flow. This helps ensure I follow my guidelines about only doing ninety-minute modules which are then broken into smaller segments of twenty minutes with only ten minutes of lecture at any given time. It also helps me stay on track with the workshop time allotted.

Here is what the time flow for the first few hours of The Bob Pike Group's Creative Training Boot Camp looks like:

Boot Camp Timing 2016
DAY 1 — 8:30-4:00

Timing	Activity	Materials
60/60	**REDiscoveRED puzzle**	PPT
8:30- 9:30	**Number Puzzle 102 tips, tricks and techniques**	PPT
	Just one word puzzle	PPT
	Debrief puzzles	
		Nametags Markers
	Volunteer-select leader	Chart
	Nametags	
	Human Scramble to share nametag info and select a Learning Partner. We will be meeting with our partners at various times throughout these two days.	
	Move to sit at a table with your learning partner. Say Hello to your learning family.	PPT
	Get to know your family better by taking this quick survey using the clickers on your table.	
	We will be using the TP clickers periodically during these two days.	
	Family Charts:	Chart
	Now we are going to do an activity with our learning families. Person who has the most siblings will be the spokesperson for your family. Why did I open this way instead of doing the agenda and logistics first?	
Leader	Leader: person who is going on vacation the soonest.	
	We are going on a short field trip. Please bring 3 large colored dots with you for your trip. Road Map (breaks every 90 minutes-ish)/Question Board/Ground Rule posters/Concepts to Capture/Agenda dotting on your way back to your seats.	Large dots

20/65 9:30-9:50	**Volunteer (Absolute Power)** **Come up and grab workbooks for your table.** Share one idea gained this morning to earn your book. **Book flip and flag** Share one page **Book organization** Evaluation discussion. **They are due at 2:23 PM tomorrow.** Action Ideas pages	Books Page flags p. 3-6
10/75 9:50-10:00	Closer: Write down all your ideas so far this morning, starting from the moment you walked into the room. We will be going on a 13-minute break at the completion of this activity. I will put on a countdown timer, so synchronize your watches before you leave the room. I will begin when it gets to zero. Stand and share ideas with your Learning Partner. Feel free to jot down any that you missed.	p. 7

The time flow goes into our Leader's Guide and then provides enough direction and instruction on the content, activities and supplies needed for any of our facilitators who might be doing the training.

In the timing box, I show how much time is required for the activity along with how long the entire training module is. For example, I have my relevant openers beginning at 8:30 a.m. I plan to have those openers take sixty minutes which will be the entire first module of sixty minutes. In the activity field, I then put the name of the activity along with a brief description of the activity and its purpose. I may also include some script if I want to phrase the directions in a specific way. Then, in the third column, I include materials I may need such as a PowerPoint slide or markers and flip charts, and I also include which page in the student handbook corresponds with the material.

As I wrap up this chapter on design, let me share one more tip with you. When I worked as a trainer at Target Corporation, I learned the mantra "Eighty percent and out the door," and I became a believer. Think about it—if your manual has a typo, is it worth the time and expense of endlessly attempting perfection? Or can we let our learners have some fun finding our mistakes, reward them for doing so, and make the edits after the pilot of the first few classes? In the name of productivity, it is better done than perfect. Unless safety is involved, it is more productive to focus on eighty percent and out the door...and on to the next thing!

Stopping your current way of training and developing, and facilitating an ILPC program doesn't happen overnight. It will take time and practice for these principles to become naturally instilled in what you are designing, but I promise that the effort will be worth it.

In the following chapters you will discover how to best select activities such as openers and closers. The Bob Pike Group has a series of books called *SCORE: Super Closers, Openers, Revisiters, Energizers* with hundreds of activities and content frames that can help you build effective participation into your program.

Designing with the Audience in Mind

by Karen Carlson

When designing your training documents, the most important question to keep top of mind is "Who am I designing this for?" The answer should always be for the participants! That seems obvious, but more often than not, training documents, especially PowerPoint presentations, are designed to aid the facilitator, thus slide after slide is filled with bullet points. This becomes more of a crutch than an aid to the facilitator. No one enjoys sitting through a class where the facilitator simply reads from the slides. Instead, consider how or what about this slide will help the participant retain the content and apply the learning back on the job.

The participant is front and center when designing the leader's guide too. Providing the facilitator with specific directions that ensure productive discussions and activities benefits both the facilitator and the participant. Including pictures of flip charts also helps both parties. When designing the leader's materials, even consider what table toys and room decorations to include and how they will benefit the learner experience. You may even want to include notes to the facilitator that detail the why behind some of the toys or decorations. This is especially helpful for newer facilitators.

When designing the participant guide, focus on creating a document that they can refer to after the class. Fill-in-the-blank sections aid in retention far more than simply providing a copy of the PowerPoint deck. Writing aids retention. Design participant materials that encourage writing: include notes pages, reflection space, questions to answer, points to ponder and discuss. A glossary is always helpful, but an interactive glossary is even better! These can be in the form of crossword puzzles, word finds, or matching games. The internet offers several free templates for creating puzzles.

Finally, the PowerPoint...Pictures speak a thousand words, as the story goes. Design slides that tell a story through pictures instead of simply loading the slides with bullet points. Again, what will help the participant remember and apply the content being presented? We have all become too accustomed to seeing slides full of bullets. Thus, we tend to ignore most of the content. Surprise your participants with fresh looking slides that capture their attention and make them wonder what's coming next!

Taking the spotlight off the facilitator and putting it on the participant can be a hard lesson for facilitators to learn. But it is perhaps the most valuable lesson of all.

Karen Carlson was a certified train–the–trainer instructor at The Bob Pike Group and contributor to books in the SCORE *series for trainers.*

Chapter 10

OPENERS

What would you guess was the average face value for a ticket to the opening ceremonies at the 2016 Olympic Games? If you guessed any less than $2,185, you were too low. Consider, then, that tickets to individual Olympic competitions started as low as $20. Event planners know the value of a good opening and, in the case of the Olympics, they charge accordingly.

A top trainer also knows the value of a strong opening and will make sure that is part of the training design because what gets planned gets implemented. Sadly, the average trainer does not open, he just begins. He might talk about himself for ten minutes and then share about the logistics of the day, maybe even go over a few objectives. Meanwhile, the learners are contemplating their drive to work or the last meeting they had. Their thoughts are not in the room.

The goal of a strong opening is to move the participants into a place of learning as quickly as possible. Objectives and an agenda are important, but the priority should be breaking the preoccupation of those in the room in order to capture interest in the training and create buy-in. In some circumstances, trainers are required to present safety procedures as a first order of business. If this applies to you, then the opener would come immediately after completing the safety precautions.

What exactly is an opener?

An opener is a purposeful activity that is relevant to the content. There are three questions we can ask about an activity to help decide if it is a good opener or not. We refer to this as raising the BAR (Break preoccupation, Allow for networking, and Relevant to content.) If you can answer "yes" to these, the activity can qualify as an opener and not just an icebreaker.

Question 1: Is it relevant to the content?

This is the first and most critical criteria when choosing an opening activity. If the opener does not relate to the content, it is not an opener at all; it is just a random icebreaker. Have you ever done the icebreaker where someone puts a sticker on your back that says Batman, and your goal is to figure out what it says by asking questions? This works well at parties because it gets people talking to others. An icebreaker is for parties; an opener is for training.

A true opener will relate to your content and contribute to the learning process. The Bob Pike Group has several books that catalog and explain hundreds of openers, but you might also take a favorite ice breaker you know and adapt it so it applies to your content.

Question 2: Does it break preoccupation?

Recall the last time you participated in a conference session. Were you ready for learning or did you have something else on your mind? Most often we need a little help getting engaged in the session both physically and mentally. Consider also that some people in the room simply do not want to be there. They feel they have better things to do, that they already know everything, or are upset because their boss made them attend. The solution to preoccupation and negative attitudes is a powerful, attention-getting beginning that involves the participants.

I find that sales trainers do a really good job of this, especially the successful ones who have been on the front lines for awhile. They have typically seen and experienced resistance firsthand and, perhaps without any training, have had to figure out how to break through it. Trainer Brian Tracy teaches the concept of redirection where, similar to a magician, you work to shift the customer's focus away from the fear that you're going to sell something to her that she doesn't want or need.

An opener can help create redirection by moving participants away from their preoccupied thoughts to a value proposition or what is in the training for them—what will they get out of the training that will make their lives better, their jobs easier. As instructors, we are salespeople in a sense. And we need to find a way to break through the preoccupation, cast vision, create buy-in, and move participants into a state of learning as quickly as possible.

Every Bob Pike Group course is designed around experiential learning, and our unique value proposition is to learn twice as much in half the time. We teach trainers how to save time designing, preparing, and teaching all while doubling retention. This gets people's attention and actually sparks their interest. They want to see how we do what we say we can do. They become willing participants in their own learning but not until after we capture their attention.

You may need to think about this for a bit and come up with a hook and selling point that works for your organization, industry, and specific course.

Question 3: Does it facilitate networking?

Your opening activity needs to help people feel comfortable with one another because when tension goes up, retention goes down (Darke 1988, Owens et al. 2014). By allowing people to network with one another and connect, tension is reduced.

The networking also adds value to your training as it improves the likelihood that less formal training will occur between the learners when the training session is long over. I recently attended a business retreat for CEOs and business owners. While we had wonderful keynotes and facilitated sessions, I found the networking time to be as valuable, if not more valuable, than the formal offerings.

The popularity of platforms like Facebook, Twitter, and LinkedIn indicate that people value personal connection even if it's done digitally. We tried something new at our fall conference one year. We started the "networking" part of our opener before the conference even began. Every one of the nearly 200 attendees was placed on a team of twenty learners prior to the conference. One Bob Pike Group trainer was assigned to each group, and each team had an opportunity to connect through social media and technology before the conference began. This allowed conferees to begin building up their comfort levels even before stepping off the plane!

At The Bob Pike Group, we do a few specific things to increase networking at the start of the session. The use of name badges is a small but very effective way for people to connect. As an opener, we typically use a name tag scramble (see directions for this activity at the end of this chapter) as an opener because no one wants to be saying "Hey, you!" all day long.

At the end of the name tag scramble, we pair participants with the person they connected with last during the activity, and then we give them the opportunity to sit at a new table with that newfound "learning partner." This breaks colleagues up and provides at least one individual with whom they can really connect during the training. Many of our participants keep in touch with their learning partners long after the session has ended. In fact, I still keep in touch with my learning partner from a Bob Pike Group course I went through eighteen years ago. We touch base on LinkedIn and share research from time to time.

If you typically open your session with a test or an agenda, STOP! Open with your most important message. Provide opportunities for learners to feel good about themselves. Use their first names, honor their years of experience, share bits and pieces of personal information as appropriate, and say thank you when they've shared a good idea. In class, once we've had partners work together, I might tell them to give one another a high-five or fist bump or just say "thank you" to their learning partner as a way to show appreciation and build their confidence.

When do I insert openers?

Openers are done whenever a class begins or reconvenes after a break. In a common day-long class, you would have four openers: one at the beginning of the day, one after the first break, one directly following lunch, and one after the afternoon break. The idea is to create more starts and stops so as to increase the retention of the content. (See chapter five on Seven Ways We Remember Anything.)

How much time should I spend on opening?

The rule of thumb is the longer the class, the more time spent opening. Why? Because of the social component of learning. Recall that when tension goes up, retention goes down.

You want to invest more time at the beginning of the session allowing participants to feel comfortable with one another so they are able to quickly engage in exercises moving forward. This gives them a chance to connect and gets their brains in the game. More time is needed for longer classes because you want to build a stronger bond and that takes more time. By spending a few minutes on the front end of each module or session, you are ensuring that participants are right there with you and can focus on the content.

Below is a grid that gives a rough idea of how much time you should spend opening a class based on how long the class is. *This grid just shows how much time your first opener should take.* All other openers, no matter how long the workshop, should take between five and ten minutes.

Length of Class	1 Hour	Half Day	One Day	Multiple Day
Time Opening	1-3 minutes	5-10 minutes	10-15 minutes	15+ minutes
Number of Openers	1	2	4	4/day

Once you have completed the opener and are moving onto your next content piece or activity, there are more creative ways to transition without using an unexpectant "Are there any questions?" as your segue.

Try some of these as alternatives:

- What's in it for me? Allow the learners to hear the objectives and answer the question for themselves. Consider having learners share around the table what they're interested in for the next segment.

- Answer "Why should I care?" for your participants.

- Share a value proposition statement for the next piece of content. For example, "This next section of content will reduce your design time by fifty percent." I know I would start listening.

- Share why the next section is important.

- If you are co-facilitating, have your peer instructor begin the debrief. This is a natural transition and doesn't need to be stated "and now Becky will debrief." That would defeat the whole purpose.

- Ask learners to join you on a new page.

- Ask for volunteers to come up and get the next set of materials.

Quick Openers

Here are a selection of openers that will help you quickly open your session. Pick one that suits your personality, style, and learners—because if you do not feel comfortable and confident, your learners will sense your discomfort and also feel uncomfortable. Our series of *SCORE (Super Closers, Openers, Revisiters, Energizers) for Enhanced Training Results* books has a lot of opening activities you can also adapt to your content and implement.

Outline an Incident

A good incident must create curiosity or intrigue.

Determine the protagonist of the incident. The best incident is one that you personally experienced (e.g., "I was walking through the woods when…"). The next best is one that you know happened to someone else (e.g., "My neighbor Joe was walking through the woods when…"). The third option is to make up an incident (e.g., "Imagine walking through the woods when…"). Details are key. Here's an incident I might use with a train-the-trainer class as a quick opener.

Step one: Insert a few photos into PowerPoint of Janelle, a new hire trainer with little experience.

Step two: Explain that, just before Janelle does her first practice training session, master trainer Candice shares how entertaining she makes training by regaling the story of bumbling, first-time trainer Susie.

Step three: During practice, Janelle tries to be an entertainer like Candice, but it falls flat.

Step four: Talk at your tables about how Janelle can improve. The discussion leader is the newest trainer.

Ask for a show of hands

I was a brand-new teacher looking for summer work. I met a woman named Bobbi DePorter who needed good teachers to teach accelerated learning programs to junior and senior high school students in a summer camp program. These programs took place on elite college campuses like Stanford, Notre Dame, and Colorado College. I flew out to California to audition for the position. At 20 years old, I pretty much thought I knew it all and felt sure I would be offered the job.

Upon arriving, I realized I was up against some pretty amazing talent. One was the Teacher of the Year for the State of Colorado, another was the Teacher of the Year for the State of Minnesota, and the list went on. The first day, I was given a section of content on which to present in active-learning format the next day. We were assigned a section that covered the acronym HMOY. This was before Google, and I was at a loss for what those letters represented. I'll never forget when the first presenter stood up and said, "Humoy ever had trouble reading?" She continued to say Humoy as if it were a person's name instead of spelling out the acronym and saying "How many of you?"

Although I was glad I was not the first one to present and make the same mistake, it was branded on my mind that starting a session by asking for a show of hands is a very quick, effective way to begin. When I ask for a show of hands, I oftentimes invite participants to look around and see who answered just like they did and to identify those who are different, too. It is one way to get to know each another, see the experience in the room visually, and break preoccupation. After asking for a show of hands, I will often follow up with a discussion question the participants can explore in their smaller groups.

Ask a rhetorical question

A rhetorical question is a question for which you do not expect to get an answer (e.g., "Do I look like I was born yesterday?") Rhetorical questions can be used as a quick way to ignite or provoke an audience. It could be used to get people to think or reflect on a concept that you are about to share. Rhetorical questions should not be used when you want to be very clear about something.

Did you know there are many different ways you can ask a rhetorical question? Ahhh, see what I did there? I used a rhetorical question. A rhetorical question is just one way to add variety into your training. However, if an entire training session is built on rhetorical questions, there is no variety, and your learners will become passive. Most times the same concept can be shared in a different way, so use it sparingly.

Following are nine outcomes I can get by asking rhetorical questions.

Thinking

This is the go-to reason for using a rhetorical question in a trainer's toolkit. Neuroscience research shows participants need to be actively engaged and present for learning to occur. So using a rhetorical question can quickly break lecture, break preoccupation and re-engage the learner.

Inquiring

You might ask the group to think to themselves, "What if your training program totally failed?" Give them a moment to think silently and ponder the consequences of a failed program. Would jobs be lost? Would the company eventually lose clients? Would profits fall and wages freeze? Would injuries increase? By simply asking them a question that did not require any sharing, they have begun to formulate all of the reasons why it will be important to engage in the training session that is about to unfold. Instead of you selling them, they are each selling themselves on the training.

Persuading

In order to use a rhetorical question that gets an audience to agree with you, there must first be a level of trust established. Use this form of rhetorical question only after you have been presenting with the group, and they find you credible and authentic. When using this form of rhetorical questioning, you gain allies in convincing the audience of your expertise while reducing tension because they can relate to you. For example, if you represent an online assessment company and are speaking to training managers, you could ask, "Given how much time your teams put into training efforts, don't they deserve a simple tool to continue learning transfer with little effort?"

Emphasizing

This goes hand-in-hand with using statistics as a way to open. After introducing a statistic, a rhetorical question that forces higher-order thinking can make a good point. The statistic is factual while the question forces your participants to think. For example, you are speaking to the team sales reps that produce and research diabetic drugs. You could ask,

"One out of every eleven people in the United States has diabetes. Think about how many people you know—which ones would you choose to get diabetes?"

Exploring

I call this the Hail Mary approach when you talk about one thing and then take the audience by surprise by asking an opposing question. Imagine you are presenting in a sales meeting, and you attempt to get the team out of the slump and motivate them by asking, "The Association for Talent Development's annual research just came out and predicts that training budgets will be slashed next year. Does this prediction apply to us?" I can then take the presentation down the path of why it does not apply to our organization.

Evoking emotion

Stirring emotion is a way to jumpstart your session. People can relate to their own emotions and do not readily argue with their own feelings. Instead of making statements about emotions, start the session by involving their emotions. For example, suppose you are facilitating a training session at a non-profit organization. Instead of saying, "They never help us reach our donation goals," ask "What have they ever done to help us reach our financial goals?"

Answering a question

Questions can help all learners get on the same page. Ask a series of questions with the exact same answer. Some learners may not know the answer to one, but by the time you've asked three, they get the idea. For example, "What comes first: safety or fun? What matters more: safety or profits? What is our guiding principle when we're onsite with machinery?" The answer each time is safety.

Entertaining

I am the ideal weight…for a woman seven feet tall. At the beginning of a course, I might say, "Many of you agree that you don't get this good looking from just sitting around all day. It takes a lot of work to get up and get those chips and Mountain Dew! Did you know that research shows that you're smarter standing on your feet?" And then I go directly into a lecture on why standing up makes us smarter! If you are not naturally funny, this type of rhetorical question or statement may not work for you.

Addressing the elephant in the room

When you know that you have a group of people with certain perceptions walking into the room, you have your work cut out for you. By addressing the unspoken, you can gain support. This is also a technique for dealing with difficult participants. In this case, the rhetorical question will be answered immediately thereafter. For example, in a class where the training is mandatory, you might open with, "As a tenured employee, you may ask yourself, 'Why do I have to go to these mandatory harassment courses? To stay employed.'" I then say, "Take thirty seconds at your tables and share why you don't want to be here." I follow that with a two-minute table discussion on what we can get out of the session if we are willing to move past our resentment and engage with the learning. I always give more time for them to think of ways and reasons to want to be in the room.

After they're done brainstorming what they could get out of it, I have each table share aloud. If nothing else, people usually feel better because they got it off their chests.

Ask a discussion question

Because we want to include the social component of learning (see chapter eight), we want to start with discussion questions that are about the topic. These are low-risk questions that build in networking and allow people to engage with the content. People are more comfortable talking about facts than feelings, especially with colleagues. Start with questions about content, then dig deeper into how it applies to work, and then ask questions that are directed at individuals and how they will apply or change behavior. There are several kinds of discussion questions.

Connection

Connection questions should relate to the workshop you are just opening but can also be questions that allow participants to get to know one another. An example I use is "What's one thing you love about being a trainer and one thing you love to do outside of work?" It is important to give an example first when asking these types of questions, so I might say that "I love when participants have an 'A-ha' moment, and one thing I love outside of work is hanging out with my PGA golf-pro hubby and four kids." Your example will set the tone for what they share.

Dissection

Dissecting questions analyze, examine and study a topic. Each group can have a different question in order to explore different components of content to be covered. Again, dissecting questions are comfortable and safe because they relate to content and can be used to open a session. An example of a dissecting question is "What is blended learning?" To take it up a step and make it more difficult, you could ask, "How does neuroscience play a role in blended learning?" Questions that start with "how" are more difficult to answer then "what" or "why" questions.

Collection

Collection questions are designed to gather information. This looks like brainstorming. Jump right into the brainstorming process by getting both sides of the brain, the creative (right) and logic (left), warmed up.

Reflection

Reflection questions help learners draw from their past experiences. This can help with retention because it taps into long-term memory to make an association or link. This also honors the learners' experience and provides an opportunity for participants to learn from one another. Reflection questions might sound like, "Who have you seen model these techniques before?" "Can you think of a time when the principles we just covered would have been helpful?" or "What are the benefits for you in using the three keys to opening?"

Inspection

This takes the discussion to a much deeper level. These types of questions require the participant to utilize analysis and synthesis skills. These questions require reflection on the content and push learners to figure out how to adapt, adopt, and apply it to their world. It goes beyond the job, and it requires individuals to take action. Inspection questions might sound like, "What is one concept you learned today that you are struggling to understand?" or "What will be the most difficult component for you to apply?"

Use inspection questions later on in a training after participants have gotten to know one another. This might fall as an opener right after an afternoon break where people have a better chance of knowing the content and can apply it before the end of the day to conquer whatever roadblocks they may have.

Make a promise

When you make a promise, you need to be sure to keep it. Promises can include small things like, "If you remind me in each segment to share a secret web address, you'll get the five secrets every trainer should know." Now you've not only created curiosity, you have a promise that you can keep. I make promises surrounding giveaways, start and end times, breaks, and how I will answer questions.

Make an outrageous statement

"My guess is that in a group this size, half of you are prisoners." Now of course this would be an outrageous statement made in a mandatory class or training. It addresses the elephant in the room, that people are required to be there and are thus "prisoners," but it also grabs attention. Outrageous statements are memorable and quickly grab attention and focus the group. Another outrageous statement is "I'm going to share with you the five deadly sins of training." Here's a list of some exciting words that can help grab attention in your next outrageous statement:

Boost	Explosive	Significant
Brilliant	Free	Spicy
Capture	Guarantee	Striking
Clever	Incredible	Stunning
Conquer	Killer	Tremendous
Dangerous	Mega	Ultimate
Dynamite	Perfection	Unreal
Exceptional	Secrets	Wicked
Exciting	Sexy	Worst

Use an unusual statistic

At the start of this chapter, I gave an example about the cost of tickets to the opening ceremony of the Olympic games. Offering unusual statistics, and even better, having learners guess a statistic that's unusual, can create excitement and energy in a class opener. Guessing and struggling assists in the learning process.

My sister was working with educators, and she had some amazing statistics on how many kids drop out of school each year in the United States. Instead of just stating the statistic or putting the number up on a slide, she put a visual of a stadium on the slide and had learners visualize the stadium completely full with no seats left. On the next slide, she minimized the picture and put forty stadiums side-by-side and had participants imagine all of them full for the biggest game of the year. Then she made the statement, "This is how many kids in the United States drop out of school each year." It's only after we've allowed the participant to absorb the statistic that we reveal the answer. An unusual statistic can be staggering, jaw-dropping, emotional or entertaining and is a powerful way to engage the brain with curiosity.

Use a visual aid or prop
Without saying a word, you can grab attention. In one session I was teaching, I had an industrial-sized roll of toilet paper. As participants came into the room, I simply asked them to "take as much as you need." They had no idea why. As we began the course, I explained that they were going to share at their tables information they already knew about the content. Each person needed to share one idea or concept for each square of toilet paper they had taken.

The next day as they entered, I once again said, "Take as much as you need." This time, several participants took fewer squares thinking I was going to do the same thing. But this time, I said for each square you took, give yourself one point and share one concept or idea you learned yesterday. I now had a bunch of participants wishing they had taken more squares. This became a theme in the class, and they never knew how many pieces they should take!

There are a lot of different ways to use visual aids and props. Which ones do you see most commonly in your classrooms? My guess is that you see flip charts, projectors, Smart Boards, markers, nametags, posters, and perhaps books. Do any of those create curiosity? Why not add visual aids and props that are unexpected? Here are some examples that I have used successfully:

- Movie clips
- Classroom response systems (TurningPoint clicker technology)
- Individual sized whiteboards (one per table)
- Oversized dice
- Sticky notes
- Koosh balls
- Balloons
- Smart phones as a way to poll everyone
- Buzzers
- Chimes

The idea is to have a variety of visual aids and props. Consider having one for each table. Participants love to engage and be a part of using visual aids themselves versus just watching all the time. When deciding which props or visual aids to use, consider your end goal. For example, let's say the visual aid is a movie. Do not just use your favorite movie clip because it is funny; instead select a movie that draws the learner into the content you are about to teach.

Use a metaphor and analogy

Metaphors and analogies can give learners a good memory hook for new information. Mnemonics and acronyms are also good tools to use. The Bob Pike Group uses the acronym CORE which stands for closers, openers, revisiters, and energizers. It is another way to help learners access the file folders in their brains.

Regardless of which strategies you choose to use, the value is in giving participants control over their learning from the very beginning, allowing them to feel included and a part of the group through networking so they are then open to the content that will be shared in the next eighty minutes (CIO model). Make your opening Olympic by breaking preoccupation and allowing for networking but also being relevant to the concepts and content that will be taught and reinforced throughout the day.

The Social Component of Learning

The networking facilitated by openers adds value to your training as it improves the likelihood that less formal training will continue to occur between the learners when the training session is long over. Another idea to facilitate networking is to seat participants at round tables where they can interact with each other, rather than classroom style in rows (see chapter fifteen on Training Day Preparations). This encourages talking—something people do not always expect at a training. Yes, we want to encourage talking even if it is while we are talking from the front of the room. Most of the time neighbors will talk to one another about the content because they are interested in trying to better understand. [Trainer tip: only set five chairs at a standard sixty-inch round banquet table that seats eight so nobody's back is to the instructor.]

As the trainer, you set the example and tone for networking in the classroom. The instructor and any other training staff should welcome participants and be available to connect fifteen minutes before and after each class or session to help set the tone. I was on a flight recently with an administrator of a hospital in Door County, Wisconsin. In talking with him, he shared that they have been a top hospital for client satisfaction for the past ten years because of the culture they have created. They train their staff to say hi every single time they pass someone in the hallway—to patients and employees alike. The first time they say, "Hello, good morning," and the second time it might be, "Good to see you again," the third time they say, "Still looking good!" He said he told his staff it does not matter how many times you pass the same person, always acknowledge him or her.

The hospital administration also trained their employees to finish every conversation in the patient's room with, "What else can I do for you? I have time." At first, the staff was chagrined imagining their work load would become overwhelming. But the mandate was

"Make the time to provide exceptional service." The staff defined the culture, and soon the hospital became known for being the best around in patient care.

As instructors, it is our job to create a culture even if only for sixty minutes during a training session. Arrive early, leave last and start saying, "How can I help? I have time." It could make all the difference. Learners want to network with each other, but they also want to get to know you and be known by you.

ILPC training builds in time to tap into the experience in the room. During our courses, we ask learners to write down how many years of experience they have in their particular field of training. When we add up the years of experience in the room, we always see a number greater than ten times that of the instructor. This honors the experience in the room and allows participants to learn from one another as well as from the process and the content. Yes, networking happens on breaks and organically, but we choose to foster relationship building and experience-sharing in session too.

The Rockefeller Foundation has a video titled *Gather: The Art and Science of Effective Convening*. The idea is that you can go alone, but together we can go further, that three brains are better than one. Allowing opportunities for people to connect is a valuable use of time in the classroom and leads to improved learning and retention.

Folding Time™: How to Achieve Twice as Much in Half the Time for Training Professionals

by Neen James

You don't have time to do everything; you only have time to do what matters.
When was the last time you went on a road trip? There is a huge amount of planning that takes place: where to go, what route to take, what to visit, where to stay, what to wear, what snacks to pack on the trip (no matter with which audience we ask this question, snacks always comes up and makes us giggle). Once you have answered all these questions, it is then time to try and fit all the luggage and other items into the boot of your car (we call it a boot in Australia; in the United States, it is called the trunk of your car).

Which suitcases do you pack in first? You don't try and put in all the little things; you always put in the large luggage first.

Our day is like a road trip. Each day, we need to ensure we focus on the large luggage items first. Many training professionals want to just get little things done so they can cross them off a list; however, this strategy doesn't allow you to have the greatest impact. It makes you feel good in the short term because you think you got something completed, but it doesn't maximize your time.

What are your large luggage items today?

Invest fifteen minutes
If you really want to prioritize your day, invest fifteen minutes in the morning to determine your highest priority activities, and then focus on the achievement of those. We take that a

step further and write the three non-negotiable items on a Post-it note and carry it with us all day until it is complete. That one little Post-it note becomes a filtering system to help us prioritize how we complete activities and how we agree to invest time.

Ask yourself three questions

If you want to determine if the project or task you are about to embark on will have an impact, ask yourself these questions:

1. Is this the best use of my time?
2. Is this the best use of my abilities?
3. Is this the best use of my opportunities?

You may not get it right every time, however, if you answer these questions honestly, you will have a bigger impact in your day, your business, your home and your community.

Eliminate Distractions

Training professionals need to eliminate distractions to accomplish more. You know your distractions (they might include other people, social media, email, meetings, maybe even yourself). All of these are important; however, to accelerate your focus and achieve all you want to do, here are a few practical suggestions:

Use social media blocking apps

Find ways to block your technology to give you focused concentration time instead of sneaking a look at social media when you get bored or are procrastinating. We like Anti-Social for Mac computers.

Change your location

A new environment, even the local Starbucks, could assist you in completing a project or task. Consider scheduling time to work in a conference room. Out of sight, out of mind...and out of distraction.

Play a game

Treat completion of a project as a game. Set yourself a reward for completion. Once you have done it, celebrate with a nice lunch, a walk outside, calling a friend, reading an article... whatever you need to do to incentivize yourself to get it done.

Use a timer

We enjoy setting our iPhone for fifteen minutes and then achieving as much as we can in that timeframe. It works if you are scoping out a new module, writing an agenda for a training day, booking logistics for the next training day, reviewing a training calendar. You would be astounded how much you can do when you play a game to beat the clock. Try it; you'll be so glad you did!

As busy training professionals, we are constantly investing our time to develop others and our organization. Today, choose to invest time in yourself to work on the activities that will give you the greatest return on your time investment so you can make a greater impact in the world.

Our motto for our company is to "Do what we love, with people we love, in places we love." It is such an honor to do the work we do; let's invest our time in the most important things.

Remember, you don't have time to do everything, only time to do what matters.

Neen James is a high energy, Aussie leadership expert focused on productivity. The author of Folding Time™ *and* Secrets of Super Productivity, *Neen also provides one-on-one mentoring to leaders. Find out more at www.neenjames.com*

Chapter 11

CLOSERS

After the opening ceremonies, the Olympic Games closing ceremonies in 2016 had the next highest average ticket price at $2105. The Olympic Committee isn't just committed to its opener, it's equally committed to a strong close to its storied games. Conversely, most training sessions don't close strong, they just sort of end. They end because time runs out. They end because the worksheet is complete. They end in utter boredom. Imagine if the Olympics ended with this announcement: "Well, that's it. I guess that was the last game. So, thank you for coming. Have a nice weekend." Heaven forbid! Instead, they end with a celebration, an activity to lock in the experience and make it even more memorable. The opening and closing ceremonies are a wonderful picture of what it looks like to open and close well because beginnings and endings are far more memorable than the stuff that came in the middle.

Ending a session with a request for learners to fill out an evaluation is *not* making the best use of "prime real estate" in the training schedule, especially when the content and the day have gone really well. It would be like an Olympic athlete finishing the race in first place and then just walking off the field and heading back to the Olympic Village. It's anticlimactic and lacking something.

The goal in closing each session and day of training is to wrap things up with a three-to-fifteen minute activity that is designed to help lock in what was learned in class. If you want to transfer learning back to the job, there *must* be an opportunity for learners to tie things together for themselves and plan to do something differently.

What does an effective closer look like?

There are three keys components to closing out a session well, and they conveniently create the acronym ACT. If we were to be punny, we say it's the closing ACT: **A**ction planning, **C**elebration, and **T**ying things together. A single effective closing activity should embody all three of these components—it should direct participants to consider how they will apply their new knowledge; it should celebrate their hard work during the session; and it should allow participants to tie together, in their minds, the new information with their prior knowledge, and tie up loose ends of the new content into a nice neat bow.

Action Planning

A deadly sin of trainers is closing by saying, "In closing, let me summarize...." I cringe at the thought. In that situation, the person doing the talking is doing the learning. An Instructor-Led, Participant-Centered trainer would close by saying something like, "Take four minutes to work as a team at your table and brainstorm five ways you plan to implement skills or ideas you learned today." *That* is facilitating action planning—it's setting up your participants to plan how they will act on the information they've learned.

The role of instructor is to set the activity up; the participants decide on their take-aways. This reflection and planning time helps them focus on what they will do differently as a result of what they learned. Through this brief planning, they are participating with the content (promoting retention), communicating with one another, gaining a greater awareness of their next steps, and building a better attitude toward applying the content—all before they walk out the training room door.

Celebration

In closing a session, celebration does not need to be a big party or a graduation. For example, if I'm running a one day workshop, I will facilitate four closers—one before morning break, one before lunch break, one before afternoon break, and one to close the day. So how do I allow learners to celebrate before going on break or going to lunch? I use activities that encourage them to look at how they have grown in the last ninety minutes, to reflect on the new knowledge they've gained, and to take satisfaction in knowing they'll be able to do something differently on the job because of it. In some small way, they leave the session feeling impressed with themselves. It's an internal celebration.

Tying Things Together

Once the session has ended, it's natural and good for participants to continue considering bits and pieces of the material. What we don't want, however, is for them to leave with niggling questions. The "tie things together" aspect of a closer should help participants understand how all the content fits and works together. It helps them discover, if they haven't already, that they have a satisfying understanding of the material as a whole. It's like a casserole. During the session, participants learn the different parts of the content—the ingredients: the noodles, sauce, meat, and veggies. For many participants, all those ingredients will naturally come together into a satisfying whole. But for some, it won't be until the closing activity that the ingredients are all put together and baked. Participants should leave knowing the satisfaction of the casserole, not the dissatisfaction of individual ingredients. An effective closer bakes all the content elements together.

How much time should I spend on closing?

The amount of time you spend closing a session depends on the type of closer you do and what you are attempting to accomplish in your closer. For example, in a one-hour session, a closer could be ten minutes but might include some brainstorming. So take into account what types of activities you plan to do during the closer before deciding on how long your closer will be. You are the expert and best understand the outcomes for your session and your audience. The time guidelines in the grid on the next page are just a rule of thumb.

Typically closing takes a little more time than opening because it's an opportunity to action plan, which takes thought, and good thinking takes time. In a day-long session, the first three closers of the day might be quick while the final closer is the culmination of all the day's work and will take longer.

Length of Class	1 Hour	½ Day	1 Day	Multiple Day
Session Closer	3-5 minutes	3-5 minutes	3-5 minutes	3-5 minutes
Final Closer	NA	10-15 minutes	15 minutes	15-20+ minutes
Number of Closers	1	2	4	4-5/day

A closer should be the very last thing you do. All housekeeping, evaluations, giveaways, cleanup and other details should be covered prior to your final closer. If it is not going to inspire, encourage or motivate, don't waste your last moments of class doing it! You want to leave the best impression and close on a high note, just like they do in the closing ceremonies of the Olympic Games.

Closers

For the remainder of this chapter, I flesh out a number of different closers that embody ACT, making them excellent choices if you want to successfully close out an ILPC training session.

Objective Writing

A closer can involve a more formal action plan, like creating goals and objectives for the next four weeks, with learners using the ABCDs of objective writing: **A**udience, **B**ehavior, **C**ondition, and **D**egree of Mastery. Direct participants to write ABCD down the left hand side of a note card and read the following aloud:

- Audience: For whom are the objectives written? As part of a closer activity, the answer to this question will be the learner himself.

- Behavior: What needs to be done? The learner will typically begin this statement with a verb like, "Apply," "Create," etc.

- Condition: What specifically has been provided to successfully meet this goal? The answer to this question should be specific. The learner should not simply write, "Given my three days of training. . . ." Instead, the learner should specifically indicate what new information or new skill he's received during the training that will allow him to accomplish his goal. For example, "Given the nine steps to creating an effective job aid, I will . ."

- Degree of Mastery: What specifically will successful completion of this goal look like? For example, "I will have the new job aid completed and tested by three analysts by March 1st."

A quality objective completed by a participant during the closer might be, "Given the nine steps to creating an effective job aid, I will create a job aid for the branch bank tellers on closing procedures and have the aid successfully followed by three different tellers by March 1st." It is best to use a template for learners to fill in so they can complete the action plans in a few minutes' time and not feel overwhelmed. Perhaps it is just fill in the blank, like this: "Given _____(information you've gained in order to do what you need to do), I will _____ (indicate what you're going to do here, including what indicators are necessary for it to be completed successfully) by _____(indicate a reasonable deadline here).

As an alternative to, or in addition to, the fill-in-the-blank approach, you might want to ask the participants questions as a means of leading them to an objective. Questions like:

1. What do you need to take action on immediately?

2. How much time will you allocate toward making that happen?

3. What resources do you need to be successful?

4. When will you schedule a status meeting with your manager to share this plan?

5. How can your manager help you achieve these objectives?

6. What obstacles will you need to overcome to embrace your learning and change behavior?

7. Will your peers and colleagues need to know about your objectives?

Highlighting Takeaways

At the end of the session, you may simply ask participants to highlight their Top Takeaway List, numbering their highlighted takeaways in order of priority. By numbering which ones they want to start, you help them to focus better on their goals. Encourage them to give full attention to the first one and bring it to completion before moving on to the second. This is an effective way to divide the action plan list into bite-size pieces that are far more manageable. It also allows the participant to see results sooner, taste some success and feel encouraged.

Prioritizing

In 1967, Charles Hummel published a little booklet that quickly became a business classic, *The Tyranny of the Urgent*. In it, he argues, "There is a regular tension between things that are urgent and things that are important—and far too often, the urgent wins." When prioritizing, ask participants to focus on what's actually important versus tasks that are "urgent" but not necessarily important. Ask them to walk through the following three steps:

1. Think about the difference between what is urgent and what is important.

2. Review all the action ideas on your list.

3. Do what is important first.

If participants are having a hard time deciding what is important versus urgent, direct them to their company's value proposition, mission, and objectives. This can help weed out what is not important and help him or her align priorities with the company's objectives.

If there is something important on their list, but completing the task requires skills or strengths they don't possess, encourage participants to highlight it and write next to it the name of someone who could assist in making the objective come to fruition.

Diagramming

A diagram, of course, is a visual way to represent content; it allows a viewer to see how a large quantity of information is related. When using a diagram as an action plan, participants will take an empty or a partially empty diagram and fill it in with how they plan to use the content they've just learned. The diagram becomes their action plan. By ending a session using a diagram, learners connect their learning with its application which reveals potential gaps.

An example of an action plan-ready diagram might be a half completed mindmap (see chapter nine for a sample mindmap). The portion that is completed includes core content from the class, the remaining portion will contain the action plan of the participant once she's sketched out how she will apply the various content pieces back on the job. A second example might be a Venn diagram. If the course content covered two related topics—openers and interactivity—one of the circles would be labeled openers, the other circle would be labeled interactivity. At the close, participants would build their action plan in the Venn diagram, indicating how they'll apply their new knowledge of closers to their own training; how they'll apply their new knowledge of interactivity; and, where the two circles intersect, how they'll apply interactivity to closers.

Other examples of diagrams that work well for action planning might be maps, charts, blueprints, sketches, infographics, fishbone, affinity circle, or technical drawings. It could also be as simple as smart art.

When selecting an appropriate diagram to use as an action plan template for the end of your session, you must consider the content being covered. Select a diagram that works well with the amount and type of content you've taught. For example, a partially completed mindmap works well for a course covering ten to fifteen areas, and a Venn diagram works well when a course has covered information that falls into two or three main, related umbrellas.

Storytelling

A creative way to action plan is to have each individual take three minutes to write a story of how he or she will apply the learned skills in the next few weeks. Have everyone share his or her story with a partner or aloud to the group. One of my favorite ways to set up this action plan option is to provide two sets of note cards to the participants. The cards in one stack each have single, descriptive words on them. The cards in the other stack each have a picture on them. Participants grab three word cards and one or two picture cards.

Then, in less than five minutes' time, they create a story using the words and pictures on their cards, and they include as many ideas for implementing their new skills as possible. Um, I don't want to have to create word and picture cards, you say? Purchase the game Jabberjot and use the word and picture cards that come in it.

The strength of this action plan activity is that participants write quickly and creatively. It is an unassuming way to get participants to become storytellers while engaging with the content and planning for its personal application.

Assigning Roles and Responsibilities

If work teams typically attend your trainings, then it is a great idea to end the session having those teams action-plan together. I have attended sessions where I and my team have been excited, but no action was taken afterward because no one knew who was going to do what. So it is important to close with an action plan activity that invites everybody to get on the same page and assigns roles or responsibilities.

Here is one creative way to have teams create a to-do list and then assign the different roles needed to complete the tasks. Ask all participants to take two minutes to write on sticky notes everything that needs to be done moving forward based on the session. Next, have participants get with a partner to cull out duplicates and select the four most critical. Then on a wall, all partners post their four most critical tasks. The team now removes additional duplicates and chunks the tasks into related buckets. At this point, I ask if people have any additional task sticky notes back at their tables. They can add them to the appropriate bucket of tasks on the wall. Finally, have people assign themselves to particular tasks by writing their name on the chosen task sticky notes.

Scheduling Reminders on a Virtual Calendar

For this closer, participants look through the action planning page they have been adding to throughout the session, and they simply add a reminder to their virtual calendar for several of their action ideas. If they have attended the course with a peer, they can share their deadlines and help hold one another accountable, which greatly increases the likelihood that the items will get done.

This closing activity is an effective bridging technique that takes learning outside the classroom because the participants are the ones that have determined what action to take and have set the reminders. If work teams have attended the training, you can provide them with a few minutes, after participants have added action plan reminders to their calendars, to determine and add team task reminders to team members' calendars.

What, Gut, So What, Now What?

When closing out a session with this activity, you ask the participants to reflect on four questions. In combination, these questions remind them of the new content they've just learned, help them process how they feel about it and consider what it means to them, and then determine what they'll do with it. They really pack a punch!

What: This question can be addressed as simply as "What have you learned that you didn't know before?" The question, however it is phrased, should ask the learners to describe their experience or consider what just occurred or was learned in the session.

Gut: This question asks participants to do a "gut check." How are they feeling about the session? About what they've learned? About what they plan to take back to the workplace?

So What: This question asks the learner to be introspective, to consider how the learning is personally important. "So what information is important to me?" or "So what new information do I need to apply?"

Now What: This question asks learners to figure out what they'll do with the new information. How will they begin to implement and apply the messages that were taught? "Now—with the new information I've got— what will I need to do differently on the job?"

Reflection

Give people a few minutes to analyze what they've learned. This might seems like a "duh" type of activity for closing, but when we allow our minds to be still and percolate on the recent concepts, we're better able to transfer new information into something usable. One example of a reflection closer would be to put the three reflection words up on the PowerPoint: Adapt, Adopt, Apply. Then, ask participants to consider:

How they will adapt the information?

How they will adopt it into their work and planning?

How they will apply it back on the job?

Reflection requires us to be still. And with all the activity and noise of the session, a few still, quiet moments to reflect might be just the ticket.

Paired Share

This is also a simple reflection-based closer. Start by asking participants to take a couple minutes to privately reflect on their learning and action plan. Then, ask them to pair up with a neighbor and share their reflections.

Inspire

I love the "No excuses" commercial Nike used to run where Matt Scott for fifty seconds gives all sorts of excuses like "I'm too fat … I'm too thin … I don't own a bicycle," and so on. I won't ruin the end; it is so good! You can watch it here: http://bit.ly/MattScott to see for yourself. This commercial gets at what is inspiring. In this reflection-based closer, I ask my participants what excuses are in their heads that need to be pushed aside. No excuses. You can do this.

Quick Closers

If you tend to run out the training clock, never fear! Here are some simple ways to help you effectively close in a short amount of time. Some of them are done individually, some with a partner, and others as a small or large group.

Action Idea List
Include a blank page in the participant workbook where learners can record important ideas for the future. Make the page stand out by printing it on a different color paper. Throughout the session, have participants come to this page and update it with key concepts they want to capture. As you close, ask them to briefly reflect on their list and circle their top priority.

Journaling
Direct your class to write down concepts and ideas that really resonate with them. It's a peaceful and stress reducing close.

Poll
This can be done with any number of low- or high-tech tools. You can use polleverywhere.com and have participants cast their vote with their cell phones or you can use Turning-Point clickers. Either way, results are immediately displayed on the PowerPoint slide (to learn more about setting up these options, read the polling section of the chapter titled PowerPoint Design for the Classroom). Of course, one low-tech solution is just having them raise hands to vote.

Quiz
One of my favorite ways to quiz participants is to give each a red and a green 3x5 card. As I read statements, participants raise their green card if they agree and red card if they disagree. Make sure your prepared statements tie information together and drive participants to action plans. For example, one statement might be: I have an action plan for how I will use some of the knowledge I've learned in this session. Ensure that you see mostly green cards for these kinds of statements!

Peruse the Last Section Covered and Select the Top Three Ideas
It is helpful to have participants peruse the material they've just finished learning and have them look at it from an application standpoint. Have them highlight, circle, star or just note which concepts they will use first. You might also have them number the concepts in the order in which they plan to apply them.

Tackle the Torturous
There is typically something during the session that appears to be too overwhelming to apply. When taking the time to revisit, have individuals go back to their "mountain" and find ways to climb the mountain successfully.

Get One, Give One
Participants take their action idea list or prioritized plan and meet up with another person to share their best idea of the class so far and to get the other person's best idea. After each has shared, they separate and each finds a new partner and repeats the process. With each additional person, they continue down their list, sharing their second, third, fourth best ideas. The instructor identifies the time limit and rings a chime when time is up. This is a continuous activity for the time allotted. I encourage learners to bring a

pen with them and add any applicable ideas that were shared by their partners and not already on their own list.

Card Deck Connect

Place a deck of playing cards on the table. Have each person in the class take a card from the deck. Participants must find another person with a card of the same suit, color or number (you, as the instructor, would determine this). With their partner, they have three minutes to share with one another each of the segments covered in the session. This allows for them to put into their own words what they have been processing during the last ninety minutes.

Catch and Release

This activity allows participants to stand up, stretch and meet someone new. To begin, each person finds a partner from another table. Then, they grab a Koosh ball or soft object and line up down the middle of the classroom, facing each other. One partner passes the ball, and as she does, she shares one idea. Her partner passes it back to her, sharing another idea. Then both partners take one step back and repeat. As soon as they reach the wall passing the ball back and forth, they get to go on break.

Common sense will need to prevail here. If the room is too large, then you'll need to designate where the "stopping point" should be. If a room is smaller, an alternative is to have them line up at a wall, facing each other—one partner's back is against the wall, and the other partner's back is to the rest of the room. Then, once both have tossed and shared an idea, the partner whose back is to the room takes one step back.

Come on Six

This closer can also be done in small groups or as a large group but goes quickest if done in pairs. Each set of partners needs a game die and a blank piece of paper. On the paper, direct them to create six boxes, numbered one through six. Then, have them label each of the six boxes with topics you've covered in class (you verbalize the topics, and they write them down). Once this is complete, they are ready to "play." The partners roll the die. Then they address the box that corresponds with the number rolled, writing one comment, idea or concept related to the box's topic. So, for example, if a two is rolled, the partners will write in the #2 box. Then they roll the die again and repeat. If they roll a number already rolled, they must re-roll until they roll a number for a square they have not yet completed. The game ends when the first group has completed all six boxes, runs to the front of the classroom and rings a chime. This is a very high energy close that gets people laughing.

1 Openers	2 Closers	3 Revisiters
4 Energizers	5 ILPC	6 Cognition

Top Takeaway

Learners choose which of the concepts they plan to use most, and they share around the room with the large group. Takeaways can be shared in one or two sentences.

One Word Whip

Learners stand in a circle. Then, going clockwise, learners share with the group one or two words that encapsulate the information they've just learned in the session. The idea is to reflect on the day and boil it down into just a couple of words. Common words are: amazing, eye-opening, exhausting, and invigorating. I encourage participants to think of their word prior to beginning the closer. This way they are engaged in what others are saying instead of wracking their brain for a word. If everyone has their word or words ready, it truly is a quick whip around the group.

Sink or Swim

This is a small group activity to be done around their tables. To begin, each participant writes down several questions related to the content of the day. Then all participants at the table stand. One participant begins by asking the person on his right one of his questions. If the person answers correctly, she gets to "swim" by turning to the person on her right and asking one of her questions. If she answers incorrectly, she "sinks" and must sit down. The person who asks the question must then correctly answer his own question before "swimming" to the person to the right of the "sunk" participant. This is a fun one to do in teams, and sales teams especially enjoy this because it is competitive but in a non-aggressive way. To save on time, you may want to have learners write their questions down on 3x5 cards as a closer earlier in the day in preparation for this closer. You can also have them keep the 3x5 cards for other learning uses.

I cannot stress the importance of having evaluations completed earlier in the session, and reserve the last few minutes before break, lunch or the close of the day to close with action planning, celebration and time for learners to tie their learning together. The Olympians celebrate in their memorable closing ceremony; your final closer of the day should do that for your participants.

Chapter 12

REVISITERS

To review or revisit, that is the question. Reviewing content is when the instructor goes through and repeats what he just said in a condensed way. It is an opportunity to quickly ensure all his objectives have been hit.

Revisiting is when the learners do the work. They take the time to connect the dots and to put a content frame around what they just learned. It is their chance to make sense and meaning of what was said. Revisiting requires analysis and synthesis which also builds critical thinking skills. There is a time and place for both revisiting and reviewing, but in ILPC training we primarily focus on the revisiting so the learner is actively engaged in the process.

It is a great way to help space the learning and reinforce key messages. It helps to move information from our short-term memory into long-term memory. When learners don't have a chance to use their new found knowledge, it is very easily forgotten (Litman and Davachi 2008).

For it to be effective, revisiting activities need to be well designed and executed. Here are some rules.

Do not announce it, just do it.

Think back to when you were in high school and your teacher said, "We'll start by reviewing what was covered yesterday." What is the first thing that comes to mind when you hear that? I always think, "I've already written down my notes; I'm an A student. It's time for me to check out."

It is better to revisit content by starting an exercise than by introducing it as a time of review. For example, jump right in with, "Partner up and grab a deck of cards...." Notice I didn't say, "It's time to review—let's each find a partner."

Use variety

If we do the same activity over and over, we do not create curiosity, grab attention, or keep learner focus. Using variety means instructors use multiple modalities and types of creative activities to strengthen retention. This might include revisiting content through listening, demonstrations, speaking, teach-backs, viewing, discussing, experiencing, practicing, role-playing, games, quizzes, teams...you get the idea. We use thirty-three different ways to revisit content during our two-day Train-the-Trainer Boot Camp where participants learn twice as much in half the time (while having more fun than they have ever had in a workshop before).

Set learners up for success

When revisiting content, make sure that it is a true revisit. For example, it is never appropriate to call on someone that you "catch" not listening as a way of pointing out inattentive behavior. Revisiters set people up for success by keeping information and goals at the top of mind.

According to John Norcross, a professor of psychology at the University of Scranton, people who don't make an action plan for a New Year's resolution have about a zero to four percent chance of accomplishing that resolution. This compares to nearly forty-six percent of those who took their resolution seriously and were still successfully meeting their resolutions at six months.

Just like with resolutions, revisiting allows learners chances to recall what they've learned and want to accomplish and make a plan for how they will apply the new skills back on the job.

Plan for it

What is designed into the program usually happens. Make sure to include the revisiters into the schedule. It takes repeated effort for information to move into long-term memory. Of course, having the learning reviewed over time is most effective, but revisiting during class is important too.

Don't use the trainer's death sentence: "It's time to role-play"

The second that participants hear the words "role-play," eyes begin to roll and people let out sighs of disappointment. Role-playing is actually an extremely effective tool in the trainer's toolbox; unfortunately, it has gotten a bad rap. So what can you do instead of role-play? Use synonyms like practice, practical application, model, or skill practice.

Make revisiting fun

Just as inactive learning can be dreaded, so can mundane types of review like pop quizzes or making flashcards. Instead, make the revisit fun and interesting versus boring and tedious. Bring it to life by revisiting the content solo, with partners or in small groups. Allow for all learners to participate. When using a game to revisit, ensure more than one person can be a contestant. Allow for all to buzz in and engage. Watching others revisit content is really just review! You want to build and facilitate revisiters that have all participants engaged.

KISS—Keep It Super Simple

Take the time to write out clear instructions. This is one of the most common mistakes that instructors make from the front of the room. They give too many instructions and participants cannot keep up. The rule of thumb is three directions at a time. Once the participants have completed those three directions, give them the next three. In addition, you can list the directions on a flip chart or PowerPoint slide for easy reference.

Announce Time Limit
Give the exact amount of time they have to do the revisit, like thirty or sixty seconds. It lets them know that there is not a lot of time to get this accomplished.

Insert Revisiting Throughout the Session
In following the 90/20/10 rule, make sure that within every twenty-minute module there is a small segment dedicated to revisiting content. Because there is interactivity every ten minutes, revisiting doesn't have to come at the end of the twenty minutes but can be sprinkled throughout.

Prepare Materials in Advance
For any activity, make sure that you have items for everyone plus a few. For example, we use clickers and have extras in case a battery is dead. Prepare them in advance so every minute of class time is spent on core content and not creating.

Share the WHY
The human brain is wired to want to know why. Let learners know the goal of the exercise and the result they will achieve. When learners know what is in it for them, are able to see what is expected, and understand the "why" behind what they are doing, you gain buy-in to the process. Even in a quick two-minute closer, it may make sense to share the why behind the how. In general, I find this tip to be especially helpful when training left-brained groups or structured learners.

Music and Signal

When a revisit is happening, play background music to provide some white noise. This can help reduce tension or anxiety and allow for the feeling of privacy as pairs share and small groups discuss. Using a signal, like a chime, is a way to let learners know the revisiter is over and it's time to come back to the large group. Model the chime before the activity so they know what to expect. If you don't have a chime, use a glass with a fork or clap your hands. Use a signal other than your voice as voices tend to be drowned out by the group. Turning off the music can also help assist in gaining learners' attention.

The rest of this chapter explains some quick revisiters and some more robust ones. These will at least get you started in building your own. If you're looking for additional revisiter options, see The Bob Pike Group's series of *SCORE for Enhanced Training Results* books.

Having Fun with Formative Assessment

by Adrianne Roggenbuck

Although formative assessment is a necessary evil of teaching and training, it doesn't have to feel that way to the learner. Creative and fun revisiting techniques are an informal way to assess mastery without the associated tension and stress of a quiz or test.

Games are especially popular and can either be high-tech or low-tech., depending on the resources available to you. As your students are doing a revisiting activity, you have a chance to circulate and observe your learners' levels of competence. You may use an observation checklist or simply take qualitative notes. This data will help you determine if your learners are ready to move on with the content, or if clarification and further instruction is needed. Immediate feedback is provided to the learners throughout the revisiting activity in a non-threatening way. Although there may be winners and losers in a game, nobody "fails" the assessment. Wrong answers are utilized as a learning opportunity, not a punishment. When you use revisiters as formative assessments, your learners won't even realize what you are up to. They will be having too much fun!

As Director of Education at the Bob Pike Group, Adrianne Roggenbuck is responsible for designing and delivering programs to corporate and educational entities worldwide.

Quick Revisiters

Sit—Stand

Have learners push their chairs away from the table and then sit down. Then ask questions and have them stand back up if they know the answers. I start with an easy question like "I know the name of the instructor" so that I can see everyone sit down and stand back up. I then call on one participant to share the answer. Then I move into content I want to revisit like "I can name one of the keys to an opener or closer." I usually call on participants that sat down within the first few seconds with confidence and have them share back. After each question has been answered, I have partners share how they will use this back on the job. This activity can also be used as a quick energizer.

See, Say, Switch

Participants pair up and walk around the room. Partners see a poster, prop, learning element or other class-related item and share with one another what they learned about the topic or concept and how they can apply it. If it is a computer-based classroom or technical training, have learners take a minute to execute the example or have participants practice demonstrating the learning. This will take a bit longer, but the recall will be much greater. Give a fifteen-second audible warning to let groups know to finish their thoughts before ringing a chime or bell to notify learners it is time to thank their partner with a high-five and switch partners to repeat the process. Let pairs know that if they finish prior to the chime, they can find another object or chart to discuss. This keeps everyone engaged and not just standing around while one group is still going. Continue the process until time is up. Typically learners share for a minute with each partner. I have them switch three or four times.

Collective Wisdom

As the class is proceeding, a "Collective Wisdom" page is being created by each table group. On occasion, as the trainer, you pause for Words of Wisdom from individuals or teams. As new thoughts and ideas are shared, participants share the role of scribe and record the learnings on the "Collective Wisdom" page.

"Why" and "How" Cards

This is a revisit technique where learners each receive cards that have questions that all begin with either "Why" or "How." When designing your cards, keep in mind that "Why" cards are asking for comprehension and knowledge while "How" cards require high order cognition and give learners a chance to analyze, synthesize and apply what they have learned about a concept. Pair up learners to collaborate on the cards they were given. Each card should be worked on until they feel they have the right answer. In large classes, where it would be difficult for an individual instructor to do a knowledge check, short answers can be put on the back for self-assessment.

Think—Pair—Share

To begin, give learners an opportunity to reflect on what they have learned and write a few ideas down on an action idea page. After a minute, instruct learners to stand up and find a partner they haven't worked with yet and share their ideas. If they like what they hear from their peer, and they didn't already have that idea written down, they can add it to their list of ideas. Paired shares create the highest amount of energy in a room because you have the largest number of people talking. This exercise is good for times of the day when energy may be low. A pair share is also an efficient, low-risk revisiting technique.

Robust Revisiters

Graffiti Gallery Walk

Flip charts are a great way to have participants create their own visuals pertaining to the information they are learning. The flip charts can then be hung on the wall as reminders of what content we have already covered. I love using the Graffiti Gallery Walk after some time has passed in a class, and we have a number of handmade posters on the wall which then becomes our gallery. I can use it as a revisiting opener, closer, or energizer! Simply ask participants how many of them have ever been to a gallery. Ask them to share what happens when walking through a gallery. Listen for ideas like: observing art, discussing the meaning of art pieces, pondering etc. Direct them to take a marker and pair up with a partner. When the music begins, they will mill around the room moving from one chart to the next discussing with the partner what they learned in their own words and how they will use the concept. On each chart, each person should also write one thought on how they will adapt, adopt or apply the concept or content.

When the time is up, give a minute or two for participants to walk around and review the new graffiti and observe new ideas added. When they sit down, have groups spend a minute or two discussing what they found interesting, new or surprising and summarizing their experience.

A gallery walk can be used throughout the day. Learners are walking, talking and energized throughout a gallery walk, which is good way for learning to be spaced and reviewed.

Venn Diagram

This is a graphical representation of data that offers relationships between different elements, including places where those elements overlap. The most common Venn is of overlapping circles. Direct participants to work in small groups at the wall with chart paper and markers. Provide them with the two concepts they will be putting on their two Venn circles. When you start the music (I use fast-paced upbeat music in the background), they brainstorm and fill in their chart based on the two concepts you supplied, one idea in each circle. For example, on one circle I may write "online learning" and on the other "classroom." Groups quickly come up with what is similar and write those things in the overlapping space of the two circles and what is unique about each under the appropriate heading. I like to have each group brainstorm different content pieces, so that we can then do a quick graffiti gallery walk and groups get to revisit many topics all at once.

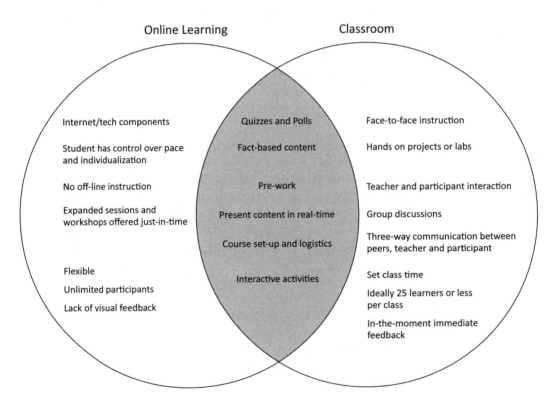

Poker Chip Pick-up

For this revisiter, each learner writes a review question on an index card with the answer on the back side. Each learner will then place a poker chip with a correlating value on top of his or her question and place it at the center of the table. For example: Red=$5 and is an easy question; Green=$10 and is an intermediate question while black=$15 and is a hard question. Instruct teams that you will put five minutes on the timer, and they should try to get through as many questions as possible. Each person at the table will read his or her own card but will not respond. The first person to pick-up the poker chip gets a chance to answer the question. If he gets it correct, he keeps the chip; if he gets it wrong, the poker chip is up for grabs again, and the question can be answered by another in the group. When time is up, each player adds together his or her chips, and the winner receives applause, high-fives or a small prize. I typically have learners collect poker chips (or some other object) throughout the day so that the fun builds.

Clicker Questions and Games like Bravo! Or Pronto! By C3Softworks

Research shows a direct correlation to using clicker questions over just hand raising or paper and pencil quizzing. Students scored significantly higher on tests over students asked questions without the aid of clicker technology. Those using clickers enjoyed a gain of approximately one-third of a grade point (Mayer et al. 2009). Who wouldn't want those kinds of results? Part of the formula is to sprinkle thought-provoking questions throughout a session. When I use BRAVO! in conjunction with TurningPoint Technology clickers or just use the clickers with questions built into PowerPoint, I usually only ask one or two questions at a time. The game builds over the session. Clicker questions help focus attention and can be effective in teaching content or revisiting it (Anderson et al. 2013). I personally like having learners discuss the questions at their tables prior to buzzing in. Once everyone has buzzed in, I then lecture on each of the wrong answers first and then expound on the correct answer.

Revisiting content is a way to space learning and allow for learners to practice and create, and it is absolutely critical to ILPC training and for successful learning outcomes. At The Bob Pike Group, we say learning hasn't occurred until behavior has changed. Time is a regular constraint, but be sure to incorporate application time so that behavior can change.

Chapter 13

ENERGIZERS

Energizers are fun activities that get people up from their chairs and moving around before getting back to work. If you ever met me, you would easily guess that energizers are one of my favorite things. I just love to see participants go from tired to pumped for what is next. I am full of energy, and I love to share it with others. People ask if I can bottle it and sell it to them. Energizers are as close to a bottle as it gets. A great energizer stimulates the mind and body all at once.

Even if you have integrated active learning throughout your course, there are certain times, such as in the afternoon after a filling lunch, where people are susceptible to being fidgety and even claustrophobic. Energizers help create learning momentum by getting the blood flowing in the body or getting the mind back on track through mental stimulation (Jensen 2000, Dwyer 2001).

An energizer can be used during a transition time, to break up a long section of content, or after a quiz. Energizers should be used any time energy in the classroom is low. Oftentimes it is late in the morning or late afternoon after candy bars or meals are processed, when participants begin to crash.

Energizers do not have to relate to the content, but they can. Sometimes I have people stand up and use their thumbs and pointer fingers to massage their ear lobes for thirty seconds. Besides feeling good, they actually trigger a stress relieving, mind-focusing effect in the body. But if you are using an energizer that does not relate to the content, make sure that it is a quick one. Many times you can find energizers that link to content you have been teaching, so it becomes a physical revisiter.

If you've noticed that your participants have been sitting for a period of time, the physical energizer provides a much needed change. By having people stand, the blood pooling in their feet is reintroduced into the blood flow. It just takes three seconds for it to flow at an optimal pace, so technically just having participants stand up as part of an exercise can be energizing.

Researchers found that when we stand, we are "smarter (Ouchi et al. 1999)." Your brain is about three percent of your body mass, but it uses just over eighteen percent of your body's blood and oxygen. When standing up, your brain is fed at an optimal rate. Think of standing up as creating a superhighway of blood flow to your brain, a straightaway blood route versus mountain switchbacks. When we sit with arms or legs crossed, we have kinks in our body, like a kinked water hose, making it more difficult for the blood to flow. Standing helps boost energy levels, engagement, learning and ultimately retention.

Psychologists and neuroscientists who study the brain tell us that the brain goes into a trance approximately thirty percent of the time and does so even more when doing mundane tasks like driving a routine route (Christoff et al. 2009, Kane 2007). This is kind of like a computer program that goes to sleep when it isn't being immediately used. When you click on the program, it takes a moment to wake it up. The research shows, however, that if subjects were actively engaged, it happened less often. When our minds wander, there is a reduction in the ability to learn and do a task (Smallwood et al. 2008).

When doing the physical energizer, keep in mind safety should always come first. You may also need to modify energizers based on ability level in the room. Physical activators get the body moving. These activities are often child-like, competitive and fun. They range from simple stretching exercises to fairly complex brain-body coordination. Some are designed to be controlled stretch breaks; they involve some questions or activities that can be related to the session content, thus creating a double win—a stretch for the participants, increased blood flow, and a learning point that is revisited or communicated.

Make sure to use these types of activities purposefully and strategically. The audience should have a sense of why you are doing them. Using simple statements like "Okay, let's get our minds focused and back on the learning process by starting with a simple poll," or "Let's wake up our brains this afternoon with this trivia test" will help participants understand why you are doing the activity or exercise.

When used correctly, mental stimulators literally create energy in the group. You can see the physical energy increase through the mental stimulation.

Quick Energizers

Here are a few energizers to add to your toolkit. Again, there are dozens of energizers in our *SCORE* book series on closers, openers, revisiters and energizers.

Three Breaths
Instruct participants to stand, rub their hands together, and take three deep breaths in unison. The instructor slowly counts out "one, two, three." Then have participants clap their hands three times and say "ready to go" at the same time. You can change the words to any three syllables like "rock and roll" or "my team rocks." That's all there is to it, yet you'll feel a definite energy change in the room.

Silent Sitdown
Select one participant to be the winker. One way to select the participant is with a deck of cards; whoever gets the ace is "it." The person who is "it" should not tell anyone. Then instruct everybody to stand up and stretch and look around the room at one another. The

person that got the ace begins winking at people. Each person who receives a wink should sit down. Once the winker has been identified by others in the room the game is over. Usually he or she is identified within sixty seconds.

Mental Vacation

Have participants close their eyes and go on a mental vacation. Allow them to think about their dream vacation for sixty seconds. Then ask them to come back from their vacation, still with eyes closed, and vacation in the room for a moment seeing what they can recall on the posters around the room, pages from the workbook, or slides from the presentation. Then have them open their eyes, stand up, and share with a neighbor either their vacation destination or one of the items they visualized from the room.

Left or Right

Tell the participants that you are going to read a paragraph. Every time they hear the word "left" they are to head to the left wall. And every time they hear the word "right" to go to the right wall. You might invent a story about *Mr. and Mrs. Right* who are going on a car ride but *left* their dog home, etc.

Team Jig

You have to consider if this one will work for your audience and your personality. Everyone at each table must agree on a single style of dance and participate in that style for fifteen to thirty seconds. I usually turn on upbeat music. I have had some people doing square dance at one table, another table doing ballet, and a final table doing moves from the 1950s. Any longer than fifteen to thirty seconds gets awkward.

Over and Under

Take any two objects that you have in the room from a roll of masking tape to a Koosh ball. Have the group form two lines. Each line becomes a team. Hand the first person in each line one of the objects and have her pass the object over her shoulders to the next person, who will then pass the object under his legs to the next person. Make it a race between the two teams. After this one is done, I ask, "What's one thing that is <u>over</u>whelming or <u>under</u>whelming from the content we learned?" Post-energizer discussion can be done in pairs, triads or a small table groups.

Cross Clap

Direct participants to stand up and clap their hands each time your hands cross one another. You, as the instructor, move your hands vertically in opposing directions (one moving upward while the other is moving downward) in a scissor-like movement so they pass the other without touching. Each time your hands pass, everyone claps. Practice this one time slowly so that participants get the idea of when to clap. Randomly alter the speed of your hands. At times, I pretend to cross but stop short. The goal is to try to trick the participants into clapping when they should not. If they clap at the wrong time, they sit down. This could also be built into a discussion on making assumptions, doing what others are doing, working ahead, and so on.

When used correctly, energizers will get participants back into a learning mode with a refreshed body and refocused mind. Although many of these activities are not content-related, most participants will make the connection between the activity and the purpose for which it was intended—to help the learning process.

ILPC During Training

Chapter 14

INTRODUCING AND TRANSITIONING BETWEEN ILPC ACTIVITIES

Have you seen the television show *The Amazing Race?* Competing pairs are given clues they must solve and challenges they must complete, usually involving global travel, in order to move onto the next part of the challenge. There are time limitations, and typically the last team to complete the challenge is eliminated.

So imagine you are a contestant on *The Amazing Race,* and you've been dropped off in a country where you do not speak the language. You know you have to complete a challenge with six steps. At the beginning of the challenge, you are given a laundry list of instructions, which you need to remember and include aspects that you do not really understand. But, you and your partner gamely set off to complete the first step of the challenge.

Midway through the challenge, you and your partner are frustrated and overwhelmed. You can't remember what you are supposed to do next, and it does not really matter because you have lost the drive to do it. It has taken far too long and it has been far too frustrating just to get to the step you are on.

Finally, you complete step five, and you are given a card with the instructions for completing the final step of the challenge. Unfortunately, the instruction is a riddle that you must solve in order to complete a scavenger hunt. You are under pressure to win, but without speaking the language, you are at a loss as to how to solve this riddle and get yourself to the end of the scavenger hunt. This feeling of frustration and exasperation can be a common one for participants in an interactive training environment.

Think about the last time you participated in scenario-based training, implemented an activity or ran discussion groups. Often there is a laundry list of verbal directions at the beginning, but if directions are unclear or the activity is poorly managed, a five-minute activity can become a twenty-minute exercise in frustration.

How can you ensure that you stay on track and get the intended outcome from ILPC training? By looking at how to best manage the process along with some of the why behind those specific steps.

There are nine distinct steps to successfully and effectively managing a discussion or activity, such as the many openers, closers, revisiters and energizers I just outlined. We've been using these at The Bob Pike Group for years, and each time we do, we get the same great results. There have been occasions where I, in haste or in an effort to save time, have chosen to skip steps, but in the end, it never saves time or improves the learners' experience, and I regret abbreviating a process I know works.

How do you set up an ILPC activity or discussion?

Use a signal or cue.
Cueing or signaling an activity is when you vocalize a starting phrase to let participants know when to begin. There are two types of learners: the quick and the analytical. The quick start the exercise before you are done with the instructions while the analytical are looking at their peers who have started and are thinking, "We're not supposed to start yet! Wait!" In order for everyone to start together, begin by cueing the activity with phrases like: "When I say 'Go,'" "When you hear music," "When I say 'begin,'" "In just a moment," or "Thirty-second discussion at your table."

Give clear directions or discussion questions and always include a time frame.
Once the chaotic energy of an activity or discussion has begun, it is difficult or impossible to regain your participants' attention to complete all the directions or to provide additional clarification. Although it is organized chaos, activities and discussions are usually loud, and it is difficult to talk over a room full of talkers. And once participants have started, they may find it frustrating to be interrupted in order to refocus their attention back on you for further instructions.

So at the outset, provide a clear question or topic to discuss or precise task to complete. Do not give more than three directions or steps at a time. If the exercise requires more than three directions or steps, chunk them. Put all of them on a flip chart, poster board, or PowerPoint slide. Your verbal instructions may sound something like this: "In just a moment, when I say 'Go,' your table group will need to take markers and a sticky piece of flip chart paper to a spot on the wall somewhere in the room. Once all groups are standing by their flipchart paper with markers at the wall, I will give further instructions. Ready, set, go." Once all groups are in position, you can continue with further instructions. If you are providing more than one question or topic for discussion, be sure to display the questions on a PowerPoint slide.

Included in your instructions should be an approximate time limit for the exercise. A thirty-second discussion limit makes each participant subconsciously aware that there is enough time for one or two thoughts. A ninety-second discussion limit will allow for three or four thoughts. The group knows there will not be enough time to hear from everyone at the table. It sets expectations and lets the "socializer" know that he or she might not get to talk this time. You can provide the timeframe in your instructions or when you are cueing up the exercise.

Assign a team leader.

Verbalize the question or topic before assigning the team leader. Why? So your participants listen because they do not know who will be the team leader. There are plenty of fun ways to designate a new team leader. It can be the newest employee, the person who most recently participated in an online survey, or the person wearing the most bling. Whether you are in a classroom or an online teaching environment, you can use the same leader selection criteria for both formats. You may be asking, "If I'm facilitating a webinar, how do I know who has the most bling?" In either the physical or virtual classroom, people can tell the truth or hide it. So in either case, the team selection of a leader is built on the honor system. If someone really doesn't want to be a team leader, he or she will get out of it, so do not expend energy on creating foolproof ways to establish team leaders.

If time is of the essence, a couple of quick ways to establish team leaders are: The person whose first name is closest to letter A (or closest to Z), or the person who has the longest/shortest name.

Whether teaching online or in the classroom, be sure to establish the team leader's responsibilities: Being the scribe, starting/leading the team discussion, and reporting back to the larger group.

Repeat the question or directions to reinforce expectations and clarify.

Participants may have forgotten the question or some of the instructions once the flurry of selecting a team leader is over, so it is best to repeat your instructions or the question for discussion. Instead of asking the typical, "Are there any questions," try "Before we start, what can I clarify for you?" People are more willing to ask a quick clarifying question like, "Where are we supposed to write down our thoughts?" and you can quickly provide the missing information.

Use music, if appropriate, during the activity.

> "Music is the electrical soil in which the spirit lives, thinks and invents."
> ~ Ludwig van Beethoven

Think of the last time your favorite song came on the radio. What did you do? Did you turn up the volume, belt out the chorus, bob your head, smile, relive the moment when you first heard it? Or all of the above? Most of us have visceral reactions to music. It affects our feelings and our energy level. When I was an undergrad coed, I used to get ready to go out with the girls while listening to Shania Twain's "Man, I Feel like a Woman." If my goal is to get pumped up, Shania's my girl, but when I need to get to a place of focus, I turn to Ray Lynch and Mannheim Steamroller's Chip Davis. This style of music preps me for a great work or brainstorming session.

Like my personal experience with music, the right music prepares, energizes or focuses your participants for successfully accomplishing the task at hand. With that in mind, never use music that is known to your participants because you do not want their minds to suddenly wander off to go dancing with the girls or dive into the dumps because the tune was their ex's favorite. Instead, use unobtrusive and unfamiliar tracks. There is research that says music inhibits learning while other research indicates it aids in the learning process (Dobbs and McClelland 2011, Hallman et al. 2002). To be on the safe side, everyone can study and learn in silence. When you have a reading activity or a study time, it is best to keep the room quiet. Use music as white noise during transitions and to create a mood in the room. Again, the ideal is to use nondescript, instrumental music. It helps learners by:

- Creating an atmosphere
- Energizing learning activities
- Adding an element of fun
- Changing brain wave states
- Resetting attention
- Improving memory when the same type of activity is always tied to the same song
- Releasing tension
- Building anticipation
- Enhancing imagination
- Aligning groups
- Developing rapport (when a genre appeals to two people, they talk about it)
- Providing inspiration
- Accentuating theme-oriented units

Music focuses learners. Baroque music, such as Bach or Handel, typically has fifty to eighty beats per minute and naturally creates an atmosphere of focus, leading learners into deep concentration in the alpha brain wave state. It is also possible to improve recall of facts and details through rhyme, rhythm, and melody or by having groups turn facts into a song, chant, poem, and rap (Kraus and Chandrasekaran 2010).

Music reduces tension. Our trainers have been using music in the classroom for thirty-five years. We use it as people enter the room to build energy and curiosity. We use it as participants are leaving the room to help maintain energy and motivation. We use it during games and activities to give participants an added sense of urgency. And we use it during discussion breakouts to add privacy. The background melody allows participants to share without feeling as though they are being overheard.

Copyright concerns. Recently I had a participant share his nightmare copyright story. He was facilitating a training for his employees and, a couple weeks later, he received a $3500 music royalty invoice, a royalty fee charged for using copyrighted music. How in the world had this happened? Someone was walking by the hotel conference room where the training was being held, heard the music and called the recording studio. Yes, the trainer paid the $3500 bill. Ouch. This cautionary tale is a painful lesson in the necessity of owning the rights to the music you use in your training classroom or using rights-free music.

Rights-free music can be found online for anywhere from free to about $40 for a single song. *I'll take free*, you say to yourself. Then you will want to search for "Creative Commons licenses." The challenge I ran up against in using free music, however, was finding the right tempo and style for my training purposes and making sure that the music could be used for commercial purposes such as a training session.

To perfectly meet your tempo and style parameters, you can create your own instrumental music using software like garageband.com. Or you can save time by purchasing our Bob Pike Group copyright-free *Training Tunes* compact discs.

Keep in mind that research has shown that music and background noise can depress learning when teaching a complex concept or attempting to help learners build understanding (Mayer 2009). This is because the audio center is overwhelmed and human working memory has a limited capacity for both visual and auditory information. Research has also found that participants "with more musical experience trained better with neutral music and tested better with pleasurable music, while those with less musical experience exhibited the opposite effect (Gold et al. 2016)."

Use a visual timer.
I prefer a large countdown timer on the screen so everyone is aware of the available time remaining. This allows the participants to police themselves regarding the amount of time spent in each task of the activity, and it saves me from having to be a nag. Be sure to give audible announcements or warnings at key times. For example, when one minute remains or even at the thirty-second mark. This helps with pacing.

End the activity at your ideal stopping point.
Depending on your training objectives, there could be several different times in which you may wish to end a particular activity. First, the activity may be a timed task. Obviously, when the countdown ends, this is the ideal point at which the activity or discussion is finished. Second, you may wish to end the activity when energy for the task remains high. If so, you'll want to listen for the peak of conversation and signal an end just after that moment. Third, it may be ideal to end the activity at partial completion. Perhaps this is when the first group finishes or maybe it's when a pre-determined percentage of groups finish. Finally, the ideal stopping point, based on your course's learning objectives, may be after completion for all groups present.

Turn off the music.
At your activity's ideal stopping point, you turn off the music. This is a subtle auditory cue that helps learners segue from the activity to a time of debriefing. I usually turn the music up several notches and then slowly decrease the volume until the music is completely muted. Finally, use a chime to signal the activity's end; this gracefully focuses the participants' full attention.

Show gratitude for participation.
Showing gratitude for participation affirms your participants, which brings us back to the research on self-compassion. After you verbally praise the participants for their engage-

ment, direct partners to give a high-five, a handshake, a knuckle bump, or just have them say thank you to one another. Imagine two grown men in a chest bump. Yes, I have seen this done in class with raucous laughter all around. Gratitude and acknowledgment builds a spirit of camaraderie, appreciation and goodwill—great feelings at the completion of a task.

Share or debrief the exercise.
Carmine Consalvo, in her book *Workplay*, describes debriefing this way, "Processing or debriefing refers to the questioning and discussion that follows the game. It strives to elicit critical reflection based on observations regarding what happened in terms of both external interactions and internal reactions (Consalvo 2010)."

The debrief is as important as the activity itself because, while the activity can take learners to a certain level of application, the debrief requires a higher level of cognition as learners analyze, synthesize or evaluate what occurred during the activity/application. Because of the essential nature of the debrief, it must be facilitated well. Here are eight guidelines for effectively facilitating an activity or discussion debrief.

1. Resist telling; be the guide. Learning and retention is higher when participants come to their own conclusions. You can and should elaborate on anything the participants are bringing up. After you have exhausted their input, you can easily add any concepts they missed, and, in a sense, you have created an interactive lecture.

2. Establish the questioning format and then ask the questions. Have team leaders share one idea at a time from each table.

3. Begin with non-threatening questions about what took place. This establishes comfort and builds energy and interest.

4. Move to questions on how learners will apply this back on the job. This generates tangible take-aways and encourages behavior modification.

5. Use application questions that ask for opinions rather than facts. Good discussion questions focus on a person's opinion, experience or feelings. An application question that works for most exercises is: "What can this exercise teach us about...?"

6. Allow learners to write down their own "take-away" ideas first, and then have them share their take-aways with their small group.

7. Close when key points of analysis and evaluation have been explored, and you have expounded on them, as necessary. The debrief is not intended to be an exhaustive (or exhausting!) time.

Although these are the mechanics of effectively debriefing a discussion or activity, you do not need to sound or act mechanical. Follow the mechanics, but make it your own.

Even when you have mastered the art of giving instructions and setting up an Instructor-Led, Participant-Centered activity, the management of the exercise doesn't end there.

Once you have verbalized the activity instructions and allowed groups to start working, ideally you will be walking around the room monitoring the participants as they engage in small groups. Your classroom meandering allows you to ensure that groups are on the right track and remain focused. It also allows groups to ask you a question or gain clarification.

Add time for working in small groups.

As you actively monitor the progress of the groups by walking around the room, you may notice that, as time is running out, groups are only halfway through the exercise. If the ideal stopping point for the activity is near or total completion, then simply ask aloud, "Would your group like three more minutes?" Each group will invariably say yes, and then you can add three minutes to the visual timer.

Attention-Getters and Resets

by Janice Horne

Participants come into training preoccupied with other things besides the training on their minds. As trainers, we need to employ techniques to break preoccupation first thing in the morning, after every break and after lunch. Below are some techniques you can use to quickly gain attention. [There are many other suggestions and activities in the chapter on Openers, too.] Make sure that whichever activity you choose to do links back to your content or message.

1. Statistics: have participants guess the actual statistic before you give it such as "How long can we listen with retention?"

2. Quotes: make sure that you give credit to the person you are quoting

3. Trivia: any trivia can be used as long as you make a tie to your content

4. Brain-teasers: these work well first thing in the morning or after a break in order to break participants' preoccupation

5. Puzzles: the principle for use is the same as for brain-teasers

6. Promise: you can say things like, "I guarantee that after this session you will be able to...." Or "I promise that today I will give you the tools to ..."

7. Outrageous statement: the statement may be outrageous, but make sure the statement is true (this could be used in conjunction with a statistic)

8. Metaphors and analogies: make a comparison between your new, and perhaps more abstract content, to something well–known

9. Stories: make sure they are real (no jokes or made-up stories)

Studies show that participants need to be actively involved at least every eight minutes. If you are lecturing or reading slides for longer than that, you risk losing the attention of your participants, possibly for the entire training. To quickly reset or re–grab your participants' attention:

1. Share a quick, real–life story or example

2. Make them laugh

3. Make a transition statement

4. Break for a question and answer segment

5. Ask for a show of hands

6. Get participants to talk

7. Get participants to write

8. Take a micro-break of two to three minutes

9. Ask for a volunteer

10. Statistics. Again, keep the statistic relevant to content and have participants try to guess the answer to the statistic before you share. For example, how often do you need to engage participants in order to keep them actively involved?

11. Quotes that are relevant to the content

12. Change something to stir things up. You might:

    a. Change the type of visual aid

    b. Use a prop

    c. Move to a different part of the room

    d. Change presenters

    e. Move tables (seats)

    f. Have participants stand

    g. Vary your voice

    h. Pause; just be silent

13. Share a metaphor or analogy

Janice Horne is a master participant-centered trainer at The Bob Pike Group and helps businesses and organizations improve results through the training function by focusing on training design and delivery.

Chapter 15

Training Day Preparations and Dealing with Difficult Participants

I had finally done it! In 1997, I graduated from college at nineteen as a certified K–12 teacher, and my first gig was as a full-time substitute teacher! I walked into Hopkins High School, home to 1,800 students in grades ten through twelve, thinking I would change the world through educating the next generation (which ironically was also my generation) and walked out that day realizing that my job for the next year would be to proactively prevent challenging behaviors in the classroom. Why wasn't classroom management a college course for future teachers?

Dave Arch, an amazing presenter and coach, taught me that eighty percent of all difficult behaviors can be prevented. Let's look at strategies that will help us minimize the appearance of difficult participants. First, let's focus on what we can do before class begins.

Before Class Begins

A big part of classroom management happens before the learner even shows up. While working with Quantum Learning on the Stanford University campus, I learned that impeccability is key. When someone walks into the room, it should be clean, prepared for learning, and organized. Wall charts should be affixed and any graphics made in-the-moment the day before during training should be recreated if necessary so they are visually appealing. The environment matters; appearing disorganized creates distraction and can create difficult participants that you then have to deal with the rest of the session.

Managers and Learners

Preparing the learner and the manager before the session increases the transfer of training after the session while creating excitement and energy before the session. Connecting with both before the session will set everyone up for success.

- Provide a welcome note to the manager with things to cover during a status update with the participant attending. In the note:

- o Share the objectives of the class and encourage the manager to share these with the participant.

- o Share manager and learner expectations.

- o Include an encouragement to provide time for the learner to prepare for the class.

- o Suggest that manager and learner work together to set goals for the class and set expectations for during and after the class.

- o Encourage the manager to talk with the learner about having co-workers cover any necessary tasks while the learner is in training.

- Send a welcome email or letter with realistic pre-work for participants with clear instructions and expectations. An example of good pre-work might be to have them listen to a podcast on a particular topic (like here: http://bit.ly/BPGpodcast) and be ready to share how they will apply the learning. Provide a rough agenda and a few objectives and ask them to identify their WIIFM. Our sample letter can be seen on the next page.

- Be creative in connecting. Prior to the session, begin to develop rapport with your learners. This can be done by sending a link to a podcast or welcome greeting or inviting them to participate in your training hashtag (example #CTTC2016) to begin engaging with others. This can also be used after the session to continue the "conversation" and learning.

Room Set Up

Choose a room set-up that is conducive to your training, usually something that facilitates collaboration and group involvement. Then send the hotel or the host location the room set-up instructions and diagram. In the accompanying diagram, you see The Bob Pike Group's preferred room set-up. From the moment a participant walks in, it suggests they will be working together. We suggest round tables that seat up to six, but have only four to five people seated at a table. None of the chairs should have its back to the presenter. Start with fewer chairs and add to each table if needed. This way everyone can have full eye contact with the presenter and see the flip charts and screen.

We specifically place the screen in the corner of the room to the presenter's dominant side as the presenter faces the audience. This way the presenter is not constantly walking in front of the projector. Unless the presenter blacks out the screen each time, it is distracting. We prefer ten-foot ceilings so we can project higher so everyone can see. The entrance to the room is at the back to reduce distractions from late arrivers or folks needing to step out for a minute.

Dear Participant:

We are delighted that you will participate in the Creative Training Techniques(TM) process. Come prepared for fun and fulfillment while learning wonderful, new training skills. Please plan on arriving promptly as the program is packed with tools that you can use immediately; you will not want to miss any of it!

Here are a few "Warm-Ups" for you to consider doing before the two-day class begins. They are optional pre-program activities that will "prime" your brain for this exciting learning experience.

· Review and share the workshop overview, purpose, objectives and take-aways with a manager or mentor.
· Write out three goals for the workshop.
· Listen to at least one of these seventy-five podcasts so you can share with peers what you learned.

Where: The Bob Pike Group
      14530 Martin Drive -
      Eden Prairie, MN 55344
      800-383-9210
When: 11/12/2016 thru 11/13/2016
Schedule:

Day 1:	8:00 AM - 8:30 AM	Registration & Continental Breakfast
	8:30 AM - Noon	Program
	Noon - 1:00 PM	Lunch is provided
	1:00 PM - 4:00 PM	Program
Day 2:	8:00 AM - Noon	Program
	Noon - 1:00 PM	Lunch is provided
	1:00 PM - 3:30 PM	Program

Helpful Information:

· Dress is business casual
· As room temperatures fluctuate, we recommend wearing layers of clothing to ensure comfort
· Be ready to have a great time in a dynamic learning environment!

Please call us if you need assistance in any way. We want to ensure that you thoroughly enjoy this unique self-development experience.

Creatively,

Becky Pluth

Refreshments are in the back of the room instead of in the hall. It keeps participants in the room, and they can quickly grab something. We have found that when a person leaves the room, he or she takes more than twice the amount of time to return than if we have the food and beverage in the room.

When I keynote or speak at a convention where groups are in rows, I still have participants work together and engage even though the seating doesn't lend itself as easily or naturally to interaction. The same is true in other common room arrangements like the traditional classroom, board-room, auditorium or U-shape.

If possible, know the space that you are being given and play to its strength by knowing its limitations. I showed up for one workshop, and there was a post directly in the center of the room! Talk about tough sight lines for some of the participants. Sometimes we set expectations, and an event planner doesn't tell us critical information about the space, and we are left in a lurch.

Depending on your activity and purpose, here are other possible room arrangements:

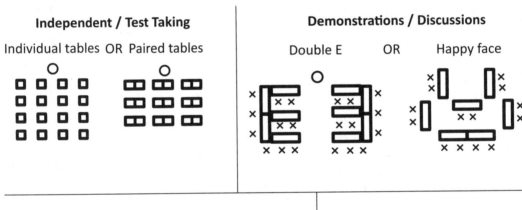

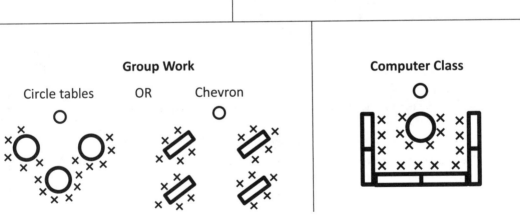

This grid shows which room set-up will maximize engagement based on your audience size and meeting purpose.

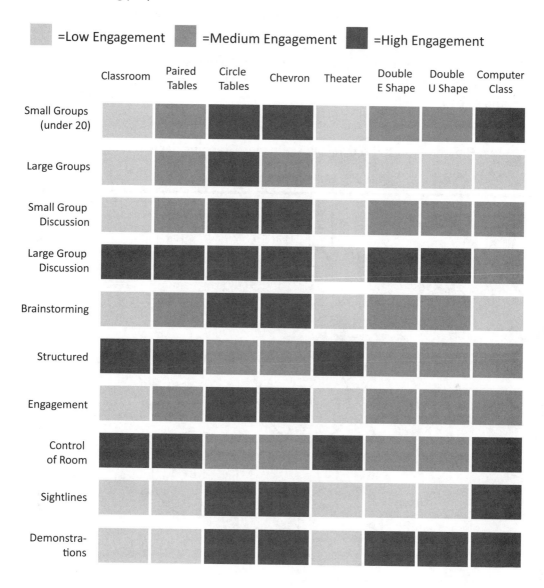

The Bob Pike Group's Workshop Meeting Room Specifications

This is our suggested layout for a right-handed trainer. A left-handed trainer would just flip the room.

A. Three skirted, rectangular tables set in room as illustrated, one accompanying bar stool for trainer, two extra chairs set aside, and a refreshment table set in the back of room near the entrance.

B. 60" to 72" Round Participant Tables. Set for four to six people per table (the number of participants will determine the total number of rounds required). Space tables a minimum of ten feet apart. Set with glasses and ice water.

C. CD/MP3 Player with built-in volume control

D. 6' x 6' Projection Screen with fully slanted projection set in left corner of room sixteen feet in front of the first row of tables. Make sure there are no lights above the screen.

E. LCD Projector

F. Two Flip Charts with three *full* pads of paper. Graphing paper on the flip chart pads is preferred.

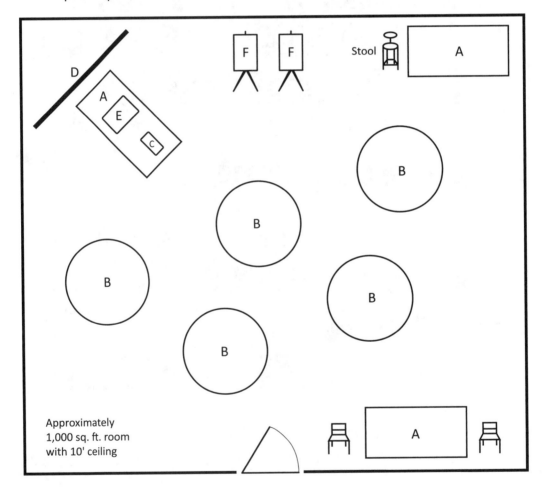

Facilitator

If preparation can minimize distractions and challenging participants, then you need to make sure you do your part to be ready. As a new trainer, I would be up until the wee hours of the morning preparing and practicing. I have since learned that is not best practice! Ideal doesn't always exist, but here are my ideal steps for before a presentation.

- Create and use a preparation checklist and include details and deadlines that are helpful for your program.

- Create and use packing lists.

  - Make one packing list that can be used regularly for sessions you run. We have a packing list for each public course and a broad checklist to select from when we are doing a customized program.

  - Design a travel packing list for items you are planning to take with you. Include items you don't want shipped like your computer, a backup USB drive with PowerPoints, chimes, a set of markers, etc. On that packing list, I also have typical items like toothbrush, hairbrush and socks. Even after doing all my travelling, I still forget basic items!

- Make or pull together handouts three weeks in advance. Review handouts for errors and make changes. Make sure loose leaf handouts have page numbers on them or are different colors for easy recognition.

- Double check hotel, car, flight and presentation room reservations a week in advance. More than once I have arrived and not had a sleeping room reserved. Luckily they have had space or I was able to bunk with another consultant, but it sure does create a panic. When booking a flight, do not book on the last flight out. This way, if there are delays or cancellations, there is still another viable option for getting there.

- Pull together contact information for the hotel and client. When you arrive, you will be able to check in with the hotel and text the client to let them know you have arrived and are excited to work together.

- Practice. And not just the night before. Pull things together as though it were the most important presentation of your life. We encourage our new consultants to invite friends and family in for a dry-run. Match content to context. If the session will be face-to-face, practice in a face-to-face environment. If the class is virtual, have a few computers logged in and record the session. After its recorded, watch it and see what tweaks need to be made.

- Once on–site, double check materials and set up the room the day or night before whenever possible. At minimum, open all boxes and make sure all materials are accounted for and not damaged. We have had potatoes stuck in hot trucks. Talk about a hot mess!

- Re-arrange the room configuration to meet your specifications. Even when we send the file of what we want, the screen will be in the middle of the room a majority of the time. If the screen is not affixed to the wall and is movable, I simply move the screen to the corner and re-set.

- Gather your flow, leader's guides, chimes, markers, PowerPoint clicker, roll of tape, etc., and make sure everything is in its place. Appearing organized is as important as being organized.

- Create a personal checklist to lessen distress and keep you on your best game. Here is a sample:

Trainer Checklist	Yes	No
Eight hours of sleep (sleep affects cortisol levels)		
Workout before class (increase energy and stress response)		
Drink five to eight glasses of water		
Eat breakfast; breakfast bars travel well		
Dress a step above your audience		
Accessorize to add, not distract, from your professional appearance		
Comfortable shoes; bring a second pair for the afternoon		
Protein at lunch to keep your energy up		
Physical stretches during break to wake up your body		
Energizing smiles for the audience		

Visuals

- Pre-make posters. If your visuals can be made ahead of time, this eliminates a lot of the drawing pauses during class time. When we slow down for something like this, it opens a door for minds to wander and phones to come out during the class. A few tips for posters are:
  - o When making posters on flip chart pads, leave a flip chart sheet between so that learners can't see the next poster.
  - o Select several posters to put on the wall or floor (ground rules go on the ground!) to grab attention when participants arrive.
  - o Write in upper and lower case. ALL CAPS IS HARDER TO READ and cursive is also challenging.
  - o Letters should be two to three inches tall.
  - o Use page flags or small sticky notes to tab pages so you can easily flip to those pages.
  - o Use teal, blue, green and purple for main marker colors. Use other colors for highlighting or emphasis.
  - o Alternate colors when creating a list on the page to make it easy to follow along.
  - o Use images; after all, a poster is a visual aid.
- Test the technology: computer, projector, sound, clicker technology (batteries do wear out!) and any software programs you will be using.

- Travel with extra workbooks, handouts and a print–out of your slides. I have arrived on-site to find the wrong workbook was sent! Because I had the correct workbook in my carry-on, I was able to copy the first twenty pages for each participant, and books arrived the morning of day two. Just this last year, one of our consultants called and shared the hotel had a two-hour fire drill. Being cool, calm and collected with thirty-five years of creative training experience, Doug McCallum asked that tables, chairs and his flip chart be brought outside, and he trained from the parking lot! Having printouts of answer sheets and workbook blanks can be a life saver. One never knows what will happen.

- Double check PowerPoint slides for accuracy and add workbook page numbers to the slides. If you have latecomers, they will be able to see where you are which reduces distractions.

During Class

During the session, there are a lot of things we can control that impact learners both positively and negatively. When you first start your training, your first goal is to move every audience member to "learner" as quickly as possible using WIIFM (What's In It For Me). Help learners answer this question by having them choose their learning goals for the session and prioritizing the content of the course. I also emphasize how the information will make them better, quicker, faster, and more competent. If someone besides you has done the needs assessment, learn as much as you can about the audience and the WIIFM they are coming into the room expecting, wanting or desiring.

Once in the room, learners subconsciously want you and other learners to "make me feel important about myself," abbreviated as MMFIAM. The basis of this is emotion and self-esteem. Building confidence can increase their interest in the course. You want your participants to leave impressed with themselves and what they are able to do versus feeling intimidated and unable to do what the trainer did.

Here are a few things you can do to impact the MMFIAM:

- Use first names
- Use polite language (no foul language or cursing)
- Provide choices
- Allow learners to pick their own topics for practice
- Greet participants before the session
- Use their words and stories in examples
- Allow them to share their expertise
- Honor their years of experience

Utilizing those few tips can help you gain learner interest quickly.

In addition, here are other strategies you can use after the opening to minimize the opportunities for difficult behaviors to emerge or to mitigate the damage of those negative behaviors and get all learners back on track as quickly as possible.

Where should you sit different types of difficult participants? Oftentimes people find people like themselves, and they end up at the very same table! Ten years ago, I was in Phoenix, Arizona, in a hotel conference room ready to present at my very first Boot Camp. Of course, no one else knew it was my first session. I had just randomly formed new groups by having people meet and greet and sit next to their new partners.

It just so happened that there were five people at each table, and there was one table filled with nay-sayers. It was a challenging first hour. Every time a group leader was to share, their group would say, "We discussed how this won't work for us because...."

I knew I had to do something. Although they had just gotten into new teams forty-five minutes prior, I decided to switch tables again. I had everyone number off from one to five and then find their new table. What this did was separate the naysayers from one another, allowing their new tables to silence the negative thought patterns and encourage open minds and thinking. It worked! This ties in with my next strategy:

Use the dynamics of the group to reduce challenging behavior.
A participant will work harder for his or her peers than for the instructor, even an amazing instructor. If an assignment is given, and learners need to share with another person, there is greater accountability and desire to make sure they have something of value to share.

Start on time.
It is a simple step that rewards those that made the effort to be there. Obviously, there are exceptions to a rule. If there are special circumstances, like weather that prevents many from being on time, you may consider a modified start.

Establish ground rules with the group to gain their buy-in.
Include in the "ground rules" a sign that says, "Thanks for putting me on silent and using me on breaks" with a picture of a cell phone. It is a quiet way to encourage what you are expecting. Try to create positive ground rules asking for what you want versus saying "Turn it off or else!" If you have a class of millennials, the texting generation, consider building into the program times for posting learnings to their favorite social media sites. For ideas on how to incorporate social media into the classroom, read the chapter Social Media in Training.

Provide breaks, even when it is only a two-hour class.
A short, one-function break allows for a nice stretch and re-focusing the mind as well as an opportunity to create more primacy-recency moments.

Genuinely thank participants and have participants thank one another.
Gratitude can be given for participants sharing with one another, coming back on time from a break or asking a question.

Use a visual timer with odd numbered break times.
Odd amounts of time are more memorable, and they require more than a gut check. Generally, people know what five minutes or ten minutes "feels" like, but when we give an eleven-minute break, it isn't a time we regularly assess, and it encourages us to look at our watch to be back on time.

Keep the classroom door closed when in session.
This lets participants know when class is in session, and it keeps distractions outside the room to a minimum. Even with the door located at the back of the room, noise from outside in the hall can be distracting.

Use small groups and rotate leadership.
The quiet or shy will naturally choose to listen and are comfortable doing so in a small group. Rotating leadership nudges them to engage in a safe way, because they know they are helping their group succeed. Rotating leadership allows a withdrawn participant to lead, and it also helps to quiet the socializer.

Use personal white boards for group responses.
This way the leader in the group can recall what was said or be the team scribe.

Use examples that are relevant and both historical and current.
This will engage the youngest to the oldest. I have been in sessions where the examples were all dated. Every "famous" quote was from two decades before my time. The opposite can also be true where all references are from after 1990 because the trainer was born in 1993. Don't have learners checking out just because of generational examples. If you don't have examples from another generation, share your example and ask the group to come up with something comparable from their generation. Using their story honors them and makes the example relevant to another group of people which closes the gap.

Use physical proximity.
Just walking by or near learners that are not engaged or are distracted can help them refocus. Pausing near the offending learner for a moment but presenting in the opposite direction is effective. It doesn't call attention to them but your near presence re-engages them.

Switch up table groups.
Have you ever selected a table and found one of your tablemates got on your nerves? Not a fun way to spend two days. The same is true for your learners. A few ways to do this creatively:

> Give everyone a playing card when they come into the class.

> Rearrange table groups by card color, number, and suit.

> Number off around the room by numbers of tables in the room. Then tell participants where the 1s, 2s, 3s and 4s will move to.

Use an app for regrouping like Team Shake. Enter participants' names into the app and have it automatically randomize the groups. Trainer tip: Shake it ahead of time until you find groupings that you like, capture the image on your phone or tablet, then shake it in front of the group and show the photo of the groupings to the class.

Ask participants to find a partner. Once everyone has a partner, announce that they will fill in the name of that partner at the 12:00 spot on a card that has a clock on it. Have everyone in the room find a new person to partner with and fill in their 3:00 spot on their clock. Repeat this for 6:00 and 9:00. Throughout the day, when you want your participants to share what they have learned or to work with a partner, ask learners to take out their clocks and find their 12:00 partner. The next time you need to do partner work, they will find their 3:00 partner and so on. You can also do this

with an image of a compass and use North, South, East and West as the spots for partners.

Go fish for your group. This is literally a "Go Fish" deck of cards where each participant receives one card. Then learners work the room to find the other three people who have cards that match his or her own.

Paint color swatches also work well for "mixing" up table groups.

Eye contact.
Sometimes just looking in the direction of the person can get his or her attention. If one person continually volunteers to share, you can look at him and simply state, "Let's get feedback from someone new on this one." This lets the person know you won't always call on him.

Private conversation.
If I have given it my best effort, and there is still a challenge in the room, I make time for discussing it privately with the person. Start with the sad card ("Is everything okay?") and not the mad card ("What do you think you are doing?"). Using words that sell work well here, too. "I understand how you feel, others have felt that way too. One thing others have found helpful...." Be relatable and empathic but at the same time convicting.

Most people don't wake up in the morning and say to themselves, "Self, what can we do to make others' lives miserable today?" However, they do find their way into our classes, and just one difficult participant can spoil a class for all the others. But these tried and true classroom management tips can help you effectively manage and redirect your difficult participants.

Managing the Energy as You Manage the Classroom

Don't wait for your participants to become difficult before you manage your classroom. Use these tactics to help create and maintain a safe and energized classroom that isn't chaotic or distracting from the learning

Getting participants into new groups. Many learners like a little variety and appreciate connecting with new people. Have learners switch table groups so they can meet others and make networking connections for long after the course.

Create healthy competition and include prizes. Prizes do not need to break the bank. Participants will gamely vie for candy and stickers.

Have a roadmap/agenda for the day up on the wall. At The Bob Pike Group, our agenda lists the topics we'll cover but does not have specific times which provides flexibility for the instructor to go longer on topics on which the learners need more time.

Fill in the blanks in the workbook. Don't put in so many blanks that it's annoying or too few so it's no longer interactive. Our minds like completion, and this is one way we can create curiosity and allow learners' brains to guess at what could be in the blank. They naturally do this without us even saying anything. Most participants want to ensure their book is completed before going home and do not like having blanks, well, blank. This ties in with the Closure Principle (we like closure) and the Zeigarnik Effect (we remember best what is incomplete).

Use a chime to get attention. You something other than your voice to quiet the room. When groups are talking, they can more easily and quickly distinguish a chime, a bell, or whistle than they can your voice.

Insert page numbers on your PowerPoint slides. This makes it easy for learners to catch up if they had to leave the room for a moment instead of distracting a neighbor to find out where you are at in the workbook.

Blackout PowerPoint. Blackout the screen when you want to have learners focus on discussion or your lecture. This is done when your computer is in PowerPoint mode by hitting the B key. If you have a clicker for your PowerPoint slides, there is usually a button that will blackout the screen.

Use the space in the room and outside the room. If you have a lot of extra space in the back of the room, use it for relay races or small group discussion space. I've even had learners take their chairs to the back of the room for a segment just for a change in scenery and focus. If you do not have very much space, consider using an empty hallway or quiet atrium for exercises. When using space outside the room, it is considered a "field trip" for the learners, and this becomes a built-in physical energizer. When the weather is nice and the out–of–doors is close by, I will teach a twenty–minute chunk of content outdoors, if there is a place for learners to sit. Otherwise, I will teach a five–minute segment and have learners stand. The fresh air does wonders to reengage and reignite.

Use scribes to write ideas on whiteboards and posters. Scribes act an extra set of hands so that you can focus on sharing content, facilitating the discussion, and asking probing questions. A little whiteboard at each table allows a team leader to be a scribe and then share the team's thoughts with the larger group. If the large group was doing brainstorming, I would have two volunteer scribes at two flipchart easels taking turns writing down the brainstorming ideas. This takes the pressure off of one person having to write as quickly as a whole group can think.

Encourage responses and guessing. Get people talking. Sometimes playing upbeat music quietly in the background makes small group discussions more inviting, or try having groups brainstorm and share back a top ten list. This provides a platform for participants to feel comfortable talking in front of the rest of the room. Let them know the expectations from the onset whether guessing or using smartphones for quick research for example is okay. Share that you recognize they may not know the answers and that's okay. If you seem to get no response when you ask questions, consider asking each small group to consider the question, brainstorm an answer for thirty seconds, and share their answers with the larger group.

Use energizers. In standing up and taking a stretch to finding a new partner in a new part of the room sharing a pattern idea to other examples throughout this book be sure to just use them to maintain attention and focus. You can read more in the Energizers chapter.

ILPC After Training

Chapter 16

TRAINING TRANSFER AND EVALUATION

Imagine back to when you attended your first train-the-trainer class. When the segment on training transfer was introduced, did you have any idea what was being discussed? As I attended my first, the jargon was like a foreign language, and even after attending, I still didn't comprehend how deeply important it was to make sure my trainees used the classroom training back on-the-job. Without that follow-through, training has no impact. And with the billions of dollars spent annually on both formal and informal training, organizations definitely want to see a return on their investment.

According to industry thought leader Robert O. Brinkerhoff, the "highest and best purpose for [training and development] is to accelerate the execution of strategic initiatives" (Brinkerhoff 2014). He also says that as much as seventy percent of companies fail due to an inadequate execution of the company's intended strategy. This means that, not only did these strategic initiative trainings not get transferred, but up to seventy percent of company failures can be tied to this lack of transfer. Yeah, training transfer is that important.

The transfer of learning, or transforming the learning into performance, is actually the whole purpose behind training and is a dynamic process that requires planning. It starts before a class begins with a solid needs assessment that identifies both perceived and real needs. Then a course is developed that covers both. Yet many trainers spend up to ninety percent of a training workshop's budget on design, development and delivery of the training, and only ten percent goes toward events before the training, like needs assessment and analysis, and reinforcement after the training, according to Jim and Wendy Kayser Kirkpatrick (Kirkpatrick 2014).

Mary Broad and John Newstrom's research indicates that before and after training is where the real "stickiness" of the training takes place. What happens at the training's bookends is really what decides whether the training will be effective in seeing the training implemented on the job and making a difference toward company goals (Broad and Newstrom 1992).

In order to provide a solid foundation for training and its effective transfer, it is critical that you become a training ambassador and gain the support of the training by company leaders. The success of the learning transfer begins with the perceived and real support of the training by company leaders and especially the training participants' managers.

Common sense would say that the people most directly involved with the success of the training are the trainer, the participant, and the participant's manager. Broad and Newstrom developed a transfer of training matrix to show which of these three players had the most impact on the training's success before, during, and after the training.

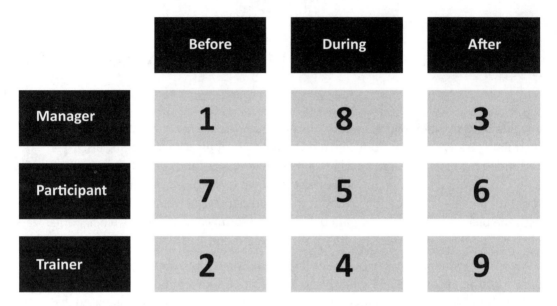

You might find it surprising that the manager's involvement and support of the training beforehand is the most important role in training transfer. Second most important is the trainer beforehand. And in third place is the manager again when he shows support and asks for follow-up on the training from the participant after the event. Believe it or not, the participant, the one actually attending the training, is fifth, sixth, and seventh most important when it comes to implementing the training on the job.

In 2006, only ten percent of learning transfer failure was actually due to the training itself, according to that year's State of the Industry report from the American Society for Training and Development (now Association for Talent Development). That means ninety percent of the failure was caused by something else in the environment.

Some of the failures were attributed to:

- A lack of executive involvement in the behavior change process.
- A breakdown in communication. If leaders support the training but do not communicate that to the learners, then the passion for the training stops at the top levels.
- A resistance to change. Change management takes time but even more so when peers are negative and outspoken.
- Interference from colleagues, managers, or peers who made it too hard to implement anything. When there is no collaboration, the few attempting to follow the new training process feel abandoned and may in turn abandon the process.

- A disconnect between the class content and the real world which made it difficult to implement.

- Participants feeling the training was poorly designed.

- Managers interrupting the participant during class for "emergencies."

- A lack or absence of appropriate needs assessment.

- A lack of collaboration between the training team and the learners' managers.

- A lack of on-the-job resources to reinforce training messages.

Training is a process, not an event. Transformational learning begins long before the "starting bell" and continues long after your training's closing ceremonies. Many of these failures could have been avoided or minimized by implementing learning transfer processes before, during and after the program.

For those companies that have molded themselves into true learning organizations and have seen an eighty percent hike in performance improvement, the responsibility and accountability of learning rests on everyone, not just the people sitting in the training room.

Following are some strategies you can use to help you think critically about what is missing in the learning transfer process and needs to be remedied.

Learning transfer strategies to use before the learning experience

Strategies for managers before

1. Recognize the performance need.

2. Shop around for best resources for providing training.

3. Involve trainees in workshop planning and preparation.

4. Meet regularly with learners before the training to discuss the training course and expectations.

5. Encourage the trainee to attend all sessions or complete all online modules.

6. Establish goals for training with the participant to make use of newly learned knowledge, skills and attitudes in an action plan.

7. Discuss what on-the-job application looks like.

8. Tie performance appraisal to training behavior and application on the job.

9. Frame the training as continuous improvement for the learner, not punishment.

10. Present positive aspects of the training to the trainee.

11. Collect baseline performance data for comparison after training.

12. Model behavior to be learned in training.

13. Arrange for backup to cover trainee work load.

14. Provide time for pre-course work to be completed.

15. Request program feedback from the trainee.

16. Provide input to the training team on important content issues.

17. Provide trainer access to needs assessment.

18. Cooperate with the training team.

19. Implement a peer mentor/coach program.

Strategies for participants before

1. Be open to new learning.

2. Review the course description and objectives.

3. List your job tasks that the training is expected to improve.

4. Identify areas that may be a challenge.

5. Consider finding a mentor or coach to help with the learning.

6. Connect with your manager on training and implementation expectations.

Strategies for the trainer before

1. Determine and develop accurate content.

2. Select relevant activities and exercises.

3. Create content relevant openers, closers, revisiters and energizers.

4. Organize content in a meaningful manner.

5. Internalize flow and content.

6. Build in peer reviews.

7. Create pre-course work or learning opportunities.

8. Begin learning cycle with tools like www.pro.mindsetter.com.

9. Proper practice and preparation prevents poor performance.

10. Send out course agenda and overview to trainees.

11. Send out pre-course learning activities.

Learning transfer strategies to use during the learning experience

Strategies for managers during

1. Communicate support for the program.

2. Plan transfer of new skills to the job.

3. Transfer work assignments.

4. Prevent distractions and interruptions for learner.

5. Prepare peers and team for new behaviors.

6. Ensure attendance.

7. Participate in the course.

8. Check in with participant at the end of each day for update.

9. Create post-training meeting with the participant.

Strategies for participants during

1. Take meaningful notes.

2. Organize new information in a usable manner.

3. Assimilate and link new concepts to prior knowledge.

4. Participate in selecting, organizing, and integrating information in the context of on-the-job tasks.

5. Identify key takeaways.

6. Verbalize key learnings.

7. Ask "How can I use this in my day-to-day?"

8. Participate fully in experiences, activities, and application time.

9. Network with others.

10. Provide self-directed learning throughout.

Strategies for the trainer during

1. Share clear work-related objectives.

2. Model and demonstrate new skills.

3. Provide relevant examples and link learning back to the job.

4. Use a variety of activities, including openers, closers, revisiters and energizers.

5. Encourage participation.

6. Use action plans.

7. Ask learners "How will you apply this?"

8. Use open-ended questions. Correct incorrect answers.

9. Provide immediate feedback.

10. Recognize learner success and participation, and celebrate achievements.

11. Share with learners what's in the training for them (WIIFM) and help them feel they are an important part of the group.

12. Demonstrate credibility. Cite resources and authorities on topics.

13. Use vocal variety.

14. Perfect pacing of your presentation.

15. Reduce tension in the room through laughter, energizers, group work to increase retention.

Learning transfer strategies to use after the learning experience

Strategies for managers after

1. Debrief the training with the learner. Ask questions about the experience and how the information will be implemented.
2. Give opportunities for the learner to use the new information six times in thirty days for reinforcement.
3. Have the trainee share her new learning in a team meeting and with peers.
4. Provide praise, encouragement and approval as the trainee implements her new learning.
5. Do periodic evaluations. Ask questions about how the learner is applying the newly learned concepts.
6. Use job aids to assess compliance and transfer.
7. Compare pre-training to post-training behavior.
8. Coach the trainee in using the new information.
9. Use mistakes as learning opportunities.
10. Reinforce best practices.
11. Model new behaviors.
12. Publicize successes.

Strategies for participants after

1. Mentor others in what has been learned.
2. Create a plan and implement the new knowledge.
3. Continue connecting with others from class.
4. Report back learning and implementation plan.
5. Teach peers the key points.
6. Implement the new learning frequently.
7. Complete follow-up training modules, emails, and exercises.
8. Create calendar reminders to check in with yourself on how well you are applying the content.

Strategies for the trainer after

1. Follow up with learners with an email or voicemail.
2. Host a live webinar to revisit key content.
3. Provide a coaching call to celebrate success back on the job.
4. Send out follow-up communication.

5. Use a tool like pro.mindsetter.com to schedule follow-up revisiting activities.

6. Create eLearning modules to support learning.

7. Connect back with the manager to ensure continued support for the trainee.

Action Planning is Step One to Achieving Follow Through

Perhaps you've heard the story of the Yale University class of 1953 where the graduates were surveyed and only three percent had written down their goals. Two decades later, the surviving classmates were once again surveyed and those three percent had amassed more financial wealth than the other ninety-seven percent of the class combined! It's a great story about writing down goals to help them get realized! The big problem with this study is that it was never done (Tabak 1996).

However, Gail Matthews, a professor in the psychology department at Dominican University of California, did do a study recently that showed there was a strong correlation with writing down goals, getting accountability for them, and achieving them (Matthews 2007).

She began with 267 participants recruited from a variety of ages, groups, backgrounds and countries. Each participant was put into one of five groups. The first group was simply asked to think about business-related goals they hoped to achieve within four weeks and "rate each goal according to difficulty, importance, the extent to which they had the skills and resources to accomplish the goal, their commitment and motivation, and whether they had pursued the goal before."

Groups two was asked to do the same thing and write down the goals.

Group three was then asked to add action commitments for each goal.

Group four was asked to do that and share these commitments with a friend.

Group five had to do all of the above and send a weekly progress report to a friend.

Of the 267 participants, 149 completed the study. At the end of the four weeks, only forty-three percent of group one participants accomplished their goals or were at least halfway there. Sixty-two percent of group four's goals had been accomplished or were at least halfway there. However, group five had seventy-six percent completion of goals, or were halfway there.

In our training sessions, to increase the odds that our learners will use their training back on the job, we have a specific page in our workbooks where learners can list actions they would like to take based on the content they have heard so far. In addition, we have them pair up with other learners, share their action ideas with one another, and exchange contact information as a way to increase their accountability to attain their goals. This is a great tactic for any classroom where follow-through is important.

If you make it easy for managers to prepare learners for the class and provide follow-up tips, it is more likely to happen. Start by drafting an email to the managers that has questions they can use with the learners to discuss the training and its implementation at status meetings.

Other transfer strategies for after the training

Informal learning
Many studies indicate that the majority of what people know about their jobs they learned through informal learning. They asked coworkers questions, they read manuals, or they simply learned through trial and error. According to Jay Cross, a champion of online learning, "formal training and workshops account for only five to twenty percent of how people learn" (Cross 2014). Cross likens informal learning to "natural" learning. Incorporate this kind of instinctive learning into your transfer plans. One way to do this would be to provide self-paced follow-up that has many options like a month-long calendar with a skill to practice in each box. Allow trainees to go out of order on the calendar, and choose seven to complete over the course of the month. This type of natural learning can make a significant impact on follow-through.

Job Aids
I believe that every training program should have a job aid that participants begin using in class and then can continue using it on the job. Be sure to write the job aids in a specific and measurable way. This helps learners know exactly what is expected of them and allows for those evaluating the behaviors later to evaluate objectively. A subjective job aid might include this expectation: The call center employee answered the phone quickly. An objective job aid would be rephrased this way: The call center employee answered the phone within three rings. Job aids should be based on behaviors that needed modification as shown during the needs assessment.

Social Media
In other areas of this book, we've discussed ways to use social media to enhance training. This is certainly one of those areas where social media can help your training live on by mimicking informal or natural training.

If you have an intranet group, a LinkedIn group or a Facebook group, you can also post applicable cartoons, thought-provoking quotes, learner questions or testimonials from learners on how they implemented a particular piece of the training. As I've said before, people like sharing their knowledge and their experience. Never underestimate the power of this kind of natural learning and the interactions that can take place if only you create the incubator for it.

Email and Voicemail
Use email to send out weekly tidbits that highlight a key piece of the training or include a new resource through a PDF. Many companies have automated phone trees. Record a brief message with a training tidbit or a tip that will help the learners on the job. Then schedule the message to go out early in the morning or late at night when the message is most likely to go directly to voicemail. The voicemail can then be saved if the listener found it particularly helpful; and many people have their voicemails sent to their emails so they have another way to file the information.

Wikis and Blogs

A wiki is a website that allows multiple people to collaborate on curating and editing the information on the site. Wikipedia is one example of a wiki. To start the wiki, use content you've already gathered such as relevant and helpful items from the training guide or data from company case studies that relate to the topic. Invite other trainers or learners who have already gone through the course to add to the information as they find new adaptations or applications to the learning. Call centers have especially found this useful as support specialists encounter new and unusual situations through their customer contacts. They can update the wiki with their new solutions, and other specialists benefit from this prior experience.

Mentoring

Mentoring connects the social component of learning with follow-up. Rich Meiss, a senior consultant at The Bob Pike Group who focuses on coaching and leadership, describes mentoring as a process where an experienced person shares knowledge or experience with a mentee. "The mentor usually has no direct supervisory role with the mentee, and the mentee is often given the choice of selecting his/her own mentor. The mentee usually sets his/her own goals, and the mentor then becomes a confidant, teacher and advisor in assisting in the accomplishment of those goals," he said (Meiss 2010).

Evaluation: Showing a Return on Investment

If you want job security and evidence that the training component of the company is critical to the company's success, then you want to follow through and do training evaluations.

Evaluation helps your organization see what is working and what needs to be changed so the whole organization can excel. In 2013, organizations reported that the cost to have one hour of learning available was $1,798 (ASTD 2013). Every hour of training is an investment either well spent or wasted. For us as trainers to show the training had an impact, we need to do more than just have happy participants fill out "smile sheets" that indicate they had a good time at training while learning something. We need to evaluate the on-the-job application of that learning and the speed at which this happened. The true success of a training program is measured by the performance improvement.

> "If we define success (impact) as sustained behavior change that is aligned with organization performance improvement goals, then almost all T&D [training and development] initiatives score less than fifty percent success, and many are a good bit lower than that; our evaluation experience shows that twenty to twenty-five percent is most typical. But some—a distressingly low number—achieve far greater success rates. As I have presented it to audiences in the past, the typical T&D endeavor invests a pound of learning for an ounce (or less) of impact. In my view, evaluation should be focused on a simple and single purpose: to turn this formula around, so that T&D initiatives regularly invest a few ounces of learning for many pounds of impact" (Brinkerhoff 2014).

Brinkerhoff says the "secret" to successful training requires transparency and involvement of the full organization. "When the value of training that worked is made clear, and when the money that was left on the table when training failed to work is made clear, and when who did what or did not do what to help it work is made clear, people take action to change things," Brinkerhoff said.

How to Evaluate

In order to show the success or failure of training and who was responsible, you need to evaluate. If you want to know if you hit your training targets or want to prove the value of your efforts, you need to evaluate.

In chapter seven, I talked about how to pinpoint training needs and how to write specific, measurable objectives before you design the training to ensure those needs were met. Just now, I showed you ways to ensure that the content you are teaching gets carried over into the workplace after the training. Those three things need to happen in order for training to be effective *and* for you to be able to show evidence of that.

Evaluation is integral to the training function, whether it is ILPC or not. Because of its vital role in training, I will cover it here briefly, but I encourage you to read Don Kirkpatrick and Jim Kirkpatrick's *Evaluating Training Programs* for a comprehensive view on how to effectively evaluate training using Don's Four Levels. Jack Phillips also builds on the Four Levels by including a fifth that shows how to calculate the ROI of training through data analysis in his book *Return on Investment in Training and Performance Improvement Programs*, if you want further reading.

As Don Kirkpatrick summarized his Four Levels, "Trainers must begin with desired results (Level 4) and then determine what behavior (Level 3) is needed to accomplish them. Then trainers must determine the attitudes, knowledge, and skills (Level 2) that are necessary to bring about the desired behavior(s). The final challenge is to present the training program in a way that enables the participants not only to learn what they need to know but also to react favorably to the program (Level 1)" (Kirkpatrick 2014). While the four levels might be seen as a pyramid with level one as the foundation, you should actually begin with Level Four in order to successfully implement this kind of evaluation.

Level Four—Evidence (not proof). This level gauges the overall organization's return on investment: to what degree did you achieve targeted outcomes as a result of the training and learning reinforcement. This is where you, as the trainer, ask questions about your overall purpose: why do we exist? What does the company want to accomplish? And how did training impact that overall mission? Then you can begin plugging those answers into your training regimen. How will your training affect these goals?

Ideally, you are planning the whole scope of training offerings when you start here, and you can see what outcomes you want before deciding which training to pursue. Even if this role is not yours, it may be in your and your company's best interests to explore this and see how each workshop, class or learning plan ties into this. If you see classes that are not in alignment with these goals, a persuasive conversation with the training department manager may be a good place to start as you sharpen focus on what will bolster the company's long-term effectiveness and get rid of the training dead weight that costs money yet produces little or no benefit to the company and its goals.

Less than thirty-seven percent of companies are measuring the business impact (return on attendance, sales increase, reduction of errors, cost savings), according to ATD (ASTD 2009). One mistake I see companies commonly making in the area of Level Four, besides the fact that only about one-third actually measure at this level, is that many companies start at level one and work their way up.

When it comes to evaluating at Level Four, look for evidence that the training made an impact, not necessarily proof. Allow time to pass for results to take place. "Intellectual capital is largely a matter of mind and relationships. It's impossible to measure directly, but you know in your heart that it's real" (Cross 2014).

Level Three—Are they using it? This level gauges the on-the-job behaviors after training: to what degree did the learners apply what they learned. It speaks directly to how well the learning was transferred. More than fifty percent of companies measure these behaviors, according to ATD, often by having learners fill out forms or having somebody use an observation checklist.

Level Two—Did they learn it? This level answers the questions "To what degree did the participants acquire the knowledge and skills put forth in the training?" Typically this level involves testing of some kind. The most often used method is using a paper and pencil test or audience response systems (ARS) clicker questions to test learners. Over eighty percent of companies are now evaluating at this level, according to ATD. However, many companies only conduct a post-training test, not a pre-training test, so viable benchmarks cannot be made. Good results on a post-test may just indicate that a learner had prior knowledge of the topic. When you evaluate at this level, create a pre-test and a post-test using different questions that cover the same information. And test as closely as you can to how participants are actually going to use the knowledge, skills or attitudes back on the job.

Level One—Did they like it? This level gauges the participants' reactions and measures to what degree the learners enjoyed the training. This is the easiest level to track, and many trainers just use "smile sheets" at the end of a program. Presumably, a smile sheet is so named because of the emoticons used on many of these evaluations: a happy face for a positive response and a frowny face for a negative one.

Survey Questions	Your Response				
Question 1 Share your response for this question	☐	☐	☐	☐	☐

This benchmark, while most frequently measured, is of the least value to stakeholders. It measures a learner's reaction to the training but little else. Because smile sheets are easy to create and easy to fill out, it is not surprising that ninety-two percent of companies are doing level one evaluations, according to ATD.

If you are going to use "smile sheet" questions, make sure these forms are reviewed and updated annually, and ask questions that give you insight into how to improve the program.

Being a great trainer is about so much more than just that moment in the workshop spotlight. It means making content memorable, usable and most of all transformational for the learner—and then showing how the training made a difference not just in the life of the learner but in the well-being of the organization as well.

Part Two

NICE TO KNOW

Chapter 17

PowerPoint Design for the Classroom

PowerPoint is one of the most misused training tools on the planet. However, when designed and used well, it is one of the most powerful weapons in a trainer's arsenal.

As we focus on digital technology for visual engagement, I don't want to "throw the baby out with the bathwater." Do not discount other visual aids such as flip charts. They have their place in ILPC training.

A trainer uses visual aids to enhance the environment. Like a computer that reboots, the human brain automatically reboots every thirty to sixty minutes. It is a subconscious physical response that cannot be stopped. A PowerPoint slide is only out for thirty seconds to a couple of minutes. And once the slide is blacked out or flips to the next slide, the visual enhancement is gone.

Now picture flip chart pages taped on the walls all around the room. Some of these are prepared by you ahead of time, others are created as participants work in small groups during the session. The posters have bright colors and maybe even pictures. Now, when your learners go on "mental vacations," they will look around the room at all of the different posters, and they're still engaged in the content. Other visuals that a trainer might use would include props, object lessons, demonstrations, matching games, colored markers, stickers, dice, preprinted posters, and a variety of others.

Okay, now back to the topic at hand. How do you build a powerful PowerPoint deck that aids you in your training effort? For the sake of those new to training or building PowerPoint presentations, I will briefly address some of the basics of best practice for the training classroom. Then, I will spend the remainder of the chapter unpacking the two traits absolutely essential for PowerPoint decks built for Instructor-Led, Participant-Centered learning.

About eighty percent of the information for PowerPoint design is applicable to both virtual and live classrooms; for the remaining twenty percent, I have clearly labeled information when it is only applicable to one type of classroom. Additional tips for designing visuals for the digital classroom can be found in the chapter PowerPoint Design for Virtual Training.

To start, here are some overarching considerations and some standard best practice information on building effective PowerPoint decks for training.

Think Billboard, Not Outline

My favorite book on PowerPoint design is *Presentation Zen* by Garr Reynolds because his ideas are simple and replicable. In his book, he talks about the elevator test, in which you view your slide as something that must get its point across within the typical duration of an elevator ride. So such a test forces you "to 'sell' your message in thirty to forty-five seconds." Although that's the typical time you may leave a slide up on the screen, I prefer to view my PowerPoint slide as a billboard. As you drive past a billboard, at a glance, do you get the main point? In the same way, it should only take three to five seconds to understand the key message of each PowerPoint slide.

Make It Stick

In *Made to Stick*, Chip and Dan Heath discuss what makes some information memorable and other concepts forgettable. Their book covers six "sticky" ideas, which spell out SUCCESs (a sticky acronym): simplicity, unexpectedness, concreteness, credibility, emotions, and stories. These principles apply not only to designing content, but also to designing visuals, more specifically PowerPoint.

PowerPoint Design Best Practice for Training Purposes

Although the following list of considerations may seem oh-so-obvious to seasoned trainers, for those who are just entering the profession, they can be a lifesaver, minimizing grief and upping the quality of their slides.

1. **Know your audience.** Are they a group of CEOs or accountants? Where are they geographically located? Are they kids, employees or a mix of generations? In knowing your audience, you can tailor your font, theme, colors and images to engage them and meet your training needs.

2. **Create a flow for your content first.** A flow to a trainer is like a storyboard to a writer—it outlines the organizational structure of your presentation and its ac-

companying slides. I highly recommend you flow using a template, as I do. This ensures you always include the title of the session, the date, the link to the webinar if appropriate, objectives, and then slides from the soft opener through content and into closing activities.

In a flow step, I also determine which slides I need to show learners for teaching them how to use the tools in the virtual platform. I'm selective here because I only want to show them a snapshot and examples of tools being used in that session so I do not overwhelm my learners with unnecessary technical information.

As you flow out your content, you will also determine how long you will talk about the content on each slide as well as how you will have learners interact with the information on the slide.

3. **Transform data into pictures.** Let your participants "see" the importance behind the numbers. This is true for both the live and virtual classroom. Take the data and compare it to something tangible. For several examples, go to noteandpoint.com and start getting some visual ideas.

    Below is a slide we used to answer the question "What percent of students entering the fifth and ninth grade are reading below grade level?"

    70% read below grade level

    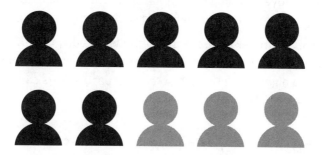

    Beyond just visual, you might also try to turn the statistic into a "story" into which your participants can put themselves.

4. **Master the basics of image editing.** Within PowerPoint, you can click on a picture or image and do some simple editing–you can remove the background, lighten it–all in an effort to make the image work best for your slide. You don't need to be a graphic designer; you just need to know the basics to capitalize on your selected images.

5. **Evaluate each slide with the learner's experience in mind.** After you have designed a slide or a series of slides covering a topic, go back and evaluate each slide by asking the following questions: How does this help participants get my message better? Is the image too little? Does it add to or detract from the message? Is the activity too simplistic? Too convoluted?

6. **Printing.** When you are printing out the slides, be aware that the paper orientation print choice impacts what is printed. If you select "landscape," only the slides will print out. If you select "portrait," both the slides and your presenter notes will print.

Here are some general considerations for individual slides:

- Reduce words but keep the meaning. Add extraneous language to your presenter notes. Make sure that you, as the presenter, add value to the session. The participants shouldn't read your entire session on your slides. Slides should simply highlight the main points. Again, each slide as a billboard not a book.

- Add interest through text animation. Do NOT use perpetually animated art which becomes an irritant as people stare at a screen for multiple minutes while you are talking. Instead, use text animation (like words flying in, being revealed, or fading away on the slide). This brings interest without irritation!

- Visually support your slide's point by using vector art. Let's be real—clip art is cheesy.

- In general, have a headline and a graphic.

- Make a watermark out of your company's logo so that you don't need to spend valuable slide "real estate" on the logo.

- It's okay to move beyond the template. In order to expand an image or document, you are going to have to get rid of the template slide, and that is okay!

- If you have a complex diagram, show the whole diagram in an initial slide, but then in subsequent slides, break the diagram down and zoom in on the portions you want to highlight and teach so that all participants can read what you are referencing.

Tips for Working with Color and Font

1. **Dark background, light font color.** When creating your PowerPoint slides, ensure you use a dark color for the background of the slide and a light color for the text font. This is easier on the participants' eyes and reduces headaches.

2. **Sharp Contrast in Color=Easier to Read.** "The most common complaint from audience members who are sitting through a presentation using PowerPoint is that they can't read the text on the slides," writes PowerPoint guru Wendy Russell on her "Presentation Software" blog. Simply put, make sure that your background color and your text color provide a sharp contrast for easy readability. If you're unsure whether participants can easily read your slides, get multiple opinions and try using a color contrast calculator to determine what works and what doesn't. Dave Paradi of ThinkOutsideTheSlide.com has developed a color contrast calculator to help, and it's a free tool. Also consider the following grid when making your color selections.

Color scheme	When to use it
Bright, vivid color (Bold, strong loud colors)	Quick message, gain learners' attention, use to highlight or as a background color
Middle tone colors (Every day colors)	Majority of slides, good for fonts combined with a darker background
Pastel, light colors (Gentle and soft)	Gently share a message
Warm colors (Reds, Oranges, Yellows)	When you want to soothe your learners When you want to engage the left or logical, analytical side of the brain
Cool colors (Blues, Greens, Purples)	To excite the senses To engage the right or creative side of the brain To attract attention To convey energy and warmth

If you're feeling locked into colors based on branding guidelines at your company, consider using different colors when it comes to images, graphs and charts.

3. **Use a sans serif font for slides, like Arial, and a serif fonts for handouts, like Times.** When looking at a screen, a sans serif font has cleaner lines and is easier to read. But when reading text on a page, it's much quicker for the eye to pick up a serif font.

4. **Use common fonts.** Use standard fonts that are found on most computers. Why? If you choose a specialty font, some participants will not be able to read the slides when you share them after the event. This frustration is easily avoided by selecting a font commonly pre-loaded on computers.

   Up to three fonts can be used per slide. One is usually used for the title at the top of the slide while the other two can be used in the main text boxes of the slide.

5. **Utilize fonts and colors that match the message of presentation.** KISS is appropriate here: Keep it super simple. Don't go crazy switching up background and font colors just because you can. It doesn't add interest; it just adds "noise" to the slides. Instead, find colors that complement the message, ensure they provide a sharp contrast (between background color and font color), and stick with them!

6. **Underline, bold and change the font color of answers.** When your slide includes fill-in-the-blanks that coordinate with a student workbook page, provide an underline for the missing word or words to be filled in. And then, when you reveal those answers, ensure they are bolded and in a different color than the rest of the

text on the page. These visual cues help participants as they glance at the Power-Point slide before filling in the blanks on their workbook page.

7. **Increase font size for readability.** General rule of thumb for live presentations is a minimum of a 36–point font. For webinars, the minimum is 24–point font. These sizes will vary dramatically depending on the nature of the slide and the character of the chosen font (for example, Arial versus Calibri). Rather than reducing font size to fit more on a slide, think "reduce words but keep the meaning."

To ensure your slide's current font size is large enough for people in the back of your classroom to read, use the six foot rule. Put your slide in presenter view and then step six feet away from your computer. If you can still read the slide, then you can be sure it will work on a big screen in your classroom.

8. **Avoid *italics* and scripted fonts.** They are just plain hard to read.

Two ingredients that are absolutely essential to a PowerPoint deck created for the Instructor-Led, Participant-Centered classroom, whether virtual or live, is that the slides must be **visual** and **engage** the participant.

Be visual

Text, Subject Title, Bullet Points, and Logos = BORING

When is the last time you heard a participant ask you for more bullets and words on the slide? Remember the PowerPoint is a visual aid for making certain core concepts memorable or "sticky."

Restraint. Need-to-know information goes in handouts.

Do NOT put every single word you are saying on the slide. Your slides should not tell the whole story; they should require you to add insights and thoughts beyond the slide. Every last word or idea can be in your learners' workbook, if needed. But each slide should reinforce a single priority message with a single visual representing a complete thought. You could also highlight key words on the slide to help focus the learner on the slide's core concept. (For webinars, this is distinctly different. The chapter on PowerPoint Design for Virtual Training takes into account this difference.)

Answer "What's the main point?" and "Why does it matter?"

You should be able to answer these two key questions about each of your slides. The main purpose of a slide may be to reinforce the message, be part of an activity, or challenge participants to act. If there's no clear purpose for the slide, delete it. For government agencies and organizations that have strict regulations concerning each word on each slide, consider dividing the content of a single slide into multiple slides until you have a singular answer to each of these two key slide questions.

When designing your slides for a classroom setting, ask yourself these additional questions: Will this slide help learners? Reinforce a key concept? Aid in retention? Link learning? Make a difference?

Keep design simple. The best design goes unnoticed.

You don't want your participants walking away saying, "I have a headache from slides," "Did you see how all the slides had both pink and red—it was awful!" or "I have no idea what the main point was, but the transitions were cool." You want the learner walking away thinking, "I wish I could make it look so easy."

It goes back to the KISS model. **Keep It Super Simple**. More animation is not better. Less is more. The same is true with color and font.

Think creatively.

When thinking about the design of your slide, it's important to get creative. One way to ignite your imagination is to think randomly. Look at pictures that are off the wall and ask yourself "How does this apply?" Or go online and look at objects that might spark thought or creativity. To trigger creativity, I will go to bigstockphoto.com and enter a key word into the search function. A lot of images will pop up; looking through them triggers additional points and broadens ideas for me.

It is important to remember that you need permission or copyright to use an image. Just because it is on Google does not make it free. When online, you can right click to see where the image originated. Go there and ensure you have usage rights. I purchase points and use them as needed to guarantee I'm legally covered. For a dollar or two, I have peace of mind and have supported the artist.

Visual does not necessarily mean photo.

Although photos are generally very captivating, there may be a specific reason to use just words or color on a slide. For example, if revisiting all of the tasks a team should stop doing, you could use a completely red slide to represent the conversation. At the same time you could choose a stop sign or a circle with a slash through it like a no smoking sign, or you could just use all capital letters STOP written in red. Four different ways to visually "say" the same thing. It comes down to knowing your audience and thinking through what would make the greatest impact or reinforce the message the best. Also take into consideration what comes right before and after that slide. If it's too big of a contrast from the slide before, it can be blinding. For example, going from a dark slide to an all-white slide is hard on the eyes. Test this concept for yourself. Create an all black slide and then an all white slide and click from one to the other and see the difference first hand.

Use vector images and photos rather than clip art.

Clipart is to the 80s and 90s as vector art and images are to the twenty-first century. So ditch clipart and upgrade your slides. Go online and search "vector art" and compare it to clip art; see the difference for yourself. Also, use photos. Your company may already own rights-free images that are quickly searchable and directly related to the content you are teaching. Another place I search for graphics is morguefile.com. These are all free to use for teaching and can be modified in any way. They do have rules around not selling their images.

Here are some before and after slides. Can you pick out which principles were used in building the "after" slides?

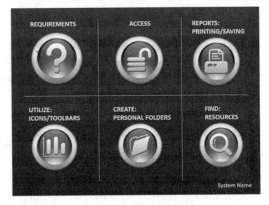

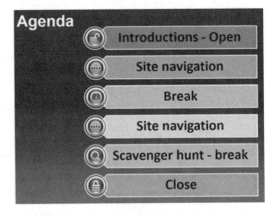

Be Interactive

The second key to effective PowerPoint design is interactive slides that create excitement and curiosity. How? There are many, MANY options.

Have you ever owned a product, like a blender, that had more bells and whistles than you ever needed or used? If you wouldn't consider yourself terribly proficient in Power-Point, then creating interactivity within PowerPoint with additional software or down-loading online game templates can be much like the additional features on the blender—overwhelming and seemingly unnecessary. So let's start with some easy ways to add interactivity to your presentation deck.

Insert Discussion Questions

By creating discussion questions in advance of your training or webinar, you are more likely to ask thoughtful and thorough questions. During training, verbalize the written question, and have small groups discuss it. (Remember that questions that begin with "How" will generally take groups into a deeper analysis and synthesis of information. Also, be sure to have group leaders assigned before you reveal the question, and let them know that they will be "reporting back" to you and the entire group once their group discussion on the question has concluded. This prepares the leader to listen to others more thoroughly and thoughtfully and perhaps even take notes.) Then show the slide with the question on it so all learners remember the question they are supposed to be answering. If groups or individuals respond via polling software (polling is discussed later in this chapter), you have the additional benefit of reaching all three kinds of learners: auditory (the spoken question), visual (the written question), and kinesthetic (the act of responding/ answering).

Create and Use Hyperlinks

Within a slide, you can create hyperlinks that, when clicked on, will take you directly to a movie clip, audio clip, website, another slide, or a file or document on your computer. Such a link makes it far more likely for you to use the audio file or visit the website because the embedded link saves you from fumbling to find those additional resources, or opting, in the heat of the training, against using them to save yourself the anxiety. With a hyperlink, there is no anxiety and no fumbling. (Although, be sure to check the links just prior to your training to make sure the links are working properly.)

To insert a hyperlink follow these steps.

1. In Normal View, highlight the text or image you want to use as a hyperlink.

2. On the "Insert" tab, in the "Text" group, select "Hyperlink" in the drop down menu.

3. In "Link to," paste the URL (web address) or file pathway to the webpage, audio, video or document file you'd like to link.

Use animated timers for in-class relays

If you want a specific time parameter for an in-class activity, prepare a pre-made timer. You can find these online for free or create slides using the animation feature in Power-Point.

For the virtual classroom: Consider using a countdown timer for not only relays but also for breaks and work time. If you are using a platform that allows for flash or HTML5, a countdown timer can be a great way for learners to know how much time is left to complete an activity or finish a discussion, especially if they are in breakout rooms. Blackboard Collaborate has a built-in timer that can be preset and will automatically begin when people are placed into breakout rooms. If your platform does not have a built-in timer, there are several free countdown timers online that you can application-share with the group in the main room. If they are in breakout rooms, the timer application may not work.

Write on slides during the presentation

In the live classroom, there are two easy ways to write on your slide in the moment when your PowerPoint is in 'presentation' mode. The first is to click on the pen icon in the bottom left-hand corner of the screen. The second is the short-cut key—pressing and holding the **Ctrl** key and the **P** key. In both instances, the cursor turns into a pen for "writing," and then you use your finger on the mouse pad to write. The writing might be messy, but this is an easy way to add spontaneity.

If I have a compliance document that needs to be accurately completed, I might place an error-riddled copy of that on the slide. Then, asking the participants to work in teams, I may have half the teams identify what is wrong with the document and the other half engineer correct solutions for the errors. After some work time, a representative from an "error finding" group will come up to the front of the class and write on the slide, circling all the errors on the slide. A team leader from a "solution finding" group will then come up and write corrections for the errors on the slide.

For the virtual classroom: One of the key components to consider when deciding on an online training platform is how easy is it for learners to write on the whiteboard. The person doing the writing is doing the learning and with participants writing on the white board, you are free to focus on your content and facilitate the session.

You can type on your slide, on the fly, too. This makes for a "prettier" finished look but the set up is a bit more involved. For a tutorial on how to type in presentation mode, go to bit.ly/typeonslide.

For the virtual classroom: Similar to the live classroom, you can easily create activities that involve writing on the slide. But unlike the live classroom, it is even easier and "prettier" to have participants engage in the actual writing because multiple participants can write on the slide at the same time, and their "writing" is actually typing, so the slide remains legible. For a "write on the slide" activity, you can develop a matching game to teach or review content.

To do this, create two slides. On the first slide, randomly place the answers to your learners' fill-in-the-blank workbook page. On the second slide, you place a copy of the learners' workbook page. When you show the first slide, tell the learners that they will be attempting to quickly fill in the blanks in their workbook page using the answers on the screen. Then, when you reveal the second slide, ask the virtual learners to type in the answers to the fill-in-the-blanks on the slide, using their recently completed workbook as reference. This gives learners a chance to preview the information that you'll be lecturing on and engages them from the beginning.

Previewing material this way really gets to the EAT model. Experience, awareness, theory. Through the *experience* of matching the words with the blanks in the workbook, they become *aware* of some of the concepts that will be taught. Then, you, as the instructor, can fill in the missing information with the *theory* behind the concepts.

Both writing and typing on a presentation slide are great ways to add interactivity and spontaneity to your PowerPoint deck and your training.

Quotations

At first blush, quotations might not seem all that exciting, but a thoughtful, thought-provoking, and well-placed quotation can be just the ticket for sparking conversation and debate. It also might not seem very interactive, especially if you're familiar with the various PowerPoint game templates with all sorts of bells and whistles. But quotations offer the opportunity for groups of participants to interact with the quotation itself, with ideas, and with how the quotation relates to a key concept or concepts. This can be especially useful as you transition from one chunk of content to another.

Here are some things to keep in mind as you transform a slide into a quotation slide or add quotation slides into your existing deck:

- Use a dark background

- Use an image that you have the rights to use

- Write the quotation on the slide, don't just verbalize it. Having the quote on the slide makes it easier for learners to recall what they are discussing and how it relates to the content. The written quotation also assists English Language Learners in their understanding.

As an example, I might use the Normal Vincent Peale quotation slide in a sales class or presentation skills class. I would reveal the slide and provide small groups an opportunity to discuss how this quotation might relate to the content. Then, I would have each team leader share back one idea. I typically get one thought per table. I might then add an idea or two as a way to transition into the new content. This interactivity does not need to take more than five or, at most, ten minutes of class time.

The trouble with most of us is that we would rather be ruined by praise than saved by criticism.
Norman Vincent Peale

Photo Norman Vincent Peale. Courtesy of the Library of Congress. No known copyright restriction.

Incorporating More Involved (But Very Cool) Interactivity into Your PowerPoint Slides

Movie Scenes

Movie scenes quickly draw people in and get them talking. It can be a breath of fresh air and a mental break while simultaneously making a powerful point or creatively helping unpack difficult content. When used well, a short movie clip can motivate, create curiosity and provide learner choice. For example, to motivate your learners, try using an emotional, inspiring or triumphant clip. To promote curiosity, try stopping a movie scene at a critical moment and asking learners to discuss what might happen next. Then resume the scene. To offer choice when using a movie scene, ask participants to focus on one character or another; let them choose. Then allow participants to work together in teams on analyzing a scene.

Here are some considerations when adding a clip to your PowerPoint deck:

- Insert the clip into your PowerPoint. If you aren't proficient in PowerPoint, consider having the animation (movie) automatically begin as the slide is pulled up.

- Be sure that you have the rights to use whatever scene you choose (see Copyright Clearance Center for corporate licenses in US and Motion Picture Licensing Corporation for non-profit, schools and countries outside the U.S.).

- Decide how the clip will be used to reset and excite your learners. Just starting a movie oftentimes does this, but if the clip does not directly connect to the content, participants quickly get frustrated with the perceived waste of time.

- Keep the movie clip under four minutes.

Where to get a movie clip? It can come from myriad movies coming out of Hollywood, but it also can come from your company's human resources team, or it can be created on an iPhone by the training team to make a point. In a module on how to create step-by-step job aids, I once used a home video of my three-year-old daughter standing on a chair making a peanut butter and jelly sandwich at the kitchen counter and talking through the necessary steps.

Don't sweat the film quality. With the invention and round-the-clock use of YouTube, almost anything goes as far as video quality is concerned for training purposes. What your participants are really looking for is the entertainment factor as well as concepts that aid their learning.

Games

The key places for adding interactive slides into your PowerPoint deck are when you need to revisit content or, less often, to blend a mixture of interactivity with lecturette (a mini-lecture of no longer than ten minutes). I use a host of different quick PowerPoint gaming options for revisiting content. Sometimes I will use longer game options, like a Jeopardy-style game, for teaching a concept. I will provide some examples to spark your thinking, but truly, there are endless gaming templates and ideas online to meet any teaching need.

Here are some specific examples for transforming your PowerPoint deck from stagnant images and content to an interactive workhorse.

Password Revisit

This interactive PowerPoint slide is simple and powerful. If you have passable proficiency in PowerPoint, you can easily create this revisit activity in a few minutes' time, transforming your dry outline of words and concepts to be reviewed into an interactive Password Revisit game.

This Password Revisit game plays out in a similar fashion to the board game Taboo or the television show Password. One person can see the term and attempts to describe the term without saying the term. His teammates attempt to guess the term correctly in the time allotted.

When you are ready to do this activity in the classroom, you will explain the game, and ensure that only the sharer of each team (the participant who will be attempting to get the rest of his team to guess the term), can see the screen. Then begin time as the sharer describes the term. All teams that guess the word before the timer expires will roll a die and receive the number of points rolled. The sharer changes for each concept so that all or most of the members of the team have a chance to be the sharer.

To create this game, you only need a single PowerPoint slide. On it, insert a text box with one of your review terms or concepts, place an opaque rectangle over the review term (hiding it from view), and insert an animated timer (see the graphic). Then add animation so that with a single click, the opaque rectangle will disappear revealing the word, and the timer will begin counting down the pre-determined length of time. You can copy this slide and change out the review term for as many terms or concepts as you'd like.

Xs and Os

Xs and Os is a tic-tac-toe style game, which can be downloaded from bit.ly/loraoneill. This is one example of an interactive slide that can be used to teach or revisit content.

To integrate this activity into your training, first create a list of questions associated with the content you need to teach. If there are fifteen people in the classroom, place seven on one team and eight on the other, and determine which team will start. Share the first question from your list and give teams a minute or two (depending on the complexity of the question) to quietly discuss and determine their answer. This draws out what they already know about the content, honors their experience and gives them an opportunity to analyze and synthesize content.

If the starting team offers a correct answer, you award them an X or O on the board, whatever they choose. You can do this by simply clicking on their color on the chosen box. [You can see in the graphic that half of the box is lighter while half is darker. Click on the lighter portion for Os and the darker portion for Xs.] If the O team answers incorrectly, give the X team a chance to answer correctly and be awarded an X in the box of their choosing. Either way, once the question has been asked and answered, whether correctly or incorrectly, you should then take some time to expound on the content associated with the question. The first group to get three in a row wins the game. A game slide, such as this, creates a natural mix of interactivity and lecturette.

You should explore and find games that add interactivity to what you are teaching in the classroom. When I create games, I use the awesome, free resources and templates put together by Lora O'Neill, a technology integration specialist, at bit.ly/loraoneill. This site is a real time saver with a host of versatile activity and game slides that can be used with any audience. In addition, here is a grid of other websites offering game templates free of charge for teaching and training purposes.

Free Games Templates for Training and Educational Purposes	
bit.ly/sandfields	Variety of games, including Darts, Hangman, Blockbusters, Millionaire, Concentration, Weakest Link scoreboard, animated PowerPoint timers, bingo number generator, and Wheel of Fortune spinner
bit.ly/loraoneill	Amazing number of PPT-based games: Includes Concentration, Jeopardy, Wheel of Fortune, Millionaire, Hollywood Squares, Balloon Game, Blast It.
bit.ly/PPTgametemplates	Variations on many of the standard game templates. Many of these templates seem more suited to a younger audience but will provide ideas.
bit.ly/lengsas	Additional different games can be found here. It also has a few tutorials if you want to create your own games.

Embed HTML5 or flash-based animation, games and graphics
In overly simplistic terms, both flash and HTML5 are building blocks for creating cool animation, games, and vector graphics. The genius of using these blocks is that someone else has already set the blocks up into cool interactives for you. You add your content to their templates and embed it into your PowerPoint. Then, during your training, your participants will play that game, vote in that poll, or comment on that idea by using their cell phones and texting the vote, answer or comment to a pre-arranged number. Before their very eyes, the polling data, or comments or answers will appear on your PowerPoint slide.

For polling: There are many places to get these animations, games and graphics to embed in your PowerPoint. Wiffiti.com provides a survey tool which allows participants to register their thoughts and comments via cell phone. Polleverywhere.com and yawn-buster.com are both polling programs that allow participants to register their votes or comments if the question is open-ended. Some of these options are free and some are fee-based.

If you are interested in teaching or revisiting some of your content through an interactive game, try raptivity.com, which has over 200 flash-based games from which to choose.

You can use HTML5 and flash files in your PowerPoint to have your learners:

- Share their examples related to the content

- Share one learning they will adapt, adopt and apply

- Brainstorm as a large group

- Ask questions or make comments in a backchannel during a lesson

- Answer questions (this has the added benefit of valuing all the learners and their collective knowledge and years of experience)

- Register their opinion on a poll

- Answer quiz questions to assess the transfer of knowledge

For the virtual classroom: The above list can easily be accomplished in the virtual classroom. Most virtual platforms already offer polling, chatting, and question options. Additionally, you can engage learners in some of the above interactions through social media outside of the virtual classroom. The easiest ones to use when starting off as a trainer are LinkedIn, a Facebook page, or Twitter.

TurningPoint

There are a lot of products out there that integrate with PowerPoint. At The Bob Pike Group, we have tried a number of "cool" products, but there always seemed to be hiccups when rolling it out to our trainers. Some products were too time consuming to learn; others were jazzy but only worked half the time. The one we settled on and have now been using for years is Turning Technologies TurningPoint clickers. They have a great product and customer service and support that far exceeds their competitors.

Turning Technologies is a polling software that integrates with PowerPoint to bring slides to life, create engagement and transform a PowerPoint deck into a robust interactive tool. It allows a presenter to ask a question and have learners respond using hand-held keypads also known as "clickers." Results are instantly displayed for the group and presenter to see. The technology collects and gathers the data in detailed reports for further analysis by the presenter after the session is done. For example, one report shows how long it takes each participant to click in or make an answer. Research shows that if it takes longer than twelve seconds to respond, the learner is likely making a guess.

Dr. Tina Rooks, chief instructional officer at Turning Technologies, analyzed data from hundreds of polling sessions. What she concluded was that twenty-five seconds was the best practice for a time limit for polling. From zero to five seconds, learners were probably still reading the question. The majority of the correct answers came between five and ten seconds, with ten to fifteen seconds still having a healthy showing but demonstrating a twenty percent drop in correct answers. At fifteen to twenty seconds, only about thirty percent had correct answers (Rooks 2016).

Based on that information, I can then review the time it takes the learners in my classroom to respond. I can assume which questions were challenging for the group by seeing how long it took them to respond, and then I can clarify that particular content the following day.

Clickers allow for all participants to engage simultaneously. They can "compete" against themselves, against others or as a team. Its immediate and competitive nature increases participation and engagement. And there are a number of effective ways to put this polling software to work for you. Here are some of the ways I use it:

- Quizzing. Use the software to quiz the learners to confirm retention of content during safety or compliance training. Be sure you don't call it a quiz as that may induce anxiety. Instead, say something like, "Are you ready to get your click on?" and make it a fun activity. After the quiz questions are answered, I will insert and display a fastest responder slide and make it a bit of a competition.

- Voting. Use TurningPoint to vote and make decisions. As an achiever and activator, I tend to run before I walk and accomplish a lot in a short amount of time. This tool allows for running—accomplishing data collection and drive for decisions quicker while still getting results that are accurate. TurningPoint allows me to get to consensus quicker. Incidentally, I also use this in meetings to save time and money and still get the buy-in necessary for the success of a project or team.

- Pre- and post-testing: One of the challenges of Kirkpatrick's level three evaluation is that, without a pre-test, it is impossible to determine if the participants learned the content during the class rather than prior to the class. With TurningPoint, I can do a short pre-test and then a post-test, compare data, and allow learners to "opt out" if they already have a solid content foundation. This can be done as a class, and I can choose to display or hide the results. In the background, the software is gathering the data, by learner, for analysis. It's a very easy way to assess your audience.

- Post-program evaluating. We sometimes use the polling software for the end-of-the-class evaluation. This eliminates the need for paper and pencil and allows for easy compilation versus manual data entry.

- Gaming. This is one of my favorite uses for clicker technology. I use TurningPoint in conjunction with BRAVO! and PRONTO! by C3 Softworks to create games that teach and revisit content. I LOVE both of these products—their flexibility and versatility—I highly recommend them for your live or virtual classroom.

Remember, PowerPoint is meant to be an interactive visual to aid in teaching and revisiting content in engaging ways. PowerPoint slides should be a breath of fresh air. It should not suck the life out of your training and your learners!

Chapter 18

Using Social Media in Training

Hardly a day goes by where I don't reference something I saw on Facebook—my sister's Darth Maul Dogs for dinner, news of the weird I saw in the trending news feed, or a pointless quiz I took to pass the time. I also post pictures of my kids for the relatives to view and play games with my mother and grandmother! It's definitely an integrated part of my life.

Of all social media sites, Facebook had forty-five percent of market share in 2015 with more than a billion active users, with YouTube coming in next at twenty-two percent (Statista 2016). Of *all* websites visited in 2015, Facebook was the second ranked site with YouTube coming in at number three (Wikipedia 2016). Google, the search engine, was the only website to beat out those two social media giants.

Obviously, websites with user-generated content that allow for networking and interaction have found their place in American society. And because people are already familiar with social media, most having integrated it into their everyday lives, it seems natural to bring social media into the training classroom to extend learning and add interactivity.

Why Use Social Media in Training?

As a trainer, I see many good reasons to use social networking in our classes. The use of social media can help bridge the time gap between formal trainings. I can easily update a Facebook group page with a relevant and timely article on our topic in between training sessions. I can also build on the classroom knowledge through information I send out on sites like Twitter or LinkedIn. Or, for example, if you are doing a technology roll-out, a lot of just-in-time tech tips can be life-saving and easily done through social media. Social media, which encompasses so many different tools and applications, is flexible enough to even be used for role-playing or practicing a task in a simulated but realistic scenario.

Perhaps the biggest benefit to utilizing social media, however, is allowing participants to connect with one another outside the classroom. I facilitate this corroboration by assigning tasks to be completed between trainings and having it become habitual for them to visit a particular social media site. Eventually, though, I want the learners to take on the responsibility for their own learning and help their peers learn, too. I want them to become a well-connected hive of learners who work together for the good of all.

In facilitating their connection outside class through social media, I help them create an extended personal learning network. Having twenty other learners available for consultation, feedback on new ideas, or answering questions about tricky work situations can lead to great relationships, more learning and extended networking. And social media works great for this because it has no time or space boundaries. Learners can communicate no matter where they are or what time of day (or night) it is.

Here are some of the other benefits to using social media in training.

- Training updates can be short—even as few as 140 characters!
- It gets around lecture.
- It allows the opportunity to learn from other likeminded people, authors or great thinkers.
- It extends your reach beyond just the classroom—and not just for your learners. Others you may not have even met can learn from you and you from them.
- And, with today's training budgets, free is a price tag people can afford.

Like just about every other training tool, however, social media is not without its drawbacks.

- Because it is technology-based, there can be quite a learning curve if some of your participants aren't already using social media websites.
- Because it is online and you are encouraging a corroborative environment, you can't always control what is posted (although there are some safeguards you can put in place to lower the risk of inappropriate matter being posted).
- Sometimes the technology will fail.
- There may be security concerns. The rule of thumb is that, if you're sharing proprietary information online, don't. With social media sites changing their security settings and privacy guidelines, it's just better to be safe than sorry.

Social Media Sites Useful to Training

Before I outline specific ways we can use social media in the classroom, I want to give you an overview of some of the social media sites I'll be referencing so you can more easily see how you can utilize these sites.

Facebook.com

Facebook allows you to create a profile that discusses what movies or music you like, where you work, and where you've traveled. You can post status updates about what you're thinking, who you are with, or even your pet peeves of the moment. Facebook also allows you to post photos, upload documents and videos, and create groups. This is where the functionality of Facebook becomes relevant to training.

With the creation of a group on Facebook, you can make the group public, closed or secret. A public group means anyone can read what you or others post in the group. A closed group will allow others to search for your group, and lurkers can also see who is in the group and who the group administrators are, but they won't be able to read any of the posts. A secret group is only visible to those who have been provided with a specific link or invitation to the group.

Creating a group on Facebook allows you to disseminate information to learners in current or past classes. It will allow others in the group to also post on the wall. They can either respond to a question you've asked or topic addressed by another group member. As part of the group, members will be notified when there is a new post. They can also set up email notifications, alerting them to new posts, if they don't go on Facebook often.

LinkedIn

LinkedIn is mainly a place to network for business. You can create a profile that shares your current position and past work experience. You can also upload a portfolio or projects that speak to your ability to do your job, and a copy of your resume. You can even customize your LinkedIn URL to make it easier for people to find you on their own or using search engines. For example, you can find me at https://www.linkedin.com/in/trainthetrainerbeckypluth.

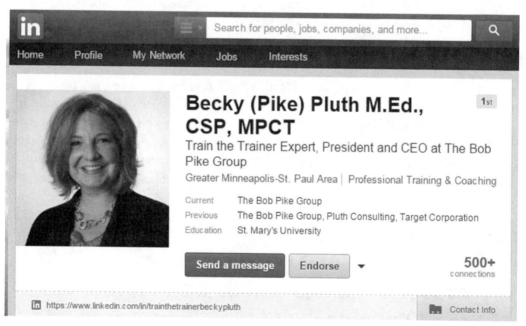

With LinkedIn, as on Facebook, you can also create an online group on a topic relevant to your learners. It could be "Creative Trainers" or "ABC Company Co-workers." You can set the security on this group so that you, as the organizer, have to approve every request to join the group or you can make it an open group which anyone can join.

YouTube

Although many people solely use it for uploading or watching videos, YouTube is considered social because people can vote on the videos or make comments about the video or respond to other comments. YouTube has an overwhelming number of useful videos; you can probably find a vast number of them pertinent to a topic you're teaching or you may post a video you make. You can even create your own video "channel" which allows other viewers to "follow" your channel and be alerted when you post new videos. Once you post a new video, you can then use other forms of social media to get the word out about it, like Facebook, LinkedIn, or Twitter. Email works, too, although it is not considered a social networking tool.

Blogger.com and Wordpress.com

Blogger.com and Wordpress.com are two blogging websites that allow you to post your own writings and photos in a letter or storytelling fashion. There are virtually no limits on how long your post can be or how many photos you can include. This method allows you to post information on your topic and have an archive of these articles for sharing through Facebook or Twitter. If you are going to blog, you need to be consistent, though. People do check in on a regular basis, and if you don't post, they will stop checking. One training blog I highly recommend, if you want to see a training blog well done, is by Brian Washburn. He posts Mondays, Wednesdays and Fridays at trainlikeachampion.com. Here is an example of an infographic he posted on his blog that I really liked.

Twitter

Twitter is called a micro-blogging site. This means your post (also known as a tweet) is limited to a maximum of 140 characters, although Twitter is looking at doing away with the character limit. And, if you want other people to re-post or re-tweet your tweet, you must limit it to only 120 characters. But a lot can be concisely communicated in that short bit, which perhaps is why it's one of the most common networking sites for trainers, according to an informal poll we did among trainers at our annual training conference.

 Becky Pike Pluth @BeckyPluth · Feb 5

90/20/10 is one of our @BobPikeGroup models. Adults can listen with retention for 20 minutes.

dash.harvard.edu/bitstream/hand…

↩   ↻ 1   ♥   •••

Many trainers use this forum to share links to interesting articles or let others know they have a new blog post published. They also use it to communicate on questions relevant to training. On Thursday nights, you can even follow a curated discussion called Learn Chat (you can search for it using #lrnchat) that discusses hot topics in our field.

With Twitter, you have the ability to lock down your twitter feed so that only specifically invited people can see your tweets. However, one caution with this is that your invited followers can read your tweets but will be unable to re-tweet or respond to a tweet, allowing others to learn from it. So in "privatizing" your feed, you dramatically reduce Twitter's power to help you network and others to network and learn through you.

Ways to Use Social Media Before Training

For introverts, breaking the ice may be one of the hardest parts of attending training. But what if you could break that ice before the class even begins? A month before the annual Bob Pike Group fall conference, we use social media to announce the fall conference learning teams and to introduce all the attendees to their fellow team members and their Bob Pike Group training coach. This allows the coach an opportunity to cheerlead and get the learners excited for the training; it also allows the learners to become acquainted with one another ahead of time. Now, on the first day of the conference, we no longer have strangers working their way through an awkward introduction—we have online friends meeting for the first time.

How do we navigate these virtual introductions and support online camaraderie? We have the coach exchange email information with those participants who are comfortable sharing it. Some of the coaches have created Facebook groups where the learners can see more about one another like how many kids they have, where they work, and what movies they like. They can also have discussions ahead of time like what the learners are hoping to get out of the conference. Some of the coaches also use Twitter as a way to share links to more information on our company website or to taunt the other coaches in good fun.

Some coaches assign pre-work such as sharing a link to an activity or an article they think will benefit the learners. They could do this on Twitter through a shared hashtag like #cttc2016 or a special LinkedIn group page. They may also upload videos to YouTube or have learners post videos that share something special to them such as brief interviews with their kids, their dogs chasing flying discs, or a brief tour of their town.

It's amazing how these virtual social exchanges heighten the anticipation of the formal learning experience, take away some of the fear of the unknown, and create a sense of belonging before learners even get to the conference. It also gets people discussing content before they're in the classroom!

Enhancing Your Training with Social Media

by Kary Delaria

With some thoughtful planning, social media can enhance the training experience for both you and your trainees, before, during, and after the training itself.

Just as you prepare to lead a training session, prepare your digital presence as well. In today's connected and mobile world, attendees will look for session leaders online. Are your profiles and feeds as ready to take the stage as you are? This is an important tip to share with trainees, too. Make sure your bio and photograph are up-to-date and reinforce your personal brand. Do a quick audit of the most recent posts in your feed to ensure they are relevant to those who will be in your session that day. Is it a post about how awesome your breakfast was or a link to download a white paper you recently wrote?

If you're unsure which social platforms will be most effective for your trainees, ask them. If possible, conduct a poll at the time of registration to find out on which social media platforms they are most active. Use this information to select platforms and activities to incorporate into the learning experience, before, during and after the session.

For example, if the majority of your trainees are highly active on LinkedIn, consider creating a group (can be public or private) in which to start discussions, introduce topics, gather feedback, and most importantly, to foster relationships between attendees—who better to learn from than their colleagues?

Perhaps you find that a significant array of your attendees are active on Twitter. If so, create a list for you and others to follow—this is a great way to get an understanding of additional challenges, successes, and interests of the group. Additionally, creating a hashtag for your training topic will help attendees quickly identify related posts.

The hashtag can also be incredibly useful as a way to gather feedback during your training session. (Be sure to include the hashtag in any and all training materials so it's easy to find and reference.) For example, if attendees are participating in training exercises, real-time feedback from others in the room (or remotely) can be more powerful than singular feedback from the instructor. Additionally, encourage those you train to always watch event hashtags for feedback on the sessions they lead as a way to continually improve their performance.

With more than a decade of experience in public relations, media relations and marketing communication, Kary Delaria has helped clients from a wide range of industries develop and manage their brand's online presence and reputation through a combination of social media analysis, monitoring and community engagement.

Ways to Use Social Media During Training

I'll admit—when Twitter first came out, I was over the top with my enthusiasm for it. But as I came back to a more balanced view, I realized how much content I was missing when I was busy tweeting out what I was learning during sessions I was attending.

Those who think they are multi-taskers really aren't. When we break from one task, like writing a book chapter, to read an email, it takes us several minutes to ramp back up to where we were and get our head focused again. Forbes has published several articles on this, including one titled "Multitasking Damages Your Brain and Your Career," that discusses the research being done at Stanford University and the University of Sussex. Google now even has laptop-free meetings so people can hear the important information without the distraction of whatever is on their laptop.

So a big caution: The use of social media *during* classroom training needs to be strategic. You don't want to use these tools to the detriment of your learners and your content.

Another consideration is in the fact that typing creates no muscle memory. Meaning, once a person has typed or texted the information, the information is easily forgotten. So asking learners to tweet their notes or create their notes digitally will not aid in retention and may be a distraction with no benefit. While social media is great, the time-worn and time-tested fill-in-the-blank notes in the old-school handouts definitely have their place.

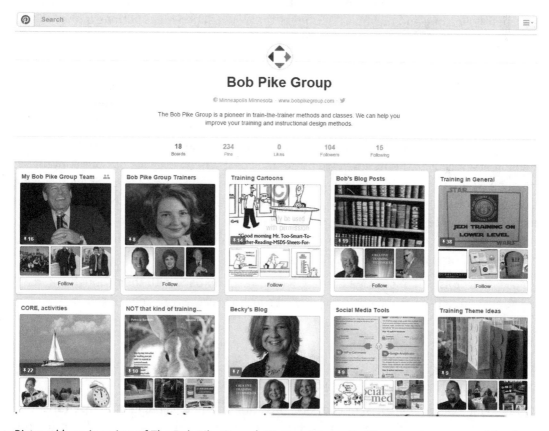

Pictured here is a view of The Bob Pike Group's Pinterest page. You'll see we have created "corkboards" for training cartoons, articles we wrote or liked, and other training related topics.

And yet there are still effective ways to engage learners and the outside world during training through social media. One way is to allow the learners time to post one key takeaway from the training so far on their favorite social media site. They can tweet it out or update their Facebook status. This has the added benefit of providing great marketing for your training. It grows anticipation in those who will be attending in the future. It piques the interest of those who have not heard about it.

You can also allow specific time for learners to capture photos of the flip charts used (if the material is not proprietary) or other visual reminders of the material covered and have them post these to the various sites, including Pinterest (an online corkboard app) or Instagram (an online photo-sharing app). This works well because it's a reminder of content covered and can again create interest and curiosity amongst the learners' contacts.

If your training is longer than one day or is done at intervals, social media can also be used to encourage reflection on the content among learners in between sessions. Perhaps you could post a provocative question about whether the learners in your class agreed or disagreed with a particular piece of content. Or simply ask them to share their biggest takeaway. Perhaps the participants already have ideas for how to use the content on-the-job that they could share with the others. By posting it and using a hashtag, other learners can follow along and maybe even update their own action ideas with new ones they see. Using social media in this way can help keep the learning momentum going.

Ways to Use Social Media After Training

Retention in learning is the whole key to training. If your learners don't retain the information, then what was the point of the training?

Social media is another tool trainers can use to extend the learning process after the training event is over. (Remember, we remember best when we space out our content revisits.) No matter which social media tool you choose to use, you can begin new conversations on the training content, post updated information, share new job aids, or continue fostering the sense of community your training began. You can revisit the content through these channels at intervals to help increase the likelihood that the information will be remembered (and hopefully applied)!

Pose questions and encourage the learners to respond back with their thoughts and applications. And, if the group got along well, it's just a great way to keep in touch.

How to Get Started

If you don't engage with any forms of social media, then dipping your toe into this arena can feel overwhelming. Let me give you a few tips to start.

1. Find one or two social networking sites that you find valuable or whose functionality suits your training purposes. Then commit to those two sites. Fill out the profiles thoroughly and post content on a regular basis. These will help you become comfortable with those platforms, which, in turn, will help you leverage them more effectively and efficiently for your training purposes.

2. Make sure your security settings are what you want them to be. If you're not sure how to do this, ask a co-worker who talks about Facebook all the time to help you.

3. Share the work; if you have other trainers doing what you do, have them become administrators of the Facebook or LinkedIn group, the training department Twitter account, the blog, or the YouTube channel. You don't have to do it yourself, and it's nice to have different voices chiming in. You can also take advantage of what social media really is—user-generated content. Invite your learners to post guest blogs or create the question of the day. The synergy and the community surrounding social media is what makes it fun, interactive and effective as a training tool.

For more information on how the different generations communicate via social media, see Appendix D.

Chapter 19

ILPC Tips for Virtual Instructors

Transitioning from classroom to virtual instructor-led training (VILT) is not as easy as taking your PowerPoint slides and uploading them to an online platform. There are distinct differences between the two environments that need to be taken into consideration.

When I was working at Target Corporation as a trainer, I was assigned to do a technical webinar on how product designs would be electronically delivered overseas and the new process for retrieving, printing and returning specs for those products. The participants were primarily in Asia, and English was a second language. I was nervous, as this was the first time I had ever done a webinar. After spending hours designing beautiful slides, all of which had lots and lots of content on each and were branded beautifully, I practiced presenting. All went well...so I thought.

My webinar design and execution had several fatal errors. There was too much content for the three-hour webinar. Not once did I practice with a participant from one of the foreign countries where I would have discovered I had bandwidth issues. I had too many words on each slide and didn't include graphics to support all that text. I didn't have a handout with all of the need-to-know information for participants to have after the completion of the live session. I had no evaluation for feedback, the webinar was almost entirely lecture, and I had not taken into consideration the time zone differences. I could go on.

Upon completion of that webinar, I told everyone in my department that the webinar had been a great success. Why? The technology didn't fail; all the participants "showed up," and they were still on when I finished. A slightly older and hopefully wiser Becky can resoundingly say that there is so much more to a successful webinar than having the technology work for a majority of the time!

Considerations When Building your Conversion Strategy

There are many aspects to consider as you look to successfully transition or begin building new courses for the virtual space. Here are nine:

> **1. Involve:** The first step in transitioning to or creating a first course in the virtual space is to gain management support. Many of us have years of education and experience in training but little idea on how to effectively influence stakeholders, so I will walk you through the ins and outs of this step.

Moving content online can be a shift for some companies. Let's say as a designer and trainer you see the value of moving from an actual classroom to a virtual one, but no one at your organization has done much virtual training even with free webinar platforms. There are many reasons that it makes more sense to do the training online, and you have those documented. What do you do next? Get stakeholder support and buy-in before designing your virtual, instructor-led training. If you are unsure where to start follow these five steps to secure the necessary support.

Point of persuasion	Example
Show the cost and time savings	• Savings gained by moving from face-to-face to webinar training • Provide data of savings for an individual class as well as the savings over the course of the year's worth of classes • Show savings in resources, time and energy • Anticipate and prepare for objections
Highlight the ability to expand offerings	• Show the increased flexibility you would have by being able to offer the training just prior to the information being needed/implemented by the participants (Just-in-time training) • Increased productivity through less travel for trainers
Point out the increased ability to meet training demands	• Describe the ability to expand training offerings rapidly and offer classes to teams/divisions that are not currently receiving development
Indicate the added flexibility	• Indicate how this virtual training can reach different markets at different times and with a variety of different arrangements that work for each audience.
Provide evidence	• Rely on what others are doing and how they have been successful • Consider finding a peer to your stakeholder that has implemented virtual training and can provide anecdotal proof

Calculate annual cost savings.

Calculate savings for your stakeholders by using the following formula.

1. Identify the cost of the virtual platform and any participant material costs that would be required for the virtual space but not in the physical classroom, if any.

2. Then, add up the face-to-face training investment (this is what it would cost for participants and the trainer to travel, including meals, lodging, expenses for a training room if off-site, etc.).

3. Finally subtract the virtual training total from the face-to-face investment total. This is your annual savings.

Annual Cost Savings Formula

F2F investment - Cost of Virtual Platform = Savings

Example with 15 participants 1 day
Travel/Participant $500/plane, $200 hotel, $120 food

$12,300 - $1,000 = $11,300

$11,300 X # of sessions =

For example, let us assume you train a single day (eight-hour) training course, and the cost of the virtual platform for eight hours is $1000 (with no additional course materials needed). For the face-to-face option, we will assume you train the one-day course for fifteen participants. If the travel per participant is $500 for airfare/car, $200 for hotel accommodations, $120 for food, and nothing for the training room (we'll assume it is at your headquarters), you are looking at a total cost of $12,300. So to complete our formula: $12,300 - $1000 = $11,300 cost savings by moving a single course from face-to-face to online. Once you've determined how many sessions you'll train through the online platform, you can multiply that number by $11,300 to get an annual savings. This formula does not even include the opportunity costs and savings related to travel time and lost productivity of being out of the office.

I've used the price tag of $1000 for the virtual training platform for simplicity's sake as I walked you through the cost savings formula. But in reality, the annual cost of virtual trainings can have a dramatic range. It can vary based on the size of your corporation, the number of licenses needed, the cost of the platform selected, and the man hours required for the trainer to create a course using the platform's tools. Some virtual platforms are free but have very limited tools and require a significant time investment on your part. On the other hand, platforms can cost hundreds of thousands of dollars per year for large corporations, but such a platform would invariably come with all the bells and whistles which can dramatically decrease your time investment.

Some organizations decide to start with a free tool as a transition to online training, but you may discover later that it is not as robust as it needs to be for training. At that point, your facilitators will need to unlearn the free platform and relearn a new tool. This can be stressful and costly (man hours required by facilitators to learn a new platform and build/ create new activities based on the wider array of interactive options offered in a more expensive, more robust platform).

The total cost of virtual training may seem sizable at first glance, but once it's compared to the cost of face-to-face training, it becomes a financial no-brainer in favor of virtual training.

The following is a short worksheet that can guide you as you prepare to persuade your stakeholder(s). It takes into consideration who your stakeholders are, what the company's cost savings would be, how the company could expand course offerings by moving to virtual training, how virtual training can better meet current and future demand, and how it may positively impact flexibility. The worksheet basically builds a value proposition, which highlights for stakeholders what is "in it for them" when it comes to transitioning to virtual training.

Preparing Worksheet for Stakeholder Conversation

My stakeholders:

1

2

The company's savings for one course:

$_____ - _____ = _____

Cost of single face-to-face course   cost of single virtual training   total cost difference

How can virtual training expand our training offerings?

What is the current demand and how can/will virtual training better meet it?

What are the estimated future training demands; how does virtual training position us to meet it?

How can/will virtual training provide increased flexibility?

Anecdotal proof:

2. Anchor: The second consideration in successfully moving courses to (or newly building courses in) an online format is how such movement directly ties into the business' strategic plan. Creating clear objectives and having a measurable value proposition will greatly help in this. Regularly refer back to the value proposition you created for your stakeholder buy-in meeting to ensure you have not inadvertently changed direction and fallen into a "scope creep" that does not tie back into the over-all business plan. (Scope creep is when the original project was determined but during additional meetings other ideas, that may be only tangentially related to the initial project and/or the business plan, were suggested and then added to the project.)

3. Share information: In this step, schedule regular meetings with the subject-matter experts and intended participants for the virtual course. This begins the buy-in and change management process with these key players. If the virtual course will have a substantial impact on these players, then the sooner they know it is coming, the more time they have to embrace it.

4. Prepare and plan: Once you have stakeholder buy-in, and you have established that the virtual courses directly support the overall business strategy, it is time to prepare and plan your first virtual course. Pictured on the next page is a checklist to help keep you, as the facilitator, focused, and your producers ready for success. Taking each of the steps seriously will help show the return on investment for the project. This list isn't intended to be comprehensive but a general list of ideas to follow.

If this is your first time creating a webinar and the above explanations and worksheet don't offer the details you need to successfully navigate building and executing a virtual course, you may want to refer to *Webinars with Wow Factor* for a comprehensive how-to for successfully preparing and leading Instructor-Led, Participant-Centered (ILPC) virtual training.

5. Pilot: This is your dry run of the program, not only to practice but also to get a feel for the flow. This occurs prior to the rollout and should be early enough in the development schedule to allow time for enhancements to or revisions of the curriculum before the "go live" date.

6. Evaluate Everything: The evaluation criteria for the virtual course is determined during your planning and preparing stage; however, the data analysis and compilation occurs after your dry run/pilot and the launch of the program. Create separate and distinct evaluations for each of the key players in the virtual course: the trainer, the manager, the participant and the producer. This allows you to receive evaluation on the program from each of these distinct individual perspectives. Not all evaluative questions will be valuable for each role. For example, don't ask participants about how well the producer executed his role as most participants will have no idea what the producer's role was or how well it was executed.

Checklist for Virtual Training

Prepare and Plan

- ☐ Determine what computer will be used and practice with that computer. Make sure there is plenty of memory on the hard drive to meet minimum technology requirements for the virtual platform you select. An example of the platform we use is Blackboard Collaborate.

- ☐ Have a second computer available to log into as a user so that you can see what your participants are seeing. It also works as a backup should anything happen to your main computer.

- ☐ Ensure you have a reliable internet connection. Whether wired or wireless, it needs to first and foremost be reliable.

- ☐ Internet backup plan. I have a wi-fi hotspot ready to go just in case my main internet connection goes down. I have only had to use this once in the past decade.

- ☐ Telephone Connection or Voice Over Internet Protocol (VOIP)? Determine which you plan to use and practice setting it up and using it. Come up with a contingency plan for your audio connection and your headset.

- ☐ Prepare trainers
    - o Review platform dos and don'ts
    - o Schedule a training to go over the platform and learn it
    - o Practice using technology with an expert
    - o Learn to teach online (take a class)

- ☐ Prepare course
    - o Start with a course that will make an impact and provide ways to save the bottom line
    - o Prepare a workbook and PowerPoint slides with virtual training in mind

- ☐ Determine who supports the webinar as a moderator/producer or technical support person. This can be another trainer or an admin who has learned the platform and is technically capable of helping others work through the most common technical challenges

- ☐ Prepare evaluation/measurement documents

Two Weeks Before Webinar

- ☐ Send out a welcome letter or email that includes the course information, webinar link and passcodes, conference call numbers and other details

- ☐ Prepare presenter notes and any notes you might have for your moderator or producer

- ☐ Print out workbook, presenter notes, slide deck and participant list

- ☐ Practice the session several times before going live

One Week Before Webinar

- ☐ Practice the session with moderator/producer or do a walk-through of expectations

- ☐ Send out reminder notice with attachments, handouts and workbooks

Day Before Webinar

- ☐ Check and double check this list, including the time zones of your participants

- ☐ Review last minute changes, training notes, and back up plans

- ☐ Charge any electronics to be used including: computer, headset, tablet

- ☐ Send out final reminder notice to participants. [Think this is overkill? It isn't. The day of the class we always have someone asking for this information.]

- ☐ Clear the cache on your computer (in a search engine look for "how to clear cache" and it will walk you through how to do this.

Day of the Webinar

- ☐ Login 30-60 minutes prior to start time

- ☐ Set up a private workspace to easily find notes

- ☐ Have a glass of water nearby

However, you will want to ensure that the producer's evaluation includes questions that evaluate the trainer, and the trainer's evaluation includes questions that evaluate the producer. In the following evaluation are some example questions you could ask. I always ask if the participant completing the evaluation was present and actively participating as well as if he or she would refer this class to others. I pick one or two other questions depending on what the session requires. This can be done in-the-moment as a poll or after the class. At The Bob Pike Group, we do all of our evaluations in the moment to get the highest rate of responses. Giving away prizes randomly helps increase results. Here is a sample of an evaluation we have participants complete.

YOU THE PARTICIPANT	Strongly Agree				Strongly Disagree
I was fully present and actively participated	5	4	3	2	1
My co-participants were actively involved and supported the learning process	5	4	3	2	1
I would refer this workshop to others	5	4	3	2	1
My manager helped prepare me to get the most from this class ☐ Yes ☐ No ☐ N/A					
Comment_____					

CONTENT	Strongly Agree				Strongly Disagree
The materials I received will be an ongoing resource	5	4	3	2	1
The layout and design of the materials was effective	5	4	3	2	1
The design and use of visual aids was effective	5	4	3	2	1
I understand the importance of Need to Know, Nice to Know and Where to Go	5	4	3	2	1
I can explain the Instructor-Led, Participant-Centered models (CPR, EAT, 90/20/8)	5	4	3	2	1
One suggestion for improving the program content: _____					
Comment_____					

THE INSTRUCTOR	Strongly Agree				Strongly Disagree
Demonstrated knowledge of content	5	4	3	2	1
Incorporated Instuctor-Led, Participant-Centered Techniques	5	4	3	2	1
Created a comfortable learning environment (open to questions, receptive, etc.)	5	4	3	2	1
Effectively used technology (PowerPoint, Audience response system, electronic game)	5	4	3	2	1
Provided feedback on the mastery of learning outcomes	5	4	3	2	1
Comment_____					

A producer is a second person on the webinar who can handle some of the technical issues that arise for learners. She can also help field some of the questions on the topic. Sometimes chat goes so quickly, I can't get to all the questions. Having a second person is a huge help.

Here is what a polling slide might look like:

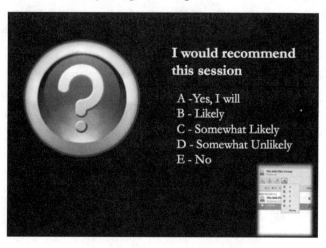

7. Launch: In this phase, you officially rollout the virtual program. Double check your company and organizational calendars to ensure that rollout does not overlap with other important events. I once scheduled a rollout of an online program on the same dates as two major company initiatives—a companywide sales meeting and a managers' off-site day. Oops. I had not realized these events were occurring because I was not in a sales role or a manager. However, it is my (and your) job to ask those attending or impacted by virtual training to help with calendaring.

8. Prioritize: After you have successfully launched a particular class online, don't be surprised to discover that an excited, anxious or overzealous manager or stakeholder may wish to have you immediately begin launching additional virtual courses. At this point, prioritize the list of requests and roll them out in the order that has the greatest positive impact on the organization.

9. Publish Successes: In this final step, take time to follow up with your key stakeholders, managers, and participants to share the evaluative, anecdotal and behavior-change results of the virtual course. If you fail to do this, it is likely that no one else will. But this is an essential aspect of successfully launching a new virtual course because others need to know the return on investment and the course's realized learner impact. This can easily be accomplished through email, a written communication, or even via video testimonials from participants. E-communication is usually the most expedient way to get the word out.

Now, in those nine steps, obviously I left out a significant quantity of other things you need to do, but many of those are the same things you do for a classroom training: needs assessment, create objectives, analysis, etc. And while we still use the basic adult learning theories we discussed in other chapters, we do need to do some modification of our content and presentation for online training. So let's take a step back and go over a few things that are done differently for the online world.

Modification for Virtual Training

One big change is that we need to build in participation every *four* minutes (the 90/20/4 rule) to keep people engaged. This comes from my own experience, having done webinars for more than a decade. I find that I get a lot less engagement from people if I go on for my usual ten minutes. Many have already checked out and are checking email by then.

On the Virtual Training Planner on the next page, you'll notice I include a soft opener. A soft opener is a relevant activity that starts before the webinar does. I encourage people to login to the workshop early to make sure all the technology is working properly for them beforehand. If it's not, it gives me or my producer time to help fix their volume, their login issues or whatever else the technology may throw our way.

The soft opener is for those who login early and don't have any technical issues. They can get some bonus information or activity so they are already engaged in the content instead of just staring at a blank webinar room screen.

Virtual Training Planner

Virtual Training Name:		Group/Size:	
Date:	Time/Duration:	Location:	Room Set-up:
Purpose: (Why meet?)		Outcome: (What Knowledge/Product will result?)	
Agenda/Items Content: (What do participants need to know/do?)		Process: (How will involvement be built it?)	
Soft Opener:		Soft Opener:	
Opener:		Opener:	
Closer:		Closer:	
Energizer:		Energizer:	
Handouts:		Materials:	
Media: Audio/Music, Print, PPT, Video etc.			
Roles/Responsibilities:			

Module One: Designing Webinars

Handouts and other materials should be emailed to the participants ahead of time. Otherwise, be sure to have the download link available.

Having royalty-free music available to play during appropriate intervals also is handy to help engage other senses. And knowing who does what is also critical. By "who," I mean whether the trainer or the producer will be doing a task.

Another critical factor is how your slides will differ when you're doing a webinar from your classroom deck. Continue onto the next chapter to find out.

The more preparation, planning and practice you have done for your webinar, the more confident you will be. In the beginning, it may feel a bit awkward or uncomfortable, but in time, you will gain comfort in your ability to handle the technology and manage a virtual training.

Ten Virtual Classroom Team Teaching Tips: The Instructional Producer

by Jennifer Hofmann

Last week I delivered a one-hour webinar to a global group of more than 100 learning professionals for a client. The content was very well received, but do you know what impressed them the most? My producer! She managed so much more than the technology; she acted as my instructional partner and convinced our client that she needed to add producers to her virtual learning team.

A producer can help transform virtual training into trouble-free, fast moving, interactive events that keep learners involved and the facilitator on track. In short, the facilitator can stay focused on content while the producer takes care of everything else.

The traditional classroom facilitator is a very busy person. In addition to delivering content, he or she facilitates interaction between participants, manages tools such as the LCD projector, writes on whiteboards and flip charts, and interprets the body language of learners. Constantly gauging participants' interest and comprehension, the facilitator also makes on-the-fly adjustments to the program design: for example, shortening breaks, lengthening days, or skipping content. By any standard, the facilitator's job requires constant attention and total concentration.

In the new virtual environment, many facilitators choose to not take advantage of all of the tools available to increase interaction. They can't see themselves being able to multitask to the extent required, so they limit participant use of chat, whiteboard tools, and other interactive features of the virtual classroom. The facilitator's role is then reduced to pushing content and lecturing, instead of facilitating interactions and knowledge sharing.

The solution to this dilemma lies in the role of the instructional producer.

Virtual instructional producers act as the technological expert on the virtual plat form as well as a co-facilitator. These professionals are also familiar enough with the course content to be able to offer comments on content topics.

Using an instructional producer in a team teaching setting provides the following advantages:

Opportunity to maximize engagement. By adding to conversations, offering opinions on content, and helping to deliver some content, participant engagement can truly be increased. With multiple people taking care of their needs, learners are more likely to not feel lost in cyberspace.

A different voice to debrief exercises. Engaging virtual classroom events include activities that solicit information from participants via chat, whiteboard activities, and polls. The instructional producer should be ready to collect, summarize, and provide opinions on the results of these activities.

Advocate for the participants. If the facilitator is taking care of content and trying to process information coming from multiple channels, someone has to look out for the participants. Instructional producers keep the facilitator in check! I ask the team members that support me to let me know when I am confusing and when I am talking too much. Also, I expect advice on the customization of exercises based on the needs of the specific audience.

No learner left behind! The instructional producer should keep an eye out for all participants during the session to make sure they are engaged, and then suggest strategies to the facilitator (via a chat backchannel) to re-integrate individuals back into the session.

Creates a trouble free, fast moving environment where students are able to be engaged by the facilitator. By being flexible, the producer can add value to the class by creating in-the-moment whiteboards or breakout rooms via the facilitator's prompting to meet the NEEDS of the class.

Here are ten tips to maximize the relationship between the virtual facilitator and instructional producer:

1. **Manage communication with participants.** In virtual and blended learning situations, participants can often feel very disconnected. This circumstance can result in a very unmotivated participant. The instructional producer should create a communication plan so participants know what to expect and also have some availability to respond to or even meet with participants who require instructional or technical support.

2. **Always take the advice of your instructional producer seriously, and solicit contributions.** He/she has a different perspective than you do, and that can only add to the success of your class.

3. **Create a leader guide that specifically outlines production tasks.** For example, include instructions for writing on the whiteboard, conducting warm-up exercises, and pasting text into the chat area. The guide should be very specific and cover the 'when' and the 'why' in addition to the 'what.' Formatting the guide so that the production tasks can be quickly identified will help the facilitator be better prepared for times when a producer isn't available. Reading over the lists of tasks, the facilitator can make informed decisions about which items he is able to manage on his own and which need to be modified in the absence of that second pair of hands.

4. **Meet at least a week ahead of time to walk through and discuss the exercises.** This meeting is best held in a virtual format so that the facilitator/producer team can plan exactly how things are going to work. It will also allow the producer, who may not be a content expert, to familiarize herself with the content. During this walk-through, the facilitator should lay out how the producer should respond to content questions that arise in the chat area.

5. **Establish emergency protocols.** What happens if the facilitator drops offline and the producer is left with a room full of participants? The answer to that question needs to be determined ahead of time. The producer should know whether to call for a break or to ask participants to complete an exercise, such as typing into chat all of the questions they have for the facilitator when he returns. Or, short self-paced exercises can be included in course workbooks so that the producer can direct people to them to while they're waiting for the facilitator to return.

6. **Establish course ground rules.** The producer needs to know how to respond to participants who get to class late or leave early. For example, if someone logs on twenty minutes into a program, should the producer tell her that class has already started and provide a schedule for future offerings?

7. **Ensure that the producer has all participant and leader materials.** This will make it easier for him or her to support the facilitator and the participants.

8. **Rehearse in a realistic environment.** Consider whether the facilitator, producer, or participants will be logging on with dial-up modems or behind firewalls. If the facilitator and producer will be at remote locations during the live event, then the rehearsal should be conducted that way as well.

9. **Create an environment of trust.** The facilitator/producer relationship should represent a true team. For example, if the producer suggests that the facilitator take a moment to review the questions in the chat area, the facilitator needs to trust that there are questions there that are worth considering.

10. **Debrief the experience.** After the live event, share notes about what went well and what needs to be changed. Make sure you document lessons learned for different facilitator/producer pairs who may tackle your class in the future.

Try team teaching in your next virtual class. Although you may discover that some courses don't require two people to manage, many will be improved by the second set of hands. At the least, a second person will become familiar with the course content. At the best, team teaching can help you feel as comfortable in the virtual classroom as in a traditional one.

Jennifer Hofmann, a pioneer in the field of virtual classrooms, is the president of InSync Training, LLC, a consulting firm that specializes in the design and delivery of virtual and blended learning.

Chapter 20

POWERPOINT DESIGN FOR VIRTUAL TRAINING

PowerPoint slides should be more than just words on a page. The point of visuals is to be visual! And when designing Instructor-Led, Participant-Centered training for a digital platform you need to be visual, exciting and interactive.

The common mistake I see made when trainers move from live classroom training to online training is they use the same PowerPoint deck they used for the live classroom. But there is a huge difference between the live classroom and the virtual space. In the live classroom, the participants have plenty to look at to gain visual cues and harness understanding – other participants, the trainer, static signs and Post-its hung around the room, and the PowerPoint slides. But in a virtual classroom, the learner cannot see her fellow participants, static signs, or the trainer. The PowerPoint slides are THE primary visual aid. And with that reality, PowerPoint slides created for the live classroom are rarely visual enough for the virtual space.

If you haven't already read the chapter in this book on PowerPoint Design for the Classroom, you really should read that first. Many of the principles in there apply to design for virtual training.

Again, the two rules of PowerPoint slides still apply here: be interactive and be visual!

Be Interactive

Consider using different forms of social media outside of the virtual classroom to continue the learning or engage participants during the session. The easiest ones to use when starting off as a trainer are LinkedIn, a Facebook page, or twitter. Here are some examples of what you could do using the different types of social media:

1. Share examples
2. Share one learning they will adapt, adopt and apply
3. Brainstorming tool
4. Use it as a backchannel during a lesson
5. Have learners provide answers to a question and answer session; it honors the experience in the "room"
6. Have them work in pairs on questions and later give out points for participation

Virtual Slide Preparation Principles

The following ten principles will help you get started designing really strong slides for your next presentation. Here is the list I provided in the chapter on Designing PowerPoint slides, however, it has been modified to speak directly to virtual training. Some of the items are duplicated so that I can present the complete list here for easy reference.

1. Clear concept for each slide.
One slide. One point. Remember, you can use as many slides as you need, you just can't put a lot of words on each. I start with forty-five seconds per slide if it's interactive. In a sixty-minute session, I may have ten slides devoted to pre-session topics or a soft opening. These slides would include pictures of myself and my family or pets. It could also include upcoming seminars or session information or a puzzle or two to get learners thinking about the topic. These ten slides scroll for five to ten minutes prior to the session beginning.

For a sixty-minute session, I won't limit myself on the number of slides I can have, but I want to have enough to visually engage the learners and actively involve them. I may have one slide up for three minutes where participants are writing on the slide, and another slide may be up for ten seconds. As you begin flowing out your content, consider how long you'll talk about the slide as well as what you'll have learners doing with the slide.

2. Ask, "How does this help participants get my message better?"
After you've designed your slides, ask yourself this question for each of them. It may be that the image doesn't enhance the message or the activity might be too difficult. You need to consider the participants first and focus on their need to gain a better understanding of the content.

3. Know your audience.
Are they a group of CEOs or accountants? Where are they geographically located? Are they young kids, middle-aged or is a wide range of generations represented? Knowing your audience will help you to tailor your font and theme to best meet your needs.

4. Create flow first.
When drafting a flow, use a template. I use templates that include the title of the session, the date, the link to the webinar, objectives, soft opener, and all content and closers. In a flow, I also determine which slides I need to show learners so they know how to use tools in the platform. I only want to show a snapshot and examples of tools being used that day so I don't overwhelm my learners.

5. Experience. Awareness. Theory.
In both the classroom and online training, your main point is addressed through engagement whenever possible. This could be through emoticons, text chat, the "raise hand" icon, white boarding and so forth.

6. Create an opener that grabs attention within the first nine seconds.

Marketing experts share that we need to grab attention within the first nine seconds in order to maintain an audience. Consider how you are starting off your session. How can you grab their attention? Sometimes it's through a puzzle, other times through a statistic or a text chat. I never start the session introducing myself and objectives; rather I begin with an opener and follow it up with information about who I am and what's to come. Use images, photography and vector art. Use words plus images.

7. End with a closer.

A call to action! What will they do differently because they were with you? Sitting through the session, enjoying it, and engaging in it is one thing, but you need to make sure that you're giving them time during the session to make a commitment to themselves as to what they're going to do with the information they've just learned. It can be as simple as an action idea or "text chat your top takeaway." A closer is at the very end of the session and is the last thing that should be done. Prior to the closer, do your evaluation and your Q&A. Remember to leave those last five minutes for yourself to wrap things up using an official closer and not just ending.

8. Make statistics graphical.

Let them "see" the importance behind the numbers. This is true for the classroom as well as for a webinar. Take the data and compare it to something tangible. Earlier, we talked about the number of students dropping out of high school in the United Sates. Instead of just stating the statistic, show an image of a football stadium that seats 80,000. On the next slide, multiply that image seventeen times. Then share that's how many American students drop out of school every year. When using survey questions to discuss statistics, use different types.

9. Insert black slides as place holders for lecturettes.

Having the monitor blacked out eases the strain on eyes. Ophthalmological research on computer screens and the strain on the optical lens is not new. Knowing this, we must consider our learners staring at the screen for an hour or more depending on the length of our webinar. By building in the blank black slides for times when you want the focus to be on your webcam will help ease the strain on learners' eyes. Other considerations for your learners are: having adequate lighting in their office space or increasing the resolution on their screen to make it dimmer or larger depending on screen size. I also recommend learners sit at least a forearm's length away from twenty- inch screens and further away if the screen size is larger.

10. Draft your slides on paper first.

Print off six blank slides on one page in PowerPoint. Garr Reynolds, author of *Presentation Zen*, says we're more creative when we aren't bound to order, and we force ourselves to consider the question "What's the main purpose of each slide?" Having six slides on a page forces us to keep each slide simple. We may have more slides but our deck is stronger for it. Remember, there is no limit to the number of slides as long as each has its own concept. If the concept is complex, put it in a handout, not on the slide. Design so a presenter is necessary.

Slide Development

1. Headlines summarize a message.

2. Visually match content to context. Get permission to use images, media, music, photos, etc. Get inspired by others! Check out some well done PowerPoints. Search online for ideas that match your scripted thoughts. Here is a link to twenty-five solid free stock photo sites. bit.ly/stockphotos2016.

3. Use screen shots of websites, marketing collateral and software.

4. Clean up images to emphasize your key points.

5. Compress image files for a quicker upload to the platform.

6. Use guest speakers, audio files, or video clips that are five minutes or less.

7. Use callouts to highlight information.

8. Use animations for transitions. Don't use constant motion objects.

One the next page is a quick, visual summary of the key design points.

While there are bad, good and then even better design principles for PowerPoint slides, there is no such thing as perfect. As you begin to transform your slides for online presentation, start with just one or two of the principles so it doesn't become overwhelming. Remember, you are the expert and these are just guiding thoughts; there is always a time when one "rule" should be broken or stretched. And with new research, there is always room for improving our slide design. As you review your slides, move from good to better and consider first how learners will engage and interact with them.

Do and Do Not

Do	Do Not	
☒	☐	Make concepts graphical whenever possible
☐	☒	Send PowerPoints that duplicate your presentation deck
☐	☒	Use only text
☒	☐	Create introduction slides
☒	☐	Create slides that allow for participation
☒	☐	Use bulleted lists
☒	☐	Make bullets graphical
☐	☒	Limit your slide numbers
☐	☒	Put complex information on slides
☒	☐	Use words and images
☒	☐	Make presenter necessary
☐	☒	Use red in a financial presentation
☐	☒	Use combination of red and green
☒	☐	Use 3 – 5 colors
☒	☐	Use complimentary colors
☒	☐	Use color wheel to choose colors
☒	☐	Match colors to the message

Appendix A

GIVING AN ILPC PRESENTATION

The terms "presenting" and "training" are not really interchangeable. And the definition of each changes depending on whether you are a consultant versus professor versus speaker. I realized this firsthand when I prepared for my first keynote presentation. It was "just" an hour-long session for 125 engaged learners. How hard could it be?

I had already been in the training industry for fourteen years, and I quickly realized it took significantly more than double the effort to finesse all of my thoughts into sixty minutes. I easily spent twenty to thirty hours preparing for that presentation. Why did it take so long when I can normally design one hour of training in five to ten hours? Because presenting and training (and facilitating, for that matter) are different and each requires a different process.

When presenting, one must be concise and clear in addition to inspiring, entertaining or clever. While some nuggets of learning may occur, the main value in presenting is having learners feeling motivated to change, grow or work with their team in a new or different way. Because I am a natural teacher, my keynotes are application-based presentations. Most presenters, however, are subject matter experts who share information through stories, case studies, research findings and visual aids.

As a member of the National Speakers Association, I have many times heard that a "good" presentation requires no visual support. However, I like to include visuals and engage audiences through interaction when I present because the same adult learning theories we base our training on also applies when speaking to groups of hundreds or even thousands. I take my talks to the next level by engaging the audience in interactive question and response exercises using TurningPoint clickers—a great way to involve every participant while presenting a keynote. Clicker questions and the graphs that are created from the clicked responses allows me to get a visual on where the audience is at with my message and help me finesse as I continue to ensure the desired impact is made.

Most trainers will not present formal keynote speeches but will likely need to present information at sales meetings, board meetings or networking events. Rich Meiss, a Bob Pike Group master trainer, shares an easy method for pulling together a strong presentation. The first step? Always begin with a hook, an opening statement or story that grabs attention. Then transition into the body of the message which usually has three to five main content pieces. Then lead with the most important concept or the one that needs the most amount of time, followed by the other concepts.

Close by providing a verbal summary, and then have those in the audience engage in an activity that reinforces the message and allows them to identify an action to take. The path of a presenter is specific, linear, and clearly laid out. (See image 1.1)

Instructor-led and participant-centered is really aimed at how we learn, no matter what type of informational setting we are in. ILPC is easily adapted to any meeting, presentation or facilitation. For opener or "hook" ideas and closers, see chapters ten and eleven.

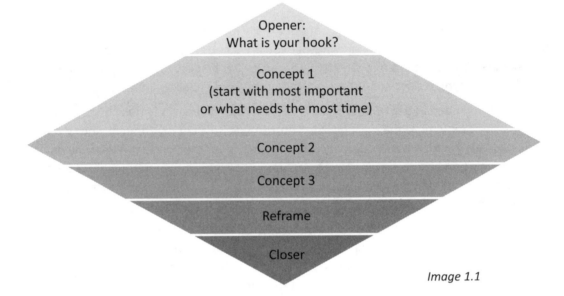

Image 1.1

Appendix B

PRESENTER VS. TRAINER VS. FACILITATOR

The roles of presenters, ILPC trainers (Instructor-Led, Participant-Centered) and facilitators vary greatly. This grid provides insight into how these roles are different along with some insight into how and why they differ.

	Presenter	ILPC Trainer	Facilitator
Purpose of the role	Present information	Increase learners' knowledge, skills and attitudes through active engagement	Lead subject matter experts through a process to achieve a common goal
Outcome of the message	Entertain, inspire, motivate, challenge	Acquire knowledge, engage, objective based	Inquire, challenge, question, draw out participants' data
When the role is required		Information is needed for transfer back on the job	To collect data, to provide information, to solve problems, to gain consensus
Group Size	Any size	Recommended between fifteen and twenty	More than fifteen
Length of the message	45-90 minutes	Any amount of time	Greater than one day
Flow of the message	Usually linear and clearly outlined	Structured for activities and application time	Process is flexible and dynamic based on group
Format of the message	Lecture	Interactive	Group work
Q&A	Answers questions	Questions used for learning and discussion	Asks open-ended questions for consensus and individuals to share
Examples of when the role is used	Business meeting, sales event, information download	Courses, workshops, classes, sessions, conferences	Brainstorming, defining annual goals, project planning
Visuals used for this type of message	Props and PowerPoint are used to clarify a point	Variety of props, objects, charts and slides aid learning	Post-its and charts used to gather and analyze data

Appendix C

PERFORMANCE SOLUTION MODEL

Sometimes, as trainers, we are order takers; someone hands us the assignment and off we go without stopping to ask questions. We just do as we are told.

If we as trainers are to move from order takers to trusted advisors, we need to slow down and think. First, determine if training is really the answer to the problem you are told to solve. Do a needs analysis using the Performance Solution Model. Here is what the model looks like at a high level.

"When performance is the question, training may not always be the answer!"

Step One **What...**	Step Two **Who...**	Step Three **How...**
Type of need	**Audience**	**Corrective Strategy**
☐ Problem (deficiency)	☐ Entire organization	☐ Systems
☐ Improvement	☐ Division	☐ Organizational
☐ Future Planning	☐ Department	☐ Development Programs
	☐ Individual	☐ Recruiting
	☐ Job	☐ Placement
		☐ Coaching
		☐ Training

www.BobPikeGroup.com

THE
BOB PIKE GROUP
Engineer Curiosity

Let's take a deeper look into each of the steps to explore how we can really become more strategic in our design process.

Step 1: WHAT

Ask stakeholders to determine what type of need exists. In general, there are three reasons we may need to look at performance.

Problem

Is there a problem or a deficiency? There's a gap between low performers and high performers. What are the high performers doing that low performers are not? What are low performers doing that the high performers are not? For example, a company has high performers and low performers in its sales department, and the gap needs to be eliminated. Multiple methods of needs assessment (surveys, on-the-job observation, task analysis, interviews, or focus groups) will help determine where the gap is and why there are low and high performers.

Opportunity for improvement

Things are fine, but there's always the opportunity to take everyone to the next level. At The Bob Pike Group, every one of our trainers averages well above 6.0 on a 7.0 scale. Yet, each of us is constantly looking for ways to be just a bit better in the work that we do. Perhaps stakeholders see an opportunity for improvement in their teams. Maybe your company wants to move from "good" to "great." The best time to do training is before there is a crisis.

Future planning

A new product is being released, a new procedure is being implemented, a new plant is coming online, new equipment is being installed, new government regulations are taking effect—each of these might indicate a need for training before the fact so that there's no slow down in performance when the changes take place.

As a trainer, meeting with stakeholders regularly and sharing the need for planning helps the entire team and makes you a stronger consultant. When leadership shares "exciting news that in the first quarter we will see big changes in the way we do business," that is a cue that a Training and Performance Solution conversation should happen quickly so that, if training is a part of the answer, it can be developed and ready.

Step 2: WHO

Determine the level of the organization impacted by Step 1. The reason performance is being examined will determine who is going to be impacted. If a new product is being rolled out, it may impact the entire organization while a Quickbooks update may only impact finance and sales.

In today's workforce, individuals may fill many different roles, so ask questions regarding not just job titles but roles. For example, if your company is rolling out a new computer-based system, it may be that training is needed for not just the people entering the data, but also those accessing the data and pulling reports.

Step 3: HOW

Determine the corrective strategy.
This is the step where we figure out if training is the answer! In forty years of helping training professionals at The Bob Pike Group, we have found that there are five other options to be considered *before* training.

Systems
Let's say you're a call center, and shift A completes 3000 calls while shift B completes only 2000. At first glance, you might assume shift B needs training: there is a performance gap. Shift B people resist and inform you that they only complete calls during four hours of their shift due to time zones and availability, and then four hours are spent researching internal issues uncovered by shift B while archiving, compression and back-up functions are completed on the computers. Who needs training? This is a systems issue which might also warrant training for shift A.

Organizational Development
Sam starts as a housekeeper. By the second week on the job, he completes his assigned twelve rooms on the seventeenth floor by noon. The supervisor informs Sam that Frank is behind schedule on his rooms and asks Sam to clean three of Frank's rooms. The scenario repeats itself for several days. By Sam's third week, it takes him until quitting time to finish his own twelve rooms. Sam, like the other housekeepers, did not receive an incentive for working more productively so he accomplished the MDR (minimum daily requirement). Due to poor policies and a lack of incentives, Sam and Frank are underproducing.

Placement
Is the wrong person in the job? Have you properly explored your employees' behavioral tendencies? Are people-oriented employees in people intensive jobs? Are your more cautious, task-oriented people in high detail, analytical jobs? People are all motivated— just by different things. Discover whether challenges and results, social recognition and people, harmony and the status quo and teamwork, or analytical attention to detail and perfection get them going. Match people's natural tendencies to the job's critical competencies for optimum productivity and satisfaction.

Coaching
Do you need a ten-day class or ten minutes of coaching? Sometimes, employees may just need a few questions answered or have a skill demonstrated. However, managers may not know how to coach. If they have never had a manager model coaching skills for them, they may not identify coaching as a vital solution. Often times, on-the-job coaching is a better return on investment than a longer learning session. Coaching provides the employee with enough information to be able to move ahead on the current project or assignment.

Recruiting

Are your recruiting efforts targeted to attract employees who start out with the basic competencies to do the job? If an organization has not clearly defined the requirements of the job and its performance standards, it may hire people who do not possess the skills necessary to meet the demands of the job. When McDonald's in New York City was faced with a dearth of applicants for counter clerk positions, it offered basic literacy classes to increase the number of potential recruits and ensure those they hired would meet the basic requirements. This is a solution to a recruitment challenge.

Training

To confirm that training is the best strategy, consider AWA. **A**ble to? Have they physically and mentally demonstrated the capability to perform the function? **W**illing to? Have they shown a desire? **A**llowed to? Are the problem factors in the workplace possibly managers or supervisors who don't give enough autonomy for the employee to do the job effectively?

We use this Performance Solution model every time a training request comes to us to ensure we are not "order takers" but are the strategic partners that our clients need us to be.

If you are inside an organization, clearly communicate that the purpose of using this model is to help and get the solution right the first time. The desire is to have a return on investment and have the training make a difference.

Appendix D

HOW THE DIFFERENT GENERATIONS COMMUNICATE VIA SOCIAL MEDIA

Each generation approaches communication differently, whether that be face to face or through technology. If you, as a trainer, want to continue the learning conversation outside of class to improve learning transfer, you want to know which communication strategies work best with each generation. For Millennials or Generation Z, send out texts with content that triggers recall with trainbycell or another texting service. Generation X and Boomers are found more often on Facebook or check email frequently. Consider creating a private social networking group for follow-up or using pro.mindsetter.com to send out additional activities via email.

Here is a high-level overview of each generation in the current workforce and the best ways to connect with them using social media and technology.

Traditionalist (1925–1945)	Boomer (1946–1964)	Gen X (1965–1979)	Millennials (Gen Y) (1980–2000)
Social Networking Communication			
• slow to share • words vs body language • face to face or written communication • everything is on purpose	• expect open, direct style, avoid controlling language • likes details and thoroughness • Present options to demonstrate flexibility in your thinking	• email rocks • short and sweet sound bites • likes to give and receive feedback • keep them in the loop • informal communication style	• use action words and challenges • resist talking down to them • email and Blackberry's rock • likes to give and receive feedback • appreciative listeners – use humor and create a fun learning environment • encourage them to take risks
Social Networking Preferred Applications			
• Email • Forward an RSS Feed link to click on • Email YouTube Links	• Blogs • Evites • Linked In • Facebook • MySpace • YouTube • Together We Serve • Plaxo • Email	• Blogs • Evites • Linked In • Facebook • MySpace • YouTube • Together We Serve • Plaxo	• Blogs • Evites • Linked In • Facebook • MySpace • YouTube • Widgets • Twitter • Together We Serve • Text Messaging/ Status Updates

Appendix E

CREATING AND MANAGING SUCCESSFUL, ENGAGING MEETINGS

by Priscilla Shumway

Principles for creative training also apply to engaging—and successful—meetings.

In order to maximize the time that you and your staff invest in face-to-face meetings, consider following this simple six-step process.

- Pre-planning
- Agenda
- Opening
- Action plan
- Closing
- Follow up

Pre-planning: Reach out to attendees prior to the meeting with logistics of the meeting and a rough draft of the agenda. Ask for their input on what else needs to be addressed. Or, as an alternative, list the topics to be covered and ask attendees to prioritize the topics. This will allow you to create buy-in. Remember, people don't argue with their own data. Who else will be taking an active role in the meeting? Guest speakers? Are different people responsible for certain sections? Be sure to engage them prior to the meeting.

Also consider the room set up. Depending on the number of attendees and the purpose of the meeting, the way in which the tables, chairs, projector, and materials are set up can affect the outcomes.

Agenda: Once the agenda is set, email it to all attendees ahead of time. Are there other people who may need to know what is being discussed but who do not need to attend? Send it to them and ask for input, thoughts, ideas and concerns.

Opening: Every meeting needs an opener to engage the attendees, help them understand the importance, and gain buy-in for future actions as a result of the meeting. Consider starting the meeting with one of the following:

- Discussion question
- Unusual statistic
- Challenging question
- Quotation
- Video

Action Plan: Every meeting needs to create a list of "to do" items. Successful action plans should include three things:

- What is the action to be done,
- when will it be done, and
- who will take responsibility.

The person recording the minutes of the meeting should capture these items on a flip chart for all to see during the meeting and then follow up with a printed version that is sent to all attendees.

Engage the attendees by allowing them to have a say at least every eight to ten minutes to keep them actively involved.

Closing: Every meeting should have a closing that allows people to accept responsibility for actions moving forward and/or recap the agreements made. An example of a meeting closer might be to have each attendee put a reminder into their calendar app (either on cell phone or laptop) to email the meeting coordinator within two weeks with progress on their action items or further comments and ideas from the meeting.

Follow up: The meeting coordinator should be responsible for any follow up items. A simple thank you email to attendees with an attachment of the action items with a time-line is important. Asking for input for future meetings is helpful at this time.

As a senior trainer for The Bob Pike Group for 14 years, Priscilla Shumway has presented semi-nars nationally, focusing on participant-centered instruction, training design, presentation skills, meeting facilitation, and adult learning theory in both public workshops and customized in-house programs.

BIBLIOGRAPHY

Anderson, L. S., A. F. Healy, J. A. Kole, and L. E. Bourne. 2013. "The Clicker Technique: Cultivating Efficient Teaching and Successful Learning." *Applied Cognitive Psychology* 27: 222–234. doi: 10.1002/acp.2899

Anderson, L.W., D. R. Krathwohl, P.W Airasian, K.A. Cruikshank, R. E. Mayer, P. R. Pintrich, J. Raths, M. C. Wittrock. 2001. *A Taxonomy for Learning, Teaching, and Assessing: A revision of Bloom's Taxonomy of Educational Objectives*. New York: Pearson, Allyn & Bacon.

Arnsten, A. F. T. 2009. "Stress Signalling Pathways that Impair Prefrontal Cortex Structure and Function." *Nature Reviews Neuroscience* 10 (6): 410-422. doi:10.1038/nrn2648.

Association for Psychological Science. 2011. "Curiosity is Critical to Academic Performance." *Science Daily*. Retrieved March 5, 2015 from sciencedaily.com/releases/2011/10/111027150211.htm.

ASTD Research. 2013. *State of the Industry 2013.* Alexandria, Va.: American Society for Training and Development.

ASTD Research. 2009. "The Value of Evaluation: Making Training Evaluations More Effective." Alexandria, Va.: American Society for Training and Development, October 2009.

Bell, M., N. Kawadri, P. Simone, and M. Wiseheart. 2013. "Long-term Memory, Sleep, and the Spacing Effect." *Memory* 1-8.

Bennion, K.A., K. R. Mickley Steinmetz, E.A. Kensinger, and J. D. Payne. 2013. "Sleep and Cortison Interact to Support Memory Consolidation." *Cerebral Cortex*. Doi: 10.1093/cercor/bht255

Brinkerhoff, Robert O. 2014. "The Growing Importance of Measuring Results and Impact." *ASTD Handbook, 2nd ed.* Alexandria, Va.; ASTD Press, 463-469.

Bloom, B.S. (Ed.), M.D. Engelhart, E. J. Furst, W.H. Hill, D. R. Krathwohl. 1956. *Taxonomy of Educational Objectives, Handbook I: The Cognitive Domain.* New York: David McKay Co Inc.

Broad, Mary and John Newstrom. 1992. *Transfer of Training*. Reading, Mass.: Addison-Wesley Publishing Company.

Brown, Peter C., Henry L. Roediger III, Mark A. McDaniel. 2014. *Make It Stick: The Science of Successful Learning.* Cambridge, Mass: Belknap Press of Harvard University Press.

Buzan, Tony. 1983. *Use Both Sides of Your Brain.* New York City: Plume.

Christoff, Kalina, A. M. Gordon, J. Smallwood, R. Smith, and J. Schooler. 2009. "Experience Sampling During fMRI Reveals Default Network and Executive System Contributions to Mind Wandering." *Proceedings of the National Academy of Sciences* 106(21): 8719–24.

Clark, Ruth Colvin. 2010. *Evidence-Based Training Methods: A Guide for Training Professionals.* Alexandria, Va.: American Society for Training and Development.

Consalvo, Carmine. 2010. *Workplay: 36 Indoor/Outdoor Activities for Leadership, Team Building and Problem Solving* HRD Press; Loose Leaf edition.

Cross, Jay. 2014. "Learning Informally in Your Workscape." *ASTD Handbook.* Alexandria, Va.: ASTD Press.

Darke, Shane. 1988. "Anxiety and Working Memory Capacity." *Cognition and Emotion 2*, no.2: 145-154. doi:10.1080/02699938808408071

Dobbs, S., A. Furnham, A., and A. McClelland. 2011.The Effect of Background Music and Noise on the Cognitive Test Performance of Introverts and Extraverts. *Applied Cognitive Psychology* 25(2), 307–313.

Dwyer, Brian. 2001. "Successful Training Strategies for the Twenty-First Century: Using Recent Research on Learning to Provide Effective Training Strategies." *International Journal of Educational Management* 15 (6): 312-18. DOI: http://dx.doi.org/10.1108/EUM0000000005910

Ericcson, K.A. 2006. "The Influence of Experience and Deliberate Practice on the Development of Superior Expert Performance." *The Cambridge Handbook of Expertise and Expert Performance.* New York: Cambridge University Press.

Glasser, William. 1998. *Choice Theory in the Classroom.* New York City: HarperCollins.

Gold, Benjamin P., M. J. Frank, B. Bogert, E. Brattico. 2013. "Pleasurable Music Affects Reinforcement Learning According to the Listener." *Frontiers in Psychology* 4: 541. *PMC.* Web. 10 Feb. 2016.

Hallman, S., J. Price, and G. Katsarou. 2002. "The Effects of Background Music on Primary School's Pupils' Task Performance. *Educational Studies 28*(2): 111-122.

Hambrick, David Z., Erik M. Altmann, Frederick L. Oswald, Elizabeth J. Meinz, Fernand Gobet, Guillermo Campitelli. 2014. "Accounting for Expert Performance: The Devil Is in the Details." *Intelligence* (February 2014), doi:10.1016/j.intell.2014.01.007

Hambrick, David Z., Brooke N. Macnamarax , Guillermo Campitelli, Fredrik Ullénjj and Miriam A. Mosingjj. 2016. "Beyond Born Versus Made: A New Look at Expertise" *Psychology of Learning and Motivation* 64: 1–55. doi:10.1016/bs.plm.2015.09.001

Hartwig, M., J. Dunlosky. 2012 "Study Strategies of College Students: Are Self-Testing and Scheduling Related to Achievement? *Psychonomix Bulletin & Review*, 19 (1): 126-134.

Heath, Chip and Dan Heath. 2007. *Made to Stick.* New York City: Random House.

Howard-Jones, Paul. "Neuroscience and Education: Myths and Messages." *Nature Reviews Neuroscience* 15 (2014): 817-824, doi:10.1038/nrn3817

Jensen, Eric. 2000. "Moving with the Brain in Mind." *Educational Leadership*, v58 n3: 34-37.

Johnson, S. and K. Taylor. *Neuroscience of Adult Learning.* San Francisco: Jossey-Bass, 2006.

Kane, M.J., L. H. Brown, J. C. McVay, P. J. Silvia, I. Myin-Germeys, T. R. Kwapil. 2007. "For Whom the Mind Wanders, and When: An Experience-Sampling Study of Working Memory and Executive Control in Daily Life." *Psychological Science* 18(7):614-21.

Kapp, Karl and Defelice, Robyn. 2009. "Time to Develop One Hour of Training," *Learning Circuits* (August 2009). Accessed November 23, 2015. http://www.astd.org/Publications/Newsletters/Learning-Circuits/Learning-Circuits-Archives/2009/08/Time-to-Develop-One-Hour-of-Training

Kirkpatrick, Donald. 1994. *Evaluating Training Programs.* San Francisco: Berrett-Koehler Publishers.

Kohn, A. 2004. "Feel-bad Education." *Education Week*, 24 (3): 44-45.

Kornell, N. 2009. Optimising Learning Using Flashcards: Spacing is More Effective than Cramming. *Applied Cognitive Psychology*, 23 (9): 1297-1317.

Krashen, S. 1982. "Theory Versus Practice in Language Training." *Innovative Approaches to Language Teaching,* 25-27. Rowley, MA: Newbury House.

Kratzig, Gregory P. and Katherine D. Arbuthnott. "Perceptual Learning Style and Learning Proficiency: A Test of the Hypothesis." *Journal of Educational Psychology* 98, no.1 (2006): 241, DOI: 10.1037/0022-0663.98.1.238.

Kraus, N. and B. Chandrasekaran. 2010. "Music Training for the Development of Auditory Skills." *Nature Reviews Neuroscience* 11: 500-505.

Lally, Phillippa, Cornelia H. M. Van Jaarsveld, Henry W. W. Potts, and Jane Wardle. 2010. "How Are Habits Formed: Modeling Habit Formation in the Real World." *European Journal of Social Psychology* 40; 998-1009. DOI: 10.1002/ejsp.674

Litman, L., and L. Davachi. 2008. "Distributed Learning Enhances Relational Memory Consolidation." *Learning and Memory*, September 8: 711-716.

Mangels, Jennifer A., Brady Butterfield, Justin Lamb, Catherine Good, and Carol S. Dweck. 2006. "Why Do Beliefs About Intelligence Influence Learning Success? A Social Cognitive Neuroscience Model." *Social Cognitive Affective Neuroscience* 1; 75-86. doi:10.1093/scan/nsl013

Mathematics Knowledge. *Applied Cognitive Psychology* 20: 1209-1224.

Matthews, Gail. "The impact of commitment, accountability, and written goals on goal achievement." Paper presented at the 87th Convention of the Western Psychological Association, Vancouver, B.C., Canada, 2007.

Mayer, Richard E. 2009. *Multimedia Learning*, 2nd ed. New York: Cambridge University Press.

Mayer, Richard E., Andrew Stull, Krista DeLeeuw, Kevin Almeroth, Bruce Bimber, Dorothy Chun, Monica Bulger, Julie Campbell, Allan Knight, Hangjin Zhang. 2009. "Clickers in College Classrooms: Fostering Learning with Questioning Methods in Large Lecture Classes." *Contemporary Educational Psychology*, Volume 34 (1): 51-57.

McEwen, B. S.. J. H. Morrison. 2013. "The Brain on Stress: Vulnerability and Plasticity of the Prefrontal Cortex over the Life Course". *Neuron* 79 (1): 16-29. doi:10.1016/j.neuron.2013.06.028.

Meiss, Rich. 2010. "Coaching, Mentoring and Counseling: Are They the Same or Different?" GiftsOfIdeas.net. Accessed March 10, 2016. http://giftsofideas.net/story.asp?story=61

Meneses, A., and G. Liv-Salmeron. 2012. "Serotonin and Emotion, Learning and Memory." *Reviews in the Neurosciences* 23 (5-6):543-53. doi: 10.1515/revneuro-2012-0060.

Miller, George A. 1956. "The Magical Number Seven, Plus or Minus Two: Some Limits on Our Capacity for Processing Information." *The Psychological Review, 63: 81-97. Accessed February 5, 2016. http://www.musanim.com/miller1956/*

Mitchell, J.P., C. S. Dodson, and D. L. Schacter. 2005. "fMRI Evidence for the Role of Recollection in Suppressing Misattribution Errors: The illusory Truth Effect." *Journal of Cognitive Neuroscience*, 17; 800-810.

Morrison, A.B., A. R. A. Conway, J. M. Chein. 2014. "Primacy and Recency Effects as Indices of the Focus of Attention." *Frontiers in Human Neuroscience* 8 (6). doi:10.3389/fnhum.2014.00006.

Mueller, Pam and Daniel Oppenheimer. 2014. "The Pen is Mightier than the Keyboard: Advantages of Longhand Over Laptop Note Taking." *Psychological Science* 25: 1159-1168. doi: 10.1177/0956797614524581

Neff, K.D., H. Ya-Ping, and K. Dejitterat. 2005. "Self-compassion, Achievement Goals and Coping with Academic Failure." *Self & Identity*, 4(3), 263-287. doi:10.1080/13576500444000317

Ojemann, G., J. Ojemann, J. Lettich, M. Berger. 1989. "Cortical Language Localization in Left, Dominant Hemisphere, an Electrical Stimulation Mapping Investigation in 117 Patients." *Journal of Neurosurgery* 109: 316-26.

Ormrod, J.E. 2008. *Educational Psychology Developing Learners.* New York City: Pearson Education.

Ouchi, Yasuomi, Hiroyuki Okada, Etsuji Yoshikawa, Shuji Nobezawa, Masami Futatsubashi. 1999. "Brain Activation During Maintenance of Standing Postures in Humans." *Brain* 122 (2): 329-338. DOI: 10.1093/brain/122.2.329

Owens, Matthew, Jim Stevenson, Julie A. Hadwin, Roger Norgate. 2014. "When Does Anxiety Help or Hinder Cognitive Test Performance? The Role of Working Memory Capacity." *British Journal of Psychology 105*, no.1: 91-101. doi: 10.111/bjop.12009.

Peatling, John. 1983. "Science, Wisdom or Wizardry?" *Religious Education*, Summer 1983.

Pillay, Srinivasan. 2011. *Life Unlocked: 7 Revolutionary Lessons to Overcome Fear.* Emmaus, Pa.: Rodale Books.

Reynolds, Garr. 2011. *Presentation Zen.* San Francisco: Peachpit.

Roemmele, Brian. "Why did Bell Labs Create Phone Numbers of 7 digits - 10 digits?" Last updated April 26, 2012. https://www.quora.com/Why-did-Bell-Labs-create-phone-numbers-of-7-digits-10-digits

Rohrer, D., and K. Taylor. 2006. "The Effects of Overlearning and Distributed Practice on the Retention of Rooks, Tina, email to the author, February 23, 2016.

Rossett, Allison. 2009. *First Things Fast*. Hoboken, N.J.: Pfeiffer.

Seifert, C. M., and A. L. Patalano. (1991). "Memory for Incomplete Tasks: A Re-Examination of the Zeigarnik Effect." In Proceedings of the Thirteenth Annual Conference of the Cognitive Science Society [refereed] (pp. 114-119). Mahwah, NJ: Erlbaum.

Sitzmann, Traci, Kenneth G. Brown, Wendy J. Casper, Katherine Ely, Ryan D. Zimmerman. "A Review and Meta-analysis of the Nomological Network of Trainee Reactions." *Journal of Applied Psychology* 93, no. 2 (2008): 280-295. doi.org/10.1037/0021-9010.93.2.280

Smallwood, Jonathan, Emily Beach, Jonathan W. Schooler, and Todd C. Handy. 2008. "Going AWOL in the Brain: Mind Wandering Reduces Cortical Analysis of External Events." *Journal of Cognitive Neuroscience* 20(3): 458-469.

Song, H. S., A. L. Kalet, and J. L. Plass, J. L. 2016. "Interplay of Prior Knowledge, Self-Regulation and Motivation in Complex Multimedia Learning Environments." *Journal of Computer Assisted Learning*, 32:31-50. doi: 10.1111/jcal.12117

Statista. "Market share of the most popular social media sites in the U.S.," accessed February 16, 2016, http://www.statista.com/statistics/265773/market-share-of-the-most-popular-social-media-websites-in-the-us/

Strickland, B., ed. 2001. "Serial Position Function." *The Gale Encyclopedia of Psychology.* Detroit: Gale. Retrieved from http://go.galegroup.com/ps/i.do?id=GALE%7C-CX3406000580&v=2.1&u=wash74137&it=r&p=GVRL&sw=w&asid=97364150ef7db-40c8358647dbd3d8a39.

Szpunar, Karl K., Samuel T. Moulton, and Daniel L. Schacter. 2013. "Mind Wandering and Education: from the Classroom to Online Learning." *Frontiers in Psychology* 4 (1): 495.

Tabak, Lawrence. "If Your Goal is Success, Don't Consult These Gurus." *Fast Company* 6 (1996/1997). http://www.fastcompany.com/27953/if-your-goal-success-dont-consult-these-gurus

Thorndike, Edward. 1911. *Animal Intelligence*. New York: Macmillan Company.

Weibell, C. J. 2011. *Principles of Learning: 7 Principles to Guide Personalized, Student-Centered Learning in the Technology-Enhanced, Blended Learning Environment.* Retrieved July 4, 2011 from https://principlesoflearning.wordpress.com.

Wikipedia. "List of most popular websites," accessed February 16, 2016, http://en.wikipedia.org/wiki/List_of_most_popular_websites

Zak, Paul. 2013. *The Moral Molecule: How Trust Works.* New York City: Plume.

Zeigarnik, B. (1927). "Das Behalten erledigter und unerledigter Handlungen." *Psychologische Forschungen,* 9, 1-85.

INDEX

Throughout *Creative Training: A Train-the-Trainer Field Guide*, author Becky Pike Pluth mentioned several resources she recommends that she either authored or co-authored. Following are some of those resources. To order, call The Bob Pike Group at 1-800-383-9210.

101 Movie Clips that Teach and Train

Using short clips from movies can relay learning points more dramatically and quicker than any lecture.

Let this award-winning book jumpstart your creativity for lesson planning or training design by providing you with the perfect movie clip for over 100 topics including discrimination, leadership, team building, and sales.

Each clip comes with cueing times, plot summary and scene context, and cogent discussion questions. All topics are cross-referenced so you can easily find the perfect clip for your teaching or training needs.

SCORE! series

The SCORE! series of books is a compilation of activities that will help engage your learners while ensuring your content is remembered long after class is over.

These activities for Closing your session with impact, Opening your session with relevance, Revisiting content creatively, and Energizing your learners will make you a learning legend and improve training retention.

Books in this series include general CORE activities as well as a focus on technical training, webinar training and one-on-one training.

Books in this series:
SCORE! Volume 3
SCORE! for Technical Training, Volume 4
SCORE! for Webinar Training, Volume 5
SCORE! for One-on-One Training, Volume 6

Webinars with WoW Factor

Death by webinar is rapidly replacing death by PowerPoint! But it doesn't have to.
Make webinars effective and engaging.

Teaching online is a different animal—requiring different skills and a different energy—that completely exposes any weaknesses in your material and preparation. In this book, Becky Pike Pluth shows trainers where to start when moving to an online platform and what pitfalls to avoid along with explaining some of the basic webinar tools trainers can use to make online training interactive. Becky includes 40 activities that will help even a novice webinar trainer create an online training that has impact and builds in long-term retention.

Creative Training Podcast

Want to continue your Creative Training education? Becky Pluth has a Creative Training podcast series with more than ninety short podcasts already archived! Each Friday, a new podcast is released. From scheduling fails to authenticity, games in the classroom to the deadly sins of team teaching, these short audio clips will continue to encourage you in your ILPC journey. You can listen to them for free at bit.ly/BPGpodcast.

Training Tunes Royalty-Free Music, Volumes 1-5

This music collection contains 80 original tracks of royalty-free music specifically designed for the learning needs of participants. Fast-paced songs for breaks and games. Songs of 90-110 beats per minutes for introductions and exits. Slow songs to enhance discussion and reflection times.

All these titles and more great resources for training effectively are available from The Bob Pike Group at www.BobPikeGroup.com/shop-products or by calling (952) 829-2658 or (800) 383-9210.